THE CONTEMPORARY WORLD

Conflict or Co~operation?

Second edition

Jim Cannon M.A. Dip. Ed.

Principal Teacher of Modern Studies
Craigmount High School, Edinburgh

Bill Clark M.A.

Head Teacher
The Academy, Galashiels

George Smuga M.A. Dip. Ed.

Depute Head Teacher,
Beeslack High School, Penicuik

Oliver & Boyd

Acknowledgements

The publishers wish to thank the following for permission to reproduce photographs (or cartoons) on the pages listed:

Keystone Press (9, 18, 19(3), 23, 34, 35, 36, 67, 120(2), 127); John Topham (12, 26 (bottom), 64, 78, 97); Camera Press (16 Leon Herschtritt; 24 Don McCullin; 26(top) James Pickerell; 47); John Hillelson (25); United Nations (35 T. Chen; 108 S. Lwin; 103 J. K. Isaac; 130); Camerapix (42); Frank Spooner (46 Brad Markel); Network (51 Mike Goldwater); Eddie Adams/TIME magazine (53); Popperfoto (60, 79); Anglo-Chinese Educational Institute (62); Commission of European Communities, London Office (80, 85); Evening Argus, Brighton (91); Owens of Wishaw (100); BMW Works, Munich (102); Dover Harbour Board (104); Scotsman Publications (104); Press Association (110); WHO/P Almasy (123); Associated Press (124).

The publishers also thank all those who gave permission to reproduce extracts from their publications, or to use their material as the basis for illustrations. Acknowledgement is given beneath extracts, tables or illustrations in the text.

Illustrated by Stephen Gibson

Oliver & Boyd
Longman House
Burnt Mill
Harlow
Essex CM20 2JE

An Imprint of the Longman Group UK Ltd

ISBN 0 05 003734 X

First printed 1979
Second edition 1985
Sixth impression 1990

Produced by Longman Group (FE) Ltd
Printed in Hong Kong

Contents

Introduction

The three parts of this book – International Relations, the European Community and the United Nations – illustrate its main theme: the alternatives facing nations in their relations with each other; whether to oppose and confront each other with the risk of destroying civilisation or whether to work together through international co-operation.

The section on International Relations concentrates on the relations between the two major powers: the USA and the USSR. It shows why these two countries are the major powers and why and how they have come into conflict. By looking at the major trouble spots it examines the variety of ways in which the Superpowers have clashed: directly in Berlin and Cuba, indirectly in Vietnam, the Middle East and Africa. This leads to a discussion of the dangers of such confrontation in a world of nuclear weapons, and the prospects for a reduction in this conflict.

The sections on the European Community and the United Nations show how these attempts at international co-operation came into being; the ways in which these organisations work and how successful they have been.

The text is designed to be followed through chapter by chapter but within each chapter the units are self-contained and can be largely understood without necessarily having studied previous units. At appropriate points there are questions based on the text or on the statistics, cartoons and photographs which accompany the text. These questions are designed to ensure understanding of the basic points in the text and to develop skill in using visual material. Also included are case studies which illustrate the meaning and impact of the events you are studying at a personal level. Some are fictional but based on fact (e.g. the units on Vietnam and migrant workers in the EEC), and others are factual (e.g. the unit on human rights).

At the end of the book you will find a Glossary and 'Who's Who' to help you understand some of the terms used in international affairs and highlight some of the principal figures who have helped shape the contemporary world.

The themes you are studying are all part of an ever-changing picture. The book aims to capture parts of this moving picture in a series of 'still photographs'. Events and personalities will inevitably change. It is up to you to keep up to date by studying outside the text-book – by use of newspapers, magazines, radio and television.

A book of this length cannot cover all the crucial issues in the contemporary world or do full justice to the complexities of the issues described, but we hope it will give an insight into the world in which you live.

Introduction to the Second Edition

This second edition has been updated to take account of the new developments and changes of emphasis in international relations during the six years since the first edition appeared. New sections include The Gulf War, Afghanistan and Central America. The sections on Africa, Eastern Europe and Cold War or Co-existence have undergone major revision. Throughout the rest of the book amendments and additions have been made to the text to take account of recent events such as the admission of Greece to the EEC, the war in Lebanon, the upsurge of terrorism throughout the world. New photographs, tables, cartoons and other illustrations have also been included to provide more up-to-date examples.

PART 1

The World in Conflict

1. The Superpowers

Russians threaten retaliation against US mainland

Mr Reagan's Reasons for Invasion of Grenada

European-American relations at a low ebb

On the edge of a new cold war

US 'producing eight nuclear weapons per day'

New China warning on Russia

US build-up prompts Syrian mobilisation

Who are the Superpowers?

The newspaper headlines on this page introduce the main theme of a large part of this book: that of international relations. These headlines are typical and although personalities and places may change, similar newspaper cuttings can be found for any period since 1945. They feature the major powers who dominate international events and whose actions determine the future of the world. Whenever they quarrel the rest of the world holds its breath; whenever they resolve their problems the rest of the world breathes a sigh of relief.

Who are these major powers who have dominated world events since 1945? Why are they so powerful? Why have they quarrelled? In which parts of the world have their quarrels taken place? Why are their quarrels so important for the rest of the world?

These are the main issues which will be dealt with in this chapter on international relations since 1945.

THE MAJOR POWERS

Which countries make up the league of major powers and what factors make them so powerful when compared to other countries?

A major power is one which has the strength to defend its own interests when these are challenged and above all the strength to exert its influence on other areas throughout the world. Certain countries have the power to do this because of their economic and military strength.

Economic Strength

Size (area), population and wealth are all indicators of a country's economic strength. The size of a country is important because this is usually an indication of the resources available to that country. A large country can be self-sufficient with regard to food, minerals, etc. whereas a smaller country, like Britain, has to rely on imported raw materials and food. Population is important as it is the workforce of a country. In times of war a country with a large population has large human resources to draw upon. The wealth (Gross National Product: **GNP**) of a country is a measure of the extent to which that country has the technology to use its resources and its workforce to full advantage.

If the four largest, the four most heavily populated and the four wealthiest countries are compared (Table 1) we can see that only two, the USA and the USSR, occur in all lists.

5

Table 1 The four strongest countries in terms of size, population and wealth

Size (Area in square kilometres)		Population (1981)		Wealth (GNP in $ billion 1981)	
USSR	22 402 000	CHINA	982 600 000	USA	2925.5
CHINA	9 561 000	INDIA	686 200 000	USSR	1212
CANADA	9 976 800	USSR	267 600 000	JAPAN	1127
USA	9 363 000	USA	230 800 000	WEST GERMANY	689

Canada is a major country in terms of land area, a large part of which is rich farmland and is rich in mineral resources. But Canada has a very small population, much smaller than that of Britain.

India has a huge population, but one which is largely poorly educated and therefore unable to contribute much to the country's economic strength. The population is increasing at a rate which is causing many problems for India's economic development. India also has a low GNP: $159.3 billion in 1981.

China has a huge land area and a huge population but falls well behind in wealth, with a GNP of $283 billion (1981).

Japan and West Germany are major industrial nations but they are dependent on imported raw materials and for political reasons have not developed a military strength equal to their economic strength.

Military Strength

Military strength is equally important as an indicator of power and can be measured in two ways: in terms of armed forces and in terms of types of weapons.

The strongest countries in terms of total armed forces are shown in Table 2.

Table 2 Armed forces

USSR	3 375 000
CHINA	2 880 000
USA	2 699 000
INDIA	980 000

Of course the size of armed force only gives us part of the picture: we need to know *how* these forces are armed. Above all we need to know the size and capability of a country's nuclear force. This, as you will see later, can be a very complicated thing to determine. The major nuclear powers in the world are shown above right.

When we examine all the relevant factors we find that three major powers stand out: the USA, the USSR and China. And of these three, the USA and the USSR are the most powerful in terms of economic strength and nuclear weapons. These two have become known as the Superpowers and have dominated world events since 1945.

The supremacy of the USA and the USSR dates from the end of the Second World War when, as leaders of the capitalist and communist worlds respectively, they built up alliances with other countries and came to control spheres of influence throughout the world.

The major nuclear powers

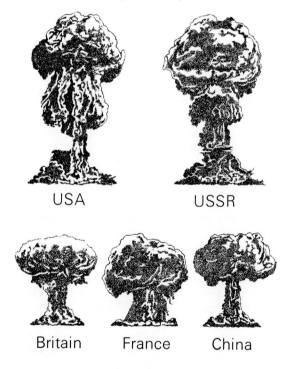

USA   USSR

Britain   France   China

Questions

1. Explain why the USA and the USSR deserve the description 'Superpowers'.
2. Why has China not yet reached Superpower status?
3. Are there any countries or groups of countries which may become major world powers in the near future?

Focus on the Superpowers

We have seen in the preceding pages why, because of the things they have in common, the USA and the Soviet Union are described as Superpowers. Yet in the context of international relations the differences between them – in their politics, economies and societies – are more important than their similarities.

The USA declared its independence from Britain on 4 July 1776 because of dissatisfaction with the government in London. After the War of Independence ended in 1783, there were 13 states; today there are 50. The USA is a vast union of states covering 9 million km² and containing many different groups of people, ideas and problems.

The Soviet Union, too, was born out of dissatisfaction with the previous form of government,

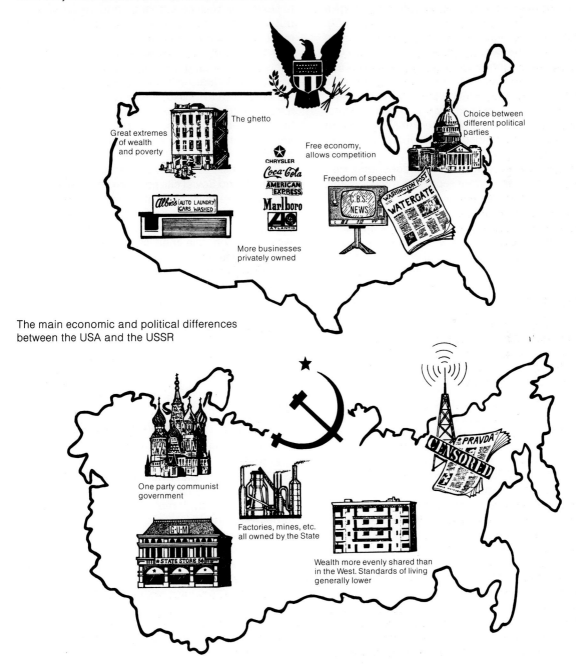

The main economic and political differences between the USA and the USSR

7

although for vastly different reasons. The overthrow of the Tsar and the Bolshevik Revolution of 1917 signalled the beginning of a new era in Russia. The Soviet Union is a huge federation of 15 republics covering one-sixth of the earth's surface and containing within its population a huge mixture of over 100 nationalities.

The people of the USA live in the wealthiest country in the world. Vast supplies of natural resources such as iron ore, oil and good farmland, coupled with an industrial and agricultural system based on mechanisation and automation, give most of the people a very high standard of living. Most Americans believe that the best way to make use of their resources is by means of what they call free enterprise: competition between individuals and private companies to exploit the resources available. They are usually wary of government interference in their lives and work. In recent years, however, the federal government in Washington has increasingly extended its control over important aspects of the people's lives, such as health and welfare, education, industrial relations and civil rights, as well as important sectors of the economy, particularly energy resources.

The Soviet Union has made remarkable progress since the Revolution of 1917. In terms of industrial power it is second only to the USA and its people benefit from advanced educational and social services. But in order to reach this position the USSR has adopted a very different method from the free enterprise of the USA. The most important difference lies in the part played by the government, or State. Through a series of Five Year Plans the State controls industry and agriculture in the Soviet Union, deciding on production targets, wages and prices throughout the country. Factories, farms and shops are owned by the State, and very little is owned privately. Although the State's control of the economy has not always been entirely successful (neither has free enterprise) the Soviet Union is an advanced industrial nation in which the vast majority of the people enjoy low-cost housing, free medical services, good pension schemes and a good educational system.

What is important is not the fact that there are differences of detail between the two societies but the more fundamental fact that they have each chosen very different ways of reaching their goals, which are very much a result of their historical and political development.

Most Americans have a basic belief in the freedom of the individual. They believe that government restrictions on, and interference with, the economy and society should be kept to a minimum. The American people believe that free elections in which the voters have a choice of candidates from different political parties is of fundamental importance. In the economy free enterprise, with its emphasis on private ownership, private profit and competition, is the accepted system. In society at large, freedom of speech and of the mass media is held to be very important.

In the Soviet Union the emphasis is rather different. Although there are elections in the Soviet Union, it is a one-party state. The Communist Party is the only political party, and voters choose people to serve in government from among the candidates put forward by the Communist Party. The government has virtually complete control of the economy and the society. It is believed that no important decisions regarding the economy should be left to private individuals or companies. Industrial and agricultural activity is for the benefit of the nation as a whole and should therefore be controlled by the State on behalf of the people. Equality and fairness are of greater importance than individual freedom of choice.

Clearly there are great differences in the lives of American and Soviet citizens. The societies in which they live have developed along very different lines. The economic systems in which they work are founded upon very different principles. The political systems which rule their lives are fundamentally different. Neither society is perfect: each has its social and economic problems.

The people of these two nations have different priorities and have chosen different ways of working towards their respective goals. Each is travelling alongs its own road towards these goals. The problem for international relations is, as we shall see, that in many cases these priorities and goals come into conflict.

Questions

1. Explain what the Americans mean by 'free enterprise'.
2. What is the role of the State in the Soviet economy and society?
3. Describe briefly three of the main differences between the lives of American and Soviet citizens.
4. Why are the different priorities and goals of the two Superpowers a problem for international relations?

The Cold War

US and Soviet troops meet in 1945

WHAT IS THE COLD WAR?

The two Superpowers, the USA and the USSR, are suspicious and afraid of each other mainly because of political, economic and social differences. This distrust leads them to quarrel and make threats against each other though trying to avoid direct war. Both the USA and the USSR are aware of the huge numbers of highly destructive nuclear weapons each possesses, and both realise that a direct war between them would have serious results, not only for them but for the whole world. Therefore they live in a state of armed, uneasy peace, facing each other in a **Cold War**.

HOW THE COLD WAR DEVELOPED

(1) The Revolution in Russia in 1917 and American opposition to the idea of a communist government in Russia led to mutual mistrust and fear.
(2) Although the USA and the USSR fought together against Germany in the Second World War, the mistrust remained and when Germany was defeated in 1945, the USA and Soviet Union faced each other, still suspicious of each other's intentions.
(3) Between 1944 and 1947 the Soviet Union gained and kept control of several countries in Eastern Europe: Bulgaria, Romania, East Germany, Poland and Czechoslovakia. The USA opposed this strongly and feared further advances by the USSR.
(4) In 1945 the USA had dropped atom bombs on Hiroshima and Nagasaki in Japan to demonstrate its military power. The USSR was afraid of this show of atomic power and of US military bases in several parts of the world.
(5) The Berlin Blockade in 1948, when the USSR tried to force the USA and its allies from Berlin, showed the seriousness of the Cold War confrontation.

HOW THE COLD WAR IS FOUGHT

Just after the Second World War an American journalist wrote, 'We are in the midst of a cold war' as his way of describing the armed confrontation

How the Cold War is fought

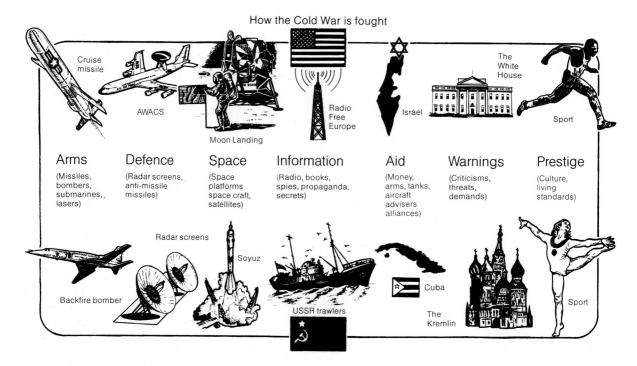

Arms	Defence	Space	Information	Aid	Warnings	Prestige
(Missiles, bombers, submarines, lasers)	(Radar screens, anti-missile missiles)	(Space platforms space craft, satellites)	(Radio, books, spies, propaganda, secrets)	(Money, arms, tanks, aircraft advisers alliances)	(Criticisms, threats, demands)	(Culture, living standards)

between the USA and the USSR. How do the two Superpowers confront each other?

(a) Each side, through fear of the other, builds up and develops its weapons in an effort to gain superiority. This 'arms race', though very costly, is vital to the balance of power between the two countries. For example, Soviet weapon developments include mobile SS-20 missiles and an 1100-kilometre range supersonic bomber (the Backfire). The USA has developed cruise and Pershing II missiles and is researching a long-range missile system (the MX).

(b) Along with the development of military equipment there is the development of defence systems in an attempt to reduce the possibility of surprise attack. One example of this is the American Airborne Warning and Control System Aircraft (AWACS).

(c) The possible advantages of military control in space give added momentum to the 'space race'.

(d) An 'information war' is waged through radio broadcasts, books and newspapers, while both sides attempt to gain information of secret military, space and industrial developments, using spies, microphones and films.

(e) Other countries become involved in the Cold War, partly because they join up with one side or the other in alliances, e.g. the USA and **NATO** 1949; the USSR and the **Warsaw Pact** 1955. The support of other countries may be bought with

aid in the form of money, military equipment or 'advisers' from either the United States or the Soviet Union.

(f) In the 'warnings race' each side complains about the other's methods and tactics. The USA criticises the USSR for the violation of **human rights** in that country while the USSR claims that the USA supports corrupt governments.

(g) In the 'prestige race' each country gives financial support to individuals and groups whose activities reflect well on their country, e.g. Soviet sportsmen and women are given well-paid jobs as instructors in their own sport, while American sportsmen and women receive university scholarships.

Questions

1. What is meant by the term 'Cold War'?
2. Why do the USA and the USSR try to avoid a direct war with each other?
3. Name four ways in which the Cold War is fought?
4. In what ways do you think space platforms might be useful to either side in the Cold War?
5. Can you give any recent examples of
   (a) the warnings race and
   (b) the prestige race?

Friend or Foe?

Operation Elder Forest

In March 1984 a jet-age 'Battle of Britain' took place in the skies over Scotland, England and Wales. More than 900 attacks were made against RAF bases, missile sites and radar stations. The main threat came from Belgian, Canadian, French, West German, Danish and Norwegian fighter planes together with a number of US Air Force Phantoms, Thunderbolts and F1-11 bombers. Helping the RAF to defend the British bases were NATO's Boeing early warning aircraft, Royal Danish Air Force Starfighters, and US Navy Tomcat fighters from the huge aircraft carrier *USS Independence*. Every RAF unit in the UK was involved, and during the battle Bloodhound and Rapier missile defences were brought into operation against the enemy.

The aim of 'Elder Forest' and similar exercises held each year is to find out just how good the North Atlantic Treaty Organisation (NATO) forces would be if the Warsaw Pact countries attacked Western Europe. The 'Elder Forest' exercise was designed to stretch to the limits the ability of the RAF to defend Britain against a long-lasting air attack from all directions. It coincided with a major sea exercise called 'Teamwork '84' in the Atlantic Ocean, North Sea and Norwegian Sea, designed to test NATO's ability to reinforce its northern flank in time of war. The Warsaw Pact countries hold similar exercises every year behind the Iron Curtain in order to try out their equipment and tactics. In recent years observers from the 'other side' have been invited to attend each other's exercises.

THE NORTH ATLANTIC TREATY ORGANISATION

NATO, which is the most important military alliance of the countries of the West, came into existence as a method of defence against the expected attempt by the Soviet Union to expand communist power and influence, particularly in Europe, after the Second World War. In 1945 the USSR was a new Superpower with armed forces of almost four million men and it had already shown its readiness to use this powerful army to set up communist rule in Eastern Europe. The setting up of NATO was designed to balance the power of the Soviet Union by combining the military strength of the countries of Western Europe with the power and wealth of the United States.

In spite of their shared aim of preventing Soviet expansion, there have been some major disagreements among NATO member countries in recent

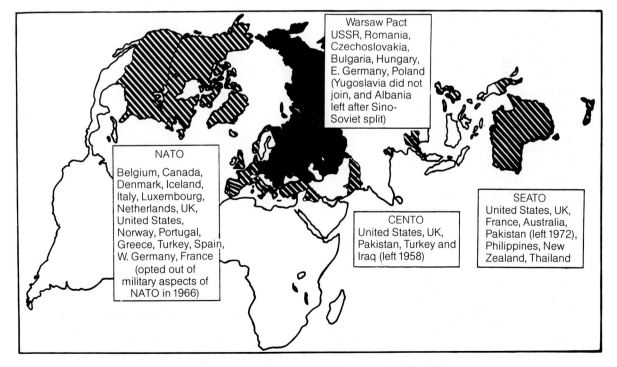

Warsaw Pact
USSR, Romania, Czechoslovakia, Bulgaria, Hungary, E. Germany, Poland (Yugoslavia did not join, and Albania left after Sino-Soviet split)

NATO
Belgium, Canada, Denmark, Iceland, Italy, Luxembourg, Netherlands, UK, United States, Norway, Portugal, Greece, Turkey, Spain, W. Germany, France (opted out of military aspects of NATO in 1966)

CENTO
United States, UK, Pakistan, Turkey and Iraq (left 1958)

SEATO
United States, UK, France, Australia, Pakistan (left 1972), Philippines, New Zealand, Thailand

Members of NATO, Warsaw Pact, CENTO and SEATO

years. NATO headquarters – SHAPE, the Supreme Headquarters Allied Powers Europe – were transferred from Paris to Mons in Belgium in 1967 as a result of a French decision to play a reduced part in the running of the alliance. More recently, the problem of fishing rights led to the so-called 'Cod War' between Britain and Iceland, and in 1974 Turkish troops invaded the island of Cyprus.

All the forces of NATO in Europe are under the direction of a supreme commander. The command, named ACE – Allied Command Europe – looks after the area from Norway in the north to the Mediterranean in the south, and from the Atlantic Ocean in the west to the eastern frontier of Turkey in the east. Forces in Europe come under this command in peace as well as in war so that they can be organised, trained and equipped as a single force ready to defend Western Europe from attack.

The belief that this attack will come from the Warsaw Pact countries is a view shared by the majority of military leaders in the NATO countries, a view which has changed very little since NATO was set up in 1949. It is summed up by General Alexander Haig, former Supreme Allied Commander in Europe, who said:

'The explosion of Soviet military capabilities . . . far exceeds the requirements of a purely defensive posture . . . The enemy is moving . . . I believe that the threat of Soviet power is greater today.'

THE WARSAW PACT

As you can see from the map on page 11, the USSR is almost totally surrounded by member-countries of the three Western military alliances. It was fear of being surrounded in this way that led the Soviet Union to bind together the Soviet satelite countries of Eastern Europe in the Warsaw Pact in 1955.

Since then, the forces of the Warsaw Pact have grown steadily and today they outnumber NATO forces by about five to three. NATO forces would find it very difficult to defend Europe against a sudden military threat from the Warsaw Pact forces. Many of the countries in the NATO alliance are cutting back on military spending as a result of economic difficulties in the 1970s. It has also been estimated that NATO may be wasting as much as a third of its effectiveness by having too many different weapons of each type, e.g. 31 different anti-tank missiles and 41 kinds of naval guns. In contrast to this, most armaments for Warsaw Pact forces are made in the Soviet Union and used by all the Warsaw Pact countries, resulting in greater efficiency.

NATO's only advantage in terms of numbers of weapons lies in tactical nuclear weapons. The United States keeps about 7000 atomic warheads in Europe, but it would face a very difficult decision about whether or when to use them. The decision to deploy cruise and Pershing II missiles in Europe from 1983 onwards strengthened NATO's ad-

A Greenham Common Peace Camp

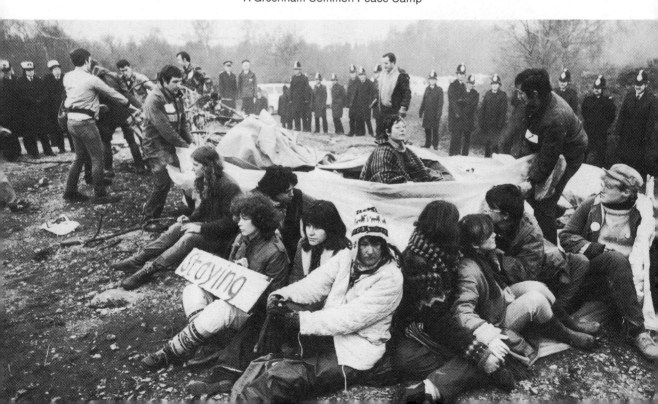

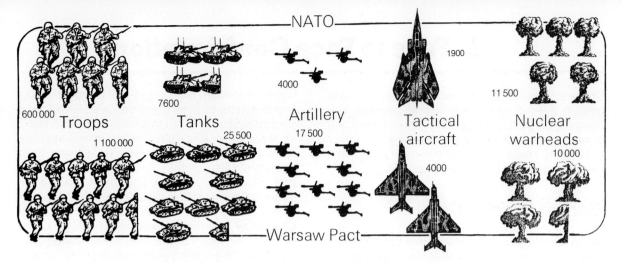

600 000 Troops

1 100 000

7600 Tanks

25 500

4000 Artillery

17 500

1900 Tactical aircraft

4000

11 500 Nuclear warheads

10 000

Warsaw Pact

The relative military strength of NATO and Warsaw Pact forces (1984)

vantage, but was the cause of widespread protests from anti-nuclear groups in Britain, West Germany and Italy. NATO also has a very important advantage in terms of advanced technology, e.g. although Soviet tanks are heavier, they are less accurate, slower and more vulnerable to attack than those used by NATO.

It is very difficult to estimate which of the two alliances would be the stronger if war did occur in Europe. But there is evidence that the Warsaw Pact conventional forces are growing much faster than those of NATO. One estimate is that the USSR now turns out a new submarine every five weeks, 800 military aircraft a year, and that in 1976 alone 2000 new tanks were built compared with only 400 in the USA. NATO commanders believe that this rate of production is too high to be purely defensive and is a serious threat to the balance of power between the forces of East and West.

Questions

1. Why do NATO forces hold exercises like Operation Elder Forest?
2. Study the map and draw up a list of the members of NATO and the Warsaw Pact.
3. Explain why the USA and the countries of Western Europe joined in a military alliance in 1949.
4. Write a short paragraph describing NATO today.
5. What evidence is there that NATO still expects any attack on Western Europe to come from the Warsaw Pact countries?
6. What persuaded the USSR to set up the Warsaw Pact alliance with the countries of Eastern Europe?
7. Why might NATO forces find difficulty in resisting a Warsaw Pact attack on Western Europe?
8. What two advantages does NATO have over the Warsaw Pact forces?

2. Face to Face Confrontation

On certain occasions the two Superpowers have been in direct confrontation with each other. The dangers of such 'face to face' involvement are immense in an age of nuclear weapons.

Two major examples of this direct conflict can be seen in crises over Berlin and Cuba.

Berlin: Divided City

On 19 March 1970, **Willy Brandt**, the West German leader, made an historic visit to East Germany to meet the Prime Minister of East Germany. The talks between the two leaders were not as important as the fact that they met at all. This first-ever meeting of the leaders of the two Germanies marked a real breakthrough in attempts to solve one of the main areas of tension between the communist and capitalist worlds. Germany, and especially Berlin, had been an area where the two confronted each other and had been the reason for a number of serious crises since the end of the Second World War.

At the end of the Second World War Germany was divided into four occupation zones by the Soviet, American, British and French allies. It was hoped that the country would be run as one under a joint administration, but this never came into being as the four victors soon began to quarrel. The capital of Germany, Berlin, which had also been divided into four sectors, lay inside the Soviet zone, and all communications with Berlin had to go through Soviet-occupied Germany.

Half of Berlin was thus an island surrounded on all sides by a communist-controlled Germany. This situation annoyed **Stalin**, the Soviet leader, who decided in May 1948 to put pressure on the western sector of Berlin by blocking all land routes – road and rail – into Berlin from the west. He hoped to lay siege to West Berlin and force the Western powers to hand over all of Berlin to his control. This became known as the Berlin Blockade.

The Western powers could have withdrawn from West Berlin or tried to force their way through the blockade and run the risk of war. Instead, they kept their sector of Berlin alive by flying in all the fuel and food needed to keep half a city operating. This 'Berlin Airlift' lasted until March the following year, supplying at its peak 13 000 tonnes of goods per day for West Berlin's 2.5 million people.

The division of Germany and Berlin after 1945

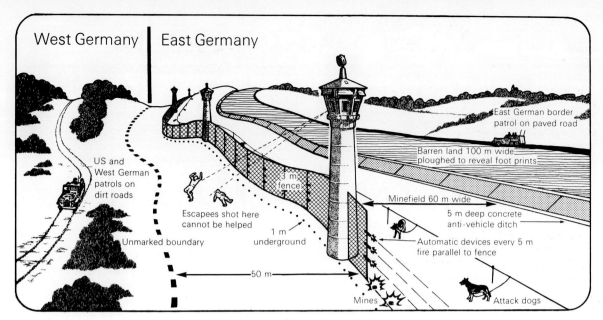

The East/West German frontier

By March, when Stalin called off the Blockade, it was clear that both Berlin and Germany would remain divided. In May 1949 the Western powers joined their three zones to form the new independent state of the German Federal Republic (West Germany). The Soviet Union replied by making its zone the German Democratic Republic (East Germany). By 1949 Germany was thus divided into two separate countries: West Germany with a population of over 50 million and East Germany with a population of 13 million. Neither country wanted to accept this division as permanent, and West Germany refused to recognise the East as a state.

West Germany began to become very wealthy. The people of East Germany were less well-off by comparison and many seemed to resent the harsh life imposed by the East German government. Many East Germans tried to escape to West Germany, especially through West Berlin. Between 1949 and 1961 over three million people fled into West Germany. Not only was this embarrassing to the East German government but it was damaging economically, as many of the refugees were skilled workers.

To cut off this outflow of refugees the East German government in 1961 built a wall of barbed wire and concrete through the city of Berlin thereby cutting the city in half. East Germans continue to risk their lives trying to escape over or under the wall but, over the years, security on the frontier has become more sophisticated, making escape almost impossible. The building of the Berlin Wall served to remind the world of the gulf between the communist and non-communist world and of the bitter divisions between the two Germanies.

TOWARDS A BETTER UNDERSTANDING

During the 1970s a number of events took place which considerably helped to reduce the tension between East and West Germany. These were very much due to the West German leader, Willy Brandt – Chancellor of West Germany from 1969 to 1974 – and his policy of **Ostpolitik** (Eastern policy).

In 1971 a Four-Power Agreement on Berlin was reached by the governments of the USA, USSR, Britain and France. The treaty secured for West Germany the right of access to West Berlin, entry into East Berlin for West Berliners, many of whom have relatives in East Berlin, and the recognition of West Berlin's links with West Germany.

In 1972 the Basic Treaty between East and West Germany was concluded. This treaty marked a major breakthrough in East and West German relations for by it West Germany recognised the existence of the state of East Germany. It created the beginnings of better relations between the two countries in the form of increased trade and cultural and personal contacts – there were to be greater opportunities for West Germans to visit the East and greater possibilities for East Germans to visit the West. In April 1972 half a million West Berliners were allowed through the Berlin Wall, for the first time in six years, to spend Easter with their relatives in East Berlin and East Germany.

These treaties opened the way for the two German states to join the United Nations in 1973.

The Berlin Wall divides the Bernauerstrasse up the middle

Above all they brought about a recognition of the division of Germany and showed that the two Germanies were at least willing to live in toleration of each other.

During the 1980s the renewed tension in international affairs has cooled relations between East and West Germany. However, both countries feel very much that they are at the 'front-line' of international tension in Europe and that continued good relations are essential for the long-term peaceful development of each state. As a result, it is likely that both East and West Germany will continue to build upon the Basic Treaty of 1972 and that this agreement between the two states will not be dropped.

EAST AND WEST GERMANY TODAY

It is now over 30 years since Germany was divided and a whole generation of Germans has grown up knowing only a divided Germany. In the East many young East Germans, who have not known a united Germany and who have only known life under a communist state, are content with their life and are often critical of the way of life in West Germany. However, there are still East Germans who do try to leave their country.

Despite the political differences between them, there are a number of important factors which the two states share. Apart from a common language and a common history, there are now close financial and trade links between the two countries. In 1982, for example, trade between East and West Germany increased by 12 per cent, with West Germany's imports from East Germany up 10 per cent and East Germany's imports from West Germany up 14 per cent. Both countries have built up strong economies, with East Germany becoming one of the wealthiest countries in Eastern Europe and West Germany becoming one of the world's industrial giants. The economic recession of the

1980s has hit both countries and West Germany has faced a major problem of rising unemployment.

Both countries are also aware of their unique position as 'front-line' states in the military and political division of Europe. There is a huge concentration of conventional and nuclear weapons in both East and West Germany. For example, half of the tactical nuclear warheads to be used by NATO in a European war are located in West Germany. The worsening international situation in the early 1980s and the controversy over the siting of such intermediate-range missiles as the Soviet SS-20 and the American cruise and Pershing missiles have led to the growth of major peace movements in both

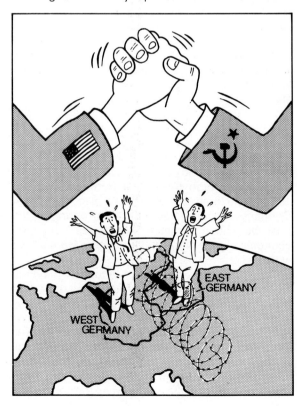

East and West Germany. The peace movement in East Germany is almost unique in Eastern Europe. In West Germany, the strength of the peace movement was seen when the Green Party, which wants an end to the nuclear arms race, gained seats in the West German Parliament during the 1983 election.

Questions

1. Explain how Germany and Berlin came to be divided in the years after the Second World War.
2. Describe in your own words the events of the Berlin Blockade.
3. Study the map and photograph of the Berlin Wall and the East/West German frontier and describe why it is virtually impossible to escape across them.
4. What was so special about Willy Brandt's visit to East Germany in 1970?
5. What is meant by describing East and West Germany as the 'front-line states' in Europe and how has this affected their relationship in recent years?

The Cuban Crisis

The second occasion on which the Superpowers confronted each other was during the Cuban missile crisis of 1962. This crisis brought the world closer to the brink of war than any other problem since the end of the Second World War.

THIRTEEN DAYS ON THE BRINK

On Tuesday 16 October 1962, a series of events began which brought the Cold War to the very brink of 'hot war'. On that day President **Kennedy** of the United States received a report that Soviet missile sites had been identified on the island of Cuba, a short distance from the coast of the USA. The President was shown photographs of the missile sites taken by a US Air Force reconnaisance plane. The President and his advisors had to decide very quickly what action they should take to counter this unexpected new threat to the USA's security: the map shows some of the major American cities and military targets which were vulnerable.

The President had three main options open to him: to do nothing; to order the immediate destruction of the missiles by the US Air Force; or to set up a barrier of American ships around Cuba to prevent more missiles and equipment being imported, i.e. a naval blockade.

Kennedy chose the last of these three ways of tackling the problem. He appeared on American television on Monday 22 October to explain the situation and announce his decision to the American people and by Wednesday 24th the US Navy was in position around Cuba with orders to turn back any ships attempting to carry further missiles into Cuba.

Kennedy had taken a firm stand and the next move was now up to the Soviet Union. Kennedy called upon the Soviet leader, **Khrushchev**, 'to move the world back from the abyss of destruction'. During the next few days as a number of ships carrying Soviet missiles approached the ring of US warships around Cuba, tension was very high. The world waited nervously for what appeared to be an inevitable clash between the two Superpowers which might lead, in a matter of hours, to all-out nuclear war. On Sunday 28 October, after a number of incidents, any one of which might have led to the much-dreaded 'hot war' (including the boarding and inspection of a Russian ship by the US Navy and the shooting down of an American U2 reconnaisance plane over Cuba) Mr Khrushchev announced in a message to President Kennedy that 'the Soviet government . . . has issued a new order, for the dismantling of the weapons which you describe as "offensive", their crating, and return to the Soviet Union'. Three hours later the radio station Voice of America broadcast Kennedy's acceptance of Khrushchev's 'statesmanlike' offer. The crisis was over, the disaster of war narrowly averted. Within eight weeks the missiles were removed from Cuba and the missile-sites ploughed over.

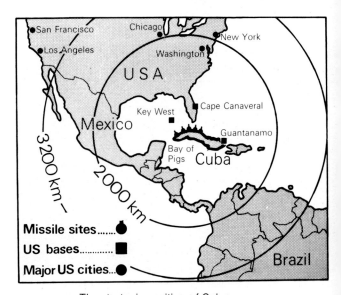

The strategic position of Cuba

Questions

1. How did the USA detect Soviet missile sites on Cuba?
2. Why were the Americans very worried about this development?
3. Explain why you think President Kennedy chose the third of the three options open to him.
4. How could the crisis have developed quickly into an all-out war?

PRELUDE TO THE CRISIS

From the description of the events outlined above it is easy to understand why the American President chose to set up a blockade around Cuba. But several important questions remain unanswered. Why did the Soviets want missiles on Cuba in the first place? Would they ever have been used in an attack on the USA? Were they there just as a threat, or to add to Soviet prestige? What did Cuba hope to gain from its Soviet connections? And why were the missiles removed with apparently little argument?

We can trace the early steps on the road which eventually led to the missile crisis back to 1953, nine years before. One day in July of that year a young lawyer, **Fidel Castro**, and 150 of his followers attacked the army barracks at Santiago de Cuba which at the time was ruled by a dictator, General Batista. Castro and his followers wanted to rid Cuba of Batista and his pro-American government, which they saw as being harmful to the interests of Cuba. After serving two years in prison, Castro went to Mexico, but returned to lead a rebellion. After a period of **guerrilla warfare** Batista fled Cuba in January 1959 and Castro and his followers took over.

Soviet missiles returning to the USSR from Cuba, November 1962

America had large investments in the Cuban economy, particularly in the telephone, electricity, railway and sugar production industries. Castro's determination to rid Cuba of American influence and his attempts to nationalise these industries led him into conflict with the then American president Eisenhower, who eventually broke off diplomatic relations with Cuba in January 1961.

During the American presidential election campaign of 1960, the Democratic candidate, John F. Kennedy, called for American support for the 'democratic anti-Castro forces in exile and in Cuba itself, who offer eventual hope of overthrowing Castro'. Kennedy, when he became President in 1961, inherited a plan, backed by the US Central Intelligence Agency, for an invasion of Cuba by Cuban exiles (the Bay of Pigs, April 1961). The attack failed and the invasion forces were destroyed on the beaches.

With American support for the attack obvious to everyone, Castro began to strengthen his links with the Soviet Union. The USSR had already agreed to buy Cuban sugar and provide financial aid for Cuba's industries and agriculture, following the withdrawal of American aid. The alliance of Cuba and the USSR became complete in December 1961, when Castro announced that he had become a Marxist-Leninist. Economic links were further strengthened, and Moscow agreed to arrange defence aid in case of further attacks on Cuba.

The determination of Fidel Castro to rid his country of American 'dollar imperialism' was the crucial factor which led to Cuba drawing further and further away from the USA and closer to Soviet influence. The error of judgment by President Kennedy in allowing American support for the Bay of Pigs invasion certainly sped up this process.

The stationing of missiles on Cuba was a new move in Soviet foreign policy. Until 1962 the Soviet Union had never stationed nuclear missiles outside its own borders. But by then the USSR was far behind the USA in the arms race and would find it difficult and expensive to catch up. If, however, some exisitng missiles were based in Cuba its power against the USA would be greatly increased: it would have powerful nuclear missiles very close to the United States, aimed at the least protected part of the country. This was why, in August 1962, SAM missiles and 5000 Soviet technicians arrived in Cuba, followed in September by Soviet Ilyushin bombers. Almost overnight the USA's warning of the approach of nuclear attack was reduced to two minutes. The ingredients for the missiles were now complete.

President John F. Kennedy   Fidel Castro   Mr Khrushchev

Questions

1. Why did Fidel Castro and his followers want to overthrow the dictator General Batista and his government?
2. What was the aim of the 'Bay of Pigs' attack and how successful was it?
3. In what three ways did the USSR and Cuba co-operate with each other after the 'Bay of Pigs' incident?
4. Explain why Mr Khrushchev wanted to have Soviet missiles in Cuba.

BEHIND THE SCENES

We have seen that each of the three countries involved in the crisis had important reasons for becoming involved. Why then did the crisis last for only 13 days and how was a solution found within that short space of time?

The confrontation between Kennedy and Khrushchev was really about two main issues: first, the USA would not tolerate the installation of more Soviet missiles in Cuba, and second the US government insisted that the Soviet missiles already in Cuba must be removed. In reply Khrushchev made a number of counter-proposals, the most important of which was the suggestion that the two Super-powers should reach a compromise: the Soviet missiles would be removed from Cuba if American missiles – which Khrushchev argued were a threat to Soviet security – were removed from America's European allies, particularly Turkey.

Khrushchev also demanded that the USA should guarantee not to invade Cuba, and never again support any groups of anti-Castro exiles in any attempt to invade the island. This request eventually gave the USSR the chance to save face and paved the way, though only after hours of tension, for the order to remove the missiles from Cuba.

The vital factor in this crisis was that each side had room for manoeuvre. Khrushchev was able to emerge from the crisis with a formal promise from Kennedy not to attack Cuba, and to appear as the man who had saved peace by withdrawing missiles whose installation was perfectly legitimate in international law. Kennedy, on the other hand, achieved the solution he had hoped for when he first set up the blockade – the withdrawal of the threatening missiles at what was really a low price: the American Jupiter missiles which were removed from Turkey were obsolete and Kennedy had already ordered their removal before the crisis developed.

Questions

1. How did the Soviet leader reply to President Kennedy's demand for the withdrawal of the Soviet missiles?
2. 'Each side had room for manoeuvre': explain the meaning of this phrase with reference to the

agreements made by the USA and USSR to end the crisis.
3. Why might President Kennedy be considered to have come out of the crisis in a stronger position than the Soviet leader?

THE SIGNIFICANCE OF CUBA

The world had survived the 'eyeball to eyeball' confrontation which had brought it so close to nuclear war. The American Secretary of State, Dean Rusk, is reported to have said, 'We looked into the mouth of the cannon. The Russians flinched.' Whether you agree with this summing up of the situation or not, the Cuban missile crisis was undoubtedly the nearest the two Superpowers have come to direct 'hot war' since 1945. The crisis developed very quickly and almost as suddenly it was over and slipped from the headlines, yet it did have a considerable effect on the course of the Cold War.

Before Cuba, the rivalry between the USA and the USSR had been the major factor in their foreign policies. As a result of the Cuban crisis, the two Superpowers were forced to recognise that the Cold War was a very delicate situation which might erupt very quickly into all-out nuclear war as a result of one misunderstanding. Having balanced precariously on the edge of destruction, they were forced to think about ways of making sure that a similar crisis did not occur again. The hot-line telephone link between Washington and Moscow was the first step towards improved Soviet–American relations.

The two Superpowers also took a step towards slowing down the pace of the potentially disastrous arms race in 1963 by signing the Moscow Test-Ban Treaty which banned the testing of nuclear weapons in the air or under water. This was the first of several agreements made between the Superpowers and other nations to try to reduce the likelihood of nuclear war breaking out.

'Cuba' shocked the two most powerful countries in the world into taking the first faltering steps along the road to better understanding of each other's position, and although there are still many differences between them today, the importance of the missile crisis should not be underestimated.

Questions

1. Why is the Cuban crisis described as an 'eyeball to eyeball' confrontation?
2. Explain why the crisis forced the Superpowers to make changes in their attitudes to one another.
3. Why might the 'hot-line' telephone link be considered an important development in Soviet–American relations?
4. What effect did the missile crisis have on the arms race?

CUBA TODAY

In 1984 Cuba celebrated the twenty-fifth anniversary of its revolution which brought Fidel Castro to power. What has 25 years of communist rule meant for the people of Cuba? How much progress has the country made since 1959? And how has Cuba managed to survive for so long as a communist state so near to the USA with its open hostility to communism?

Many of the improvements in the standard of living have been spectacular. By comparison with western countries, Cuba still appears to be economically backward. Consumer goods such as refrigerators and washing machines are only available to a few people and are very expensive. The average wage is only about $1000 a year. Yet this is not the most realistic way of judging the progress of Cuba. The fairest way of doing this is to compare present-day Cuba with other **developing countries** and with Cuba before 1959. As Table 3

Table 3 Improvements in Cuba's standard of living

1958	1984
Poor health facilities	Free health service for all Cubans 1 doctor for every 626 people
Malnutrition and infectious diseases widespread	All major 'Third World diseases' now wiped out (e.g. polio, malaria, diptheria)
Life expectancy 58 years	Life expectancy 73.5 years (similar to developed countries)
Infant mortality 7 per cent (i.e. 7 deaths per 100 live births)	Infant mortality 0.2 per cent (i.e. 2 deaths per 1000 live births)
Half of Cuba's children received no education	Free education for all. Educational spending 17.5 times greater than in 1958
1 million illiterate Cubans 1 million semi-illiterates	Literacy rate 96 per cent, one of the highest in the world
Many areas of slum housing	Few slum areas No beggars

shows, improvements in health-care, nutrition, education and housing standards have been remarkable.

Few other developing countries can claim such progress in recent years. In his speech to mark the twenty-fifth anniversary of the revolution, Castro declared Cuba to be the second best-fed country in Latin America, after Argentina. Indeed, Cuban doctors are becoming increasingly concerned about diseases resulting from smoking, fatty diets and lack of exercise: all common in countries with advanced economies.

How has Cuba achieved such progress? Without doubt, one of the main reasons has been the support received from the Soviet Union throughout these years. Cuba has become increasingly dependent on Soviet trade and financial help. In 1958 Cuba sold 55 per cent of its sugar crop to the United States, but by 1980 the Soviet Union bought 68 per cent of the annual crop at prices well above world market prices. Since joining **Comecon**, the Eastern bloc trade alliance, in 1972, Cuba has become very dependent on these countries for the supplying of goods and the purchase of Cuban sugar which remains its most important single product. It is now estimated that Soviet aid to Cuba amounts to about $4 billion every year, about half of the USSR's total foreign aid. Without this support, conditions in modern Cuba would be quite different.

As well as economic and financial links with the Soviet Union, Cuba has strong military links with Moscow. The regular Cuban army, with 150 000 troops, is dependent on Soviet equipment and a subsidy now estimated at $950 million every year. Castro is proud of the fact that some 70 000 Cubans are at work in 35 countries in Africa, Asia and Latin America as doctors, teachers, engineers and advisers. But the majority of these are Cuban soldiers who are doing jobs on behalf of the Soviet Union. It is estimated, for example, that there are 35 000

Table 4 Problems in modern Cuba

Huge foreign debts: $3.2 billion owed to Western banks, $9 billion to the Soviet Union and the Eastern bloc
Trade deficit of $700 million a year; still relies heavily on sugar exports
Strict food rationing: e.g. 1 kg of meat per month, 60 g of coffee every two weeks
Shortages of consumer goods
Over-reliance on Soviet aid
Concern about diseases resulting from smoking, fatty diets and lack of exercise

CASTRO ON SOVIET UNION

'Our revolution is a truly autonomous one. But it was fortunate for us that the Soviet Union existed. We would not have been able to survive if we had not found a market for our sugar, if we had no access to fuel and oil supplies for our country, if we had not access to a supply of weapons which we needed for defense against the threat of invasion, as in the Bay of Pigs, against assassination plots and sabotage. I'm not concerned with statements by Reagan, he's a total liar. It's a traditional charge. We have no puppet complex whatsoever. The Soviets do not have a single property in Cuba. There are mutual relationships and influences, but they are as independent from us as we are independent from them.' (*From an interview with Newsweek*)

(*Soviet Weekly*, February 1984)

Cuban soldiers in Angola helping the government against guerrilla troops backed by the West. Cuba has supported Soviet foreign policy on every issue in recent years, including Ethiopia and Afghanistan, even although this has lost Castro the friendship of some developing countries.

With such help from the Soviet Union, Cuba has felt safe from any possible military moves by the USA and has carried out a policy of offering protection and aid to other Latin American countries against US attempts to undermine them. This policy received a set-back in 1983 when the United States invaded Grenada, showing that Cuba was not powerful enough to guarantee the survival of revolutionary movements in the face of US military power. Nevertheless, Cuba remains an important military power in the Caribbean area.

Questions

1. Describe the improvements in health and education which have been made in Cuba during the last 25 years.
2. Compare these improvements with developments in other developing countries.
3. Describe the role played by the Soviet Union in Cuban affairs.
4. What are the major problems facing modern Cuba?

3. Indirect Confrontation

In certain crises and world trouble-spots the Superpowers confront each other indirectly. Instead of confronting each other face to face, one provides military and economic support to an ally, against an ally of the other. Sometimes even troops are supplied. Although the Superpowers are not in direct confrontation, there is always the danger of **escalation** into a major conflict which would involve the Superpowers directly.

Examples of such indirect confrontation are the Vietnam War, the conflict in the Middle East and various crises in Africa and in Central America.

War in Vietnam

From 1960 to 1975 the South-East Asian country of Vietnam suffered from a war which, in many respects, was as devastating to that area as the Second World War was to Europe. It has been estimated that a total of 1 800 000 people were

South-East Asia

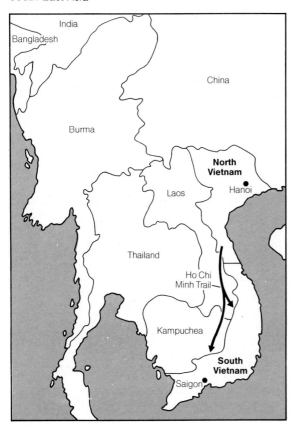

killed, 55 000 of whom were Americans. The war cost the USA some $30 000 million per year. It cost the country of Vietnam terrible devastation and misery.

What was this war all about? Why was the USA involved and to such a large extent? What was the reaction of the USSR and of China to America's involvement? The following case studies describe the war and its impact from different viewpoints. They may help to answer these questions. The people and their stories are fictitious but they are based on fact.

A North Vietnamese Soldier

'My name is Nguyen Thanh Linh. I was born in 1920 in the North Vietnamese city of Hanoi. When I was 16 I joined the Vietminh to fight against the French who were the rulers of my country. **Ho Chi Minh** was our leader. During the Second World War we fought against the Japanese, who had driven out the French to make Vietnam part of their empire. We were bitterly disappointed when after 1945 the French were allowed to return. Again we had to struggle against the French. Finally, in 1954 under the leadership of General Giap, we overwhelmed the French at the Battle of Dien Bien Phu and forced them to leave our country. However Vietnam was not to become one united independent country for it was divided into two, with only the North under Ho Chi Minh's control. The government of the South refused to hold the elections which were supposed to decide the future of our country and we were told that a final settlement could only come after another war. I had been injured at Dien Bien Phu and could no longer fight but I worked in Hanoi.

We knew that the South was being helped by the USA and we learned of the growing number of American soldiers in Vietnam. We were helped by our comrades in China and in the USSR who supplied us with weapons and equipment.

In 1964 the Americans began to bomb our cities in the North. This bombing was to continue for the next ten years. I remember the fear caused by the huge American B-52 bombers. They flew too high to be seen or heard. If there had been no air-raid warning you would have known nothing until the bombs began to drop. But, despite the bombing, we were determined never to give in. Children and our old were evacuated into the

A one-person air-raid shelter in Hanoi

countryside and industry was spread around all over the country. We carried nearly everything on bicycles. Each street in the city had its own one-person air-raid shelters. The bombing only made us more determined to win. We almost broke through during the Tet Offensive in 1968 and again in 1972 when we fought our way well into the South. The bravery of our people, who refused to be beaten by the American bombers, and the fighting courage of our soldiers convinced the Americans that they could not win and they agreed to our terms and left Vietnam in 1973.

Our country was still divided and the war was not over. In 1975, without their American protectors, the government of the South collapsed before our victorious armies and the people of the South, freed from their government's control, welcomed us as liberators. Now that the war is over we must rebuild our country.'

Questions

1. With reference to Thanh Linh's military career, outline the main events in the history of Vietnam up to 1954.
2. What happened to Vietnam after the Battle of Dien Bien Phu?
3. Who became the leader of North Vietnam?
4. Why did the government of North Vietnam believe the war would have to continue?
5. In what ways were the major powers involved in the war?
6. How did the people of North Vietnam react to the American bombing of their country?
7. What happened in 1973 and 1975 in Vietnam?

A South Vietnamese Businessman

'My name is Pham Van Troi. I was born in 1927 in the South Vietnamese city of Saigon. My parents were wealthy as my father owned a small business. We were Roman Catholic although most people in my country are Buddhist. I remember many French people coming to our house when I was young but life was terrible under the Japanese. My father was killed by them and when the French returned I was too busy building up my business to get involved in politics. After the French left in 1954 I did not want to see Ho Chi Minh and the communists take over so I supported the government of Ngo Dinh Diem. When he was overthrown, I supported President Thieu. During those years my business prospered because of all the dollars brought into Vietnam by the American soldiers and airmen. But in other ways life was growing more difficult and unpleasant. There were large areas of the South where you could not go because of the fighting and also because of the **Vietcong**. Life was dangerous even in Saigon because of them.

When the North almost broke through in 1968 and in 1972 I thought the South was finished. I knew when the Americans pulled out in 1973 that it was going to be difficult for the South to survive. But when the American Congress refused to allow President Ford the money to help us during the fighting of 1975 I knew the end was near. I arranged for myself and family to leave Vietnam and we were lucky to get to America. I know of many families who left it too late. Those who had supported the government of the South are now being 're-educated'.

My city of Saigon is now called Ho Chi Minh City. I doubt if I will ever see it again.'

Questions

1. Why did Van Troi not want Ho Chi Minh to take over South Vietnam after 1954?
2. Who were the leaders of South Vietnam?
3. How did businessmen like Van Troi benefit from the war?
4. How else did the war affect people in South Vietnam?
5. Why did Van Troi leave Vietnam in 1975?

A Member of the Vietcong

'My name is Truong Bien Tu. I was born in 1950 in a small village near the South Vietnamese city of Hue. My parents were peasants and as children we helped in the fields around our village. When I was 16 our village was taken over by American soldiers and we were taken to a special camp. We were told this was to protect us from the Vietcong. We later found out that our village and fields were destroyed to stop the Vietcong from using them. My family had lived in that village for generations and our house and fields were our only possessions. I hated the American soldiers for that.

Life in the camp was very bad. Conditions were terrible. In 1968, when the soldiers from the North captured Hue, I left the camp and joined the Vietcong. With the Vietcong I learned how to fight and how to live among the peasants so that the Americans would never know that I was one of the Vietcong. Twice I helped bring weapons from the North into the South along the Ho Chi Minh Trail. I found out the terrible destruction that had been done to my country. Large areas of forest had been stripped of their leaves. I was told the Americans sprayed these forests with chemicals in order to destroy our cover. I also saw many villages and fields destroyed. Every time the Americans increased their destruction of our land, more and more young men and women would rally to our side to join us in our fight for freedom. I remember how in 1975 we joined with the soldiers from the North and marched in victory into Saigon. Now that the fighting is over, I have gone back to where my village stood to help rebuild my area. Because I was in the Vietcong, I have been made the political leader of my village.'

A South Vietnamese soldier

Questions

1. Explain how Bien Tu came to join the Vietcong.
2. What did he do as a member of the Vietcong?
3. What reason does he give for the support given to the Vietcong?
4. What is the term used to describe fighting groups like the Vietcong?
5. Read the three Vietnamese case studies again and describe their differing experiences and attitudes to the war.

American Ex-GI and Vietnam Veteran

'My name is Robert Hall. I was born in 1946 and brought up in a small town in Michigan, USA. When I left high school I was called up for the army – drafted we call it. I was proud to be in the army and was sent to Vietnam in 1965. That was just before the real build-up of our boys there. I'm told that by 1968 there were over half a million of us there. I lost two of my best friends in Vietnam but we felt that their sacrifice was worthwhile. Somebody had to help the South Vietnamese make a stand against communism. North Vietnam was backed right down the line by China

The Domino Theory

and Russia so we had to help the South. Also if South Vietnam fell which country would be next? We had heard about the **Domino Theory**.

I was in Vietnam till 1967 and during that time most of the action we saw was in flushing out the Vietcong – VCs or 'gooks' we called them. Some of them were only kids but they were killers. This was the problem with guerrilla warfare – you never knew who was a Vietcong and who was an ordinary peasant. Trust none of them was my motto. Sometimes we worked from helicopters – it used to be exciting to see the VCs run from their cover when we flushed them out. In your helicopter armed with machine-guns it was easy to knock them out. The one thing I didn't like was napalm – I once saw a Vietnamese kid who had been caught during a raid and had been burned by it – horrible.

The other thing I didn't like was when I got home and saw all those long-haired demonstrators condemning the war. I feel if your government asks you to fight you've got to be patriotic.

I'm sorry about what happened since – we seemed to lose our nerve and look what happened. Not only did South Vietnam fall to the commies but so did Cambodia and Laos. I told you about the Domino Theory. It makes it seem as though everything was wasted.'

Questions

1. What was the maximum number of American soldiers fighting in Vietnam?
2. How does Robert Hall explain and justify American involvement in the Vietnam War? You will need to explain the reference to the Domino Theory.
3. Describe the kind of fighting Robert Hall was involved in during his period in Vietnam.
4. What is Robert Hall's attitude to events in Vietnam and elsewhere in South-East Asia since America withdrew?

The effect of defoliation in Vietnam

American Draft Dodger

'My name is John Lacey. I was born in 1945 and brought up in New York. I left America in 1967 just after leaving college. I did this to avoid being drafted. I went to Canada and then to Sweden where I lived till there was an amnesty for draft dodgers which let me return to the USA.

Was I a coward? Did I let my country down? In one way I was a coward for I left rather than go to jail for my refusal to join the army. But I wasn't afraid to fight. I refused to serve in Vietnam because we had no right to be there. We only brought untold suffering and destruction to that country. We acted like the bully of the world and used all our vast military might against a small nation of peasants.

Some people might say that I was not in a position to judge what was happening in Vietnam. However, there were many war veterans who hated the war just as much as I did. They

saw the injustices at first hand and they condemned the war too.

I'm very bitter about our government's actions. They lied to justify their actions and while they spent millions on bombing North Vietnam the problems in the ghettoes of our big cities grew worse and worse. The Vietnam War has left a deep scar on my country.'

Questions

1. What happened to John Lacey during the period of the Vietnam War?
2. Describe his attitude to his country's involvement in Vietnam and outline the reasons he gives for this attitude.
3. How do the two American case studies show the divisions of the USA caused by the war?

A South Vietnamese woman
begs a US sergeant to
save her blazing home

An anti-Vietnam War demonstration in the USA

Year	Vietnam	USA
1954	Battle of Dien Bien Phu End of French rule	
1955	Geneva Conference leads to splitting of Vietnam into North Vietnam (communist) South Vietnam (non-communist)	President Eisenhower agrees to USA aid for South Vietnam
1959		President Kennedy sends first American military 'advisers' to Vietnam
1960	Ngo Dinh Diem becomes Prime Minister of South Vietnam	
1961	Beginning of Vietnam War	American military in Vietnam number over 15 000
1962	Growing civil unrest in South Vietcong increase in number	
1963	Ngo Dinh Diem assassinated	**Lyndon Johnson** becomes President after assassination of Kennedy
1964	Gulf of Tonking naval clash	Gulf of Tonking Resolution gives Johnson full control over war effort – marks start of major US military 'escalation' in Vietnam. Beginning of US bombing in North Vietnam
1967	Nguygen Van Thieu becomes President of South Vietnam	Half a million American soldiers in Vietnam
Jan 1968	'Tet Offensive' – heavy communist attack on South	
April 1968		President Johnson announces he will not stand for re-election Bombing of North Vietnam halted
Nov 1968		**Nixon** elected President
Jan 1969	Beginning of peace talks in Paris	
June 1969		Nixon announces that he will begin to pull out US troops from Vietnam
Sept 1969	Ho Chi Minh dies	
April 1970		American troops enter Cambodia
1971		The USA renews bombing of North Vietnam
April 1972	Major North Vietnamese offensive against the South	American bombing of North Vietnam becomes intensive Port of Haiphong mined
Jan 1973	Ceasefire eventually agreed	In return for release of all American prisoners of war Nixon withdraws all American forces and bases
April 1975	Major North Vietnamese offensive against the South Cambodia falls to communist Khmer Rouge forces South Vietnamese government surrenders after fall of Saigon	

AFTER THE WAR

Vietnam Today

Years of war obviously left great scars on Vietnam. After re-unification the new communist government had to tackle the major task of 'reconstruction'. The expansion of agriculture to overcome the shortage of foodstuffs became a priority. 'New econonomic zones' were set up to restore agriculture in those areas which had been devastated by the war. In the south land was taken from private landlords and put into state ownership. During the war years many people in the south had fled to Saigon and other cities for safety. The new government moved large numbers of people from the towns into the country-side to help agriculture.

There have also been major political changes, especially in the south. Those who had supported the Americans and the government in the south before re-unification were made political prisoners and taken to special camps for 're-education'. The economic and political changes have driven many southern Vietnamese to flee their country and seek refuge abroad. These refugees have become known as 'the boat people'.

Vietnam has developed very close ties with the USSR with whom it has formed an alliance. The USSR supplies Vietnam with most of its foreign aid and regards it as a close friend in South-East Asia. Within Indochina, Vietnam has come to dominate its two neighbours, Laos and Kampuchea (formerly Cambodia). In 1978 Vietnam invaded Kampuchea and set up a pro-Vietnamese government. China saw this as a means of extending Soviet influence in the area, and in 1979 invaded north Vietnam to 'teach it a lesson'. The Chinese forces remained in Vietnam for about one month and then pulled back. Since then relations with China have remained cool, although no new fighting has broken out.

The Vietnam Factor in US Foreign Policy

The war in Vietnam had, for a period, a marked effect on American foreign policy. Since 1947 the USA had been dominated by the fear of commun-ism spreading throughout the world. This led America into forming a world-wide system of al-liances and intervening throughout the world to protect the 'free world' from communism. It also led it into defending the governments of unpopular and often corrupt dictatorships. Following the failure in Vietnam, American politicians re-examined their country's role as 'world policeman' and proposed a less interventionist role for the USA. President **Carter** summed this up in 1977 thus: 'We are now free of that inordinate fear of communism which once led us to embrace any dictator who joined our fear. This approach has failed – with Vietnam the best example of its intellectual and moral poverty.'

Foreign policy under President **Reagan** has moved back to a more traditional pattern with the USA being prepared to use its power to intervene to stop 'the spread of communism'. This change of policy became noticeable in American policy to-wards Central America, although a full-scale inter-vention there has not been encouraged for 'fear of another Vietnam'.

Questions

1. What economic and political changes have taken place in Vietnam since re-unification?
2. What role has Vietnam played in South-East Asia and why has this brought it into conflict with China?
3. What short-term and long-term effects has the Vietnam War had on US foreign policy?

Conflict in the Middle East

The Middle East has been a major area of conflict for centuries. Since the end of the Second World War and the founding of the new state of Israel in 1948, there has been renewed hostility between the Arab and Jewish people in this area.

But other major conflicts have also taken place. In this unit we shall look at two of these – the Gulf War between Iran and Iraq, and the Soviet invasion of Afghanistan – in addition to the Arab–Israeli con-flict. These three areas of confrontation have one thing in common: indirect involvement by the two major Superpowers which has developed at some stage into direct involvement, or the threat of direct involvement, by one or the other.

ARAB v. ISRAELI: THE PROBLEMS

The main cause of the conflict in the Middle East is the refusal of the Arab countries to accept Israel's right to exist. Until President **Anwar Sadat**'s visit to Jerusalem in 1977, not one Arab country had recognised officially that Israel existed. The reason for this lies in the way in which the state of Israel was set up in 1948.

For centuries the Jews had been scattered throughout the world. Many millions of Jews set up home in Europe and in the USA, but many held on to the dream of returning one day to their homeland in the Middle East. During the First World War Britain captured Palestine from Turkey and was given the task of looking after it for a period of 30 years and for making arrangements for the setting up of a Jewish homeland in the area. In the 1920s and 1930s thousands of Jews settled in Palestine, looking forward to the day when the homeland would be a reality. The Arab inhabitants of Palestine did not welcome these new settlers and violent incidents took place.

By 1947 Britain decided that it could no longer accept responsibility for the area – the violence had increased – and the problem was handed over to the United Nations, which appeared to be the most suitable organisation to deal with the problem. The UN drew up a plan to partition or divide Palestine. The new state of Israel which was established in 1948 included parts of Palestine: in the north-east, on the coast and in the south. The remainder of Palestine was divided among the neighbouring Arab countries. Not surprisingly, the Palestinian Arabs were opposed to the new state and went to war with Israel. As we shall see, the problem of the Palestinian Arab refugees who fled from the area is the biggest obstacle to peace, even today.

KEY

UN Zones

Areas occupied by Israeli forces since 1967 war:

1 Sinai Peninsula (returned to Egypt, April 1983)
2 West Bank of R. Jordan
3 Golan Heights

▲ Jewish settlements
★ PLO command posts
➤ Syrian missile batteries

Lebanon
Beirut
Sidon
Tyre
Syria
Tel Aviv
Mediterranean Sea
Amman
Jerusalem
Gaza Strip
ISRAEL
Jordan
Egypt
Sinai Peninsula
Saudi Arabia
Gulf of Suez
Red Sea

The Middle East, 1983–4

Questions

1. Why do many Arab countries refuse to recognise Israel's right to exist?
2. Explain why the UN was given the task of dividing Palestine.
3. What happened to Palestine as a result of the partition plan?
4. How did the Arab people react to the partition?

WAR IN THE MIDDLE EAST

Full-scale war in the Middle East has erupted five times since 1948.

1948–9: the First Middle East War

On the very first day that the new state of Israel came into existence in May 1948, Arab armies invaded from the north, south and east. The new Israeli forces fought fiercely and captured much of the land that had been allocated to the Arab countries in the United Nations partition plan. By 1949 the Arab countries were forced to admit defeat, although the agreement which ended this outbreak of war was only a ceasefire, not a full peace settlement. This was a remarkable defeat for the forces of Egypt, Jordan, Lebanon and Syria at the hands of the infant Israeli nation.

1956: the Suez Canal Crisis

War broke out again in 1956, but this time the war was not a simple one of Arab versus Israeli. This time British and French forces became involved. The crisis began when President Nasser of Egypt nationalised the Suez Canal, a vital communications link for the countries of Western Europe, in retaliation for the withdrawal of American financial support for the Aswan Dam project in Egypt. Britain and France made a secret agreement with Israel to launch a joint attack on Egypt. When Israel attacked in October 1956 and quickly captured the whole of the Sinai Peninsula, British and French forces attacked Egypt, supposedly to separate the Israeli and Egyptian armies and keep the Suez Canal open as an international waterway.

After the intervention of the UN, Britain and France withdrew, and the Israeli forces left Sinai. A United Nations Emergency Force was sent to preserve peace in the area by placing itself between the Egyptian and Israeli forces.

1967: the Six-Day War

After 11 years of uneasy peace, President Nasser demanded that the UN peacekeeping force in Sinai should be withdrawn in May 1967. When this was done, Egyptian troops moved into positions near the Israeli army. To complicate matters, Syria believed that it was about to be attacked by Israel.

Tension between Israel and its Arab neighbours grew daily until the Israeli government, deciding that attack was the most effective form of defence, launched a sudden attack on Egypt. Within a few days the Egyptian air force was destroyed, and in quick succession the armies of Egypt, Jordan and Syria were defeated. As a result, Israel captured the Sinai Peninsula from Egypt, a large stretch of Jordanian territory along the West Bank area of the River Jordan, and the Golan Heights, which were of great strategic value, from Syria. In the short space of six days, Israel had heavily defeated its three powerful Arab neighbours.

1973–4: the Yom Kippur War

Full-scale war broke out again in October 1973, when Arab forces, now re-equipped with modern Soviet weapons, attacked on the Egyptian and Syrian fronts. Again the Israelis, with American help, captured territory from Syria and even crossed the Suez Canal into Egypt. The UN eventually managed to persuade the two sides to agree to a ceasefire in December 1973, and once more a UN Emergency Force of some 7000 men went to act as a buffer

between the opposing armies. By May 1974 both Egypt and Syria agreed to withdraw their troops from the battle lines, and since 1974 faltering attempts have been made to try to find a lasting solution to the Middle East problem through the Peace Conference on the Middle East, meeting in Geneva.

1982: War in Lebanon

When Israel's ambassador to Britain, Shlomo Argov, was shot in London in June 1982 by an Arab student, reprisals were expected. When they came, they were sudden and overwhelming. Within hours of the shooting, the Israeli Air Force bombed PLO strongholds in Beirut, signalling the start of Israel's biggest military operation since the Yom Kippur War. The aim was to destroy, once and for all, the PLO, an estimated 6000 of whom had found refuge in Lebanon and used it as a base from which to launch terrorist attacks on Israel.

Israel claimed that in spite of the invasion it had no ambition to expand permanently into Lebanon. What it sought was the elimination of the terrorist threat, and the setting up of a strong and stable Lebanese government. It also wanted the protection of a 40-kilometre-wide buffer zone policed by an international peacekeeping force. While most of its western allies (including the USA and Britain) agreed with Israel's long-term aim to preserve its own security, they criticised the methods used, in particular the high civilian casualty rate and the Israelis' apparent lack of humanitarianism.

But these outbreaks of war, which cost a great deal in lives and money, do not tell the complete story of the Arab–Israeli conflict. There has never been real peace in the Middle East since 1948. The periods in between the wars have seen many terrorist attacks, border raids, bombings and hi-jackings which have caused much damage and taken a terrible toll of human lives.

Questions

1. How many outbreaks of war have occurred in the Middle East and when did they happen?
2. What territorial changes have resulted from these wars?
3. When and how have the Superpowers been involved in the Middle East wars?
4. What was the outcome of the latest in the series of wars?
5. Describe the other outbreaks of violence which have happened in the Middle East.

LEBANON: A CASE STUDY

The Background

Lebanon became an independent country in 1943 and was relatively free from war until the 1970s, by which time its capital, Beirut, had become the financial and commercial centre of the Middle East. After Israel was set up in 1948 many Palestinian refugees fled to Lebanon and in the 1970s PLO guerrilla groups expelled from Jordan also arrived. But the presence of the Palestinians was only one complication in a country which contained many different rival groups or factions (*see* Who's Who in Lebanon?).

In 1975–6 a bitter civil war was fought between the Christians and the National Movement, a coalition of Muslim and Palestinian groups. After intense fighting, a ceasefire agreement was reached in October 1976 and a large Syrian force arrived to supervise the agreement, thus adding yet another group to the already complicated situation in Lebanon. From 1979 to 1982 Major Saad Haddad and his followers maintained an 1100-square-kilometre area of 'independent free Lebanon' with Israeli support in the southern part of the country.

Lebanon

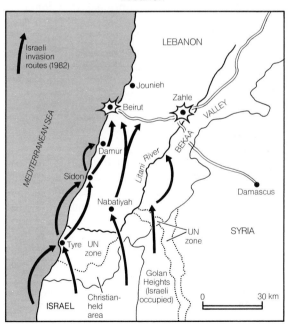

Who's Who in Lebanon?

Lebanese Army: Weakened by the civil war and not a strong fighting force but since 1983 has increased in strength as a result of heavy recruitment, American arms and training. Most of its officers are Christians and ordinary soldiers are mainly Muslim.

Shia Muslims: The largest (1.1 million) group in Lebanon, but also the poorest and least represented in government. Traditional home is the Bekàa Valley and southern Lebanon but many now live in and around Beirut. They want a greater share of power and wealth.

Amal: The defence force of the Shia Muslims. It is very militant and controls the southern suburbs of Beirut. It is split internally, however, some groups being pro-Syria and some pro-Soviet Union.

Druze Muslims: A group of about 200 000 who have splintered from the Shia Muslims and live mainly in the Chouf mountains, south-east of Beirut. The Druze have a long history of being tough mountain warriors and have little say in the political system. Led by Walid Jumblatt, they too want a greater share of political power. The Druze Militia, about 5000 soldiers, is heavily armed by Syria but has also received weapons from Israel, and controls the Chouf mountain area.

Sunni Muslims: A community of about 750 000 who are followers of mainstream Islam and live mainly in the cities, e.g. Tripoli and Beirut. They are powerful in Lebanese politics and the post of Prime Minister is usually filled by a Sunni Muslim in agreement with the Christians. The other Muslim groups distrust the Sunnis.

Maronite Christians: The largest (900 000) Christian group in Lebanon. They have been very powerful in government and were largely responsible for building up the wealth of Lebanon, and acquiring wealth themselves in the process. Not always a united group, the Phalange Party led by the Gemayel family defeated rival Christian groups in 1975–6 to emerge as powerful leaders of the community. Amin Gemayel is President of Lebanon.

Phalange Militia: This group of 10 000–15 000 troops was formed to maintain Christian supremacy by President Gemayel's brother. From 1976 it received weapons and training from Israel. It was thought to be responsible for the massacre of hundreds of Palestinian refugees in the camps at Sabra and Chatilla in 1982. It was defeated by the Druze in its attempts to control the Chouf mountains but is still powerful and difficult to bring under control.

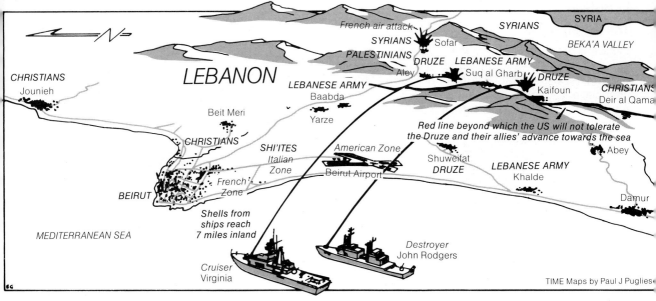

Labels on map:
French air attack
SYRIANS
SYRIA
SYRIANS
BEKA'A VALLEY
PALESTINIANS
Sofar
DRUZE
LEBANESE ARMY
CHRISTIANS
Jounieh
LEBANESE ARMY
Aley
Suq al Gharb
DRUZE
CHRISTIANS
Deir al Qama
LEBANON
Baabda
Kaifoun
Beit Meri
Yarze
Red line beyond which the US will not tolerate
the Druze and their allies' advance towards the sea
CHRISTIANS
SHI'ITES
Italian
Zone
American Zone
Shuweifat
DRUZE
Abey
LEBANESE ARMY
Khalde
French
Zone
Beirut Airport
BEIRUT
Damur
Shells from
ships reach
7 miles inland
MEDITERRANEAN SEA
Destroyer
John Rodgers
Cruiser
Virginia
TIME Maps by Paul J Puglies

Positions in Lebanon

The Multinational Peacekeeping Force

Size		Tasks	
	FRANCE 2000	Tasks	To bring stability
	ITALY 2100		to Lebanon, work
	USA 1200		towards a
	UK 100		ceasefire and
			reduce tensions
			so that Lebanon
			can return to
			peace.

Problems

Difficult to appear neutral. American force increasingly seen as helping the Christians because it supported the Lebanese army which is largely Christian. As a result, suicide attacks on French and US military headquarters killed 56 French and 230 American soldiers and marines in October 1983. This followed the destruction of the US embassy in Beirut in April 1983, killing 62 Americans. Responsibility for the attacks was claimed by the Free Islamic Revolutionary Movement. Syrian and/or Iranian forces were suspected of giving assistance in the attacks.

Chances of success

Very slim because of the very complicated situation in Lebanon. In late 1983 and early 1984 there were demands in Britain and the USA for the withdrawal of the peacekeeping force. All four countries had withdrawn their troops by March 1984. A UN peacekeeping force was suggested as a replacement, but UN troops had been in Lebanon for years and were powerless to stop Palestinian guerrilla activity and the 1982 Israeli invasion.

The Prospects for Lebanon

In spite of a partial withdrawal of Israeli troops, the prospects for a peaceful, long-lasting solution to the problems of Lebanon are not good. Quarrelling among the many different factions is likely to continue. In addition, the continued interest of Syria in the area and Syria's opposition to the Lebanese government and its attempts to reach agreement with Israel can only lead to continued instability.

THE PALESTINIANS

One of the saddest problems of the Middle East and one of the biggest obstacles to any peace settlement is the fate of the Palestinians. They are the three to four million Arab people made stateless and scattered throughout the Middle East during the fighting of the last 30 years. One million of them live in the Israeli-occupied territories of the West Bank and Gaza Strip, another million live in East Jordan.

Since 1967 the Palestinian Liberation Organisation has developed as the most important voice of these people. The PLO, under the leadership of **Yasser Arafat**, wants to replace the state of Israel by a new democratic state in which the Palestinian Arabs and some of the Israelis presently living in Israel would live together and have equal rights. But the PLO is divided on how the Palestinians should achieve these rights. Some groups have said they are prepared to settle in the short term for a

The Superpowers in Lebanon

Palestinian mini-state bordering Israel on the West Bank and the Gaza Strip. Others refuse any compromise with Israel; indeed, they refuse even to recognise that Israel has any right to exist as a nation.

As far as the Israeli attitude towards the Palestinians is concerned, there are two basic problems. In the first place the creation of a mini-Palestine as a new state is not acceptable to Israel, which says that a solution to the Palestinian problem must be achieved within a general peace settlement. Secondly, although many Israeli officials agree that the Palestinians should eventually be involved in any peace talks, they insist that the PLO must be excluded. They are not prepared to talk about peace in the Middle East at the same table as the PLO, who have caused much death and destruction in their terrorist attacks in Israel.

In November 1974 the General Assembly of the UN adopted a resolution recognising 'the inalienable rights of the Palestinian people in Palestine' to national independence and sovereignty. It repeated the right of the Palestinians to return to their homes and property, and recognised them as one of the most important groups involved in the setting up of a just and lasting peace. For the first time the PLO was invited to take part in the sessions and work of the UN General Assembly as an observer.

In the 1980s, however, the problems of the Palestinians, and the PLO in particular, have increased. By allowing the Lebanese Christian militia into areas where there were Palestinian refugees, Israel was partly responsible for the massacre of hundreds of refugees in the camps of Sabra and Chatila. The Israelis also arrested thousands of Palestinians and kept them under detention during the war in Lebanon.

Following the 1982 invasion of Lebanon, the PLO forces were dispersed into neighbouring Arab countries including Syria, Jordan, Sudan and Tunisia. By late 1983 divisions within the PLO and opposition to Yasser Arafat had become major issues. Yasser Arafat and about 4000 of his followers were then evacuated from Tripoli, where he had set up his new headquarters after being besieged by a Syrian-backed PLO faction and shelled by the Israeli navy. He went to Egypt where he found support from President **Hosni Mubarak**.

Yasser Arafat, head of the PLO at the UN General Assembly in 1974

Questions

1. Who are the Palestinians?
2. What are the political aims of the PLO?
3. Describe Israel's attitude to the PLO and its policies.
4. What evidence is there to suggest that the PLO became more accepted as the official representative of the Palestinians in the 1970s?
5. Describe what has happened to the PLO since the Israeli invasion of Lebanon in 1982.

Table 5 Middle East peace plans and the Palestinians, 1979–82

Proposals for:	Camp David 1979	Saudi Plan 1981	Fez Plan 1982	Reagan Plan 1982
West Bank and Gaza	Within a month of Treaty being ratified, negotiations to begin on Palestinian 'autonomy'. Elections to appoint a self-governing authority: Israeli withdrawal over a five-year period. Talks in abeyance since mid-1982	Israeli withdrawal. UN control for a period of a few months. The establishment of an independent Palestinian state with Jerusalem as capital.	Based on Saudi plan; reports spoke of a call for a 'mini-state' under PLO, which would have a 'guiding role'. UN forces as peacekeepers.	Palestinians to be given complete autonomy 'in association with Jordan'. Opposition to further Israeli settlements. No mention of PLO, or independent state. King Hussein speaks of Jordanian–Palestinian 'federation'.
Jerusalem		Key role as capital of independent state.		Reagan rules out division of Jerusalem.
Sinai	Israeli withdrawal in three years. UN peacekeeping force to be set up in buffer zone.	As elsewhere, immediate Israeli withdrawal required.	*Israeli withdrawal completed April 1982.*	
Recognition of Israel	Recognition of Egyptian and Israeli territorial integrity and rights to live in peace.	Confirmation of right of all countries of the region to live in peace.	As in 'Saudi plan'.	Israel's security to be guaranteed by the US.

Source: 'The Palestinians'. Report No. 24. Fourth Edition published by the Minority Rights Group Ltd, Benjamin Franklin House, 36 Craven Street, London WC2N 5NG.

Arab SAM missile near the town of Suez

Israeli troops advance on the Golan Heights

TERRORIST MOVEMENTS

Of all the guerrilla groups involved in the Middle East conflict, the one which has caused most death and destruction is the Palestinian 'Black September' movement.

In September 1972 eight terrorists forced their way into the Olympic village in Munich during the Olympic Games, took 11 Israeli athletes hostage, and demanded that the Israeli government release 200 imprisoned Palestinians and that the West German government should grant them safe conduct to an unnamed Arab country. An attempt by the West German police to free the hostages resulted in a bloodbath in which 17 people died, including all the hostages and five of the terrorists.

The President of West Germany, speaking at the funeral service in the Olympic stadium, asked:

'Who is responsible for this black deed? In the forefront is a criminal organisation which believes in hatred and murder as political weapons.'

The Palestinian 'Black September' movement is a secret organisation dedicated to attacking Israel by any means at its disposal. They hope that their actions will focus the attention of the world on the plight of the Palestinian refugees.

The Israelis have met the threat of the Arab guerrilla movements with strong measures. The Israeli air force has attacked and destroyed terrorist camps in Syria and Lebanon. These attacks often cause many civilian casualties as the guerrillas' policy is to make their camps in the middle of villages, which provide camouflage and protection. The most spectacular success achieved by the Israelis against terrorists was the raid on Entebbe in 1976, when an Israeli commando force freed the hostages from a hijacked airliner at Entebbe Airport in Uganda. In a raid lasting only 40 minutes, Israeli troops, in three aircraft, freed more than 100 Jewish hostages who had been held for almost a week after their Air France jet was hijacked by Palestinian guerrillas on a flight between Athens and Paris. During the raid, three hostages, one of the Israeli commando leaders and 20 Ugandan soldiers were killed, along with seven of the ten hijackers, and 11 Ugandan air force planes were destroyed. The raid showed that Israel could take swift and effective action against terrorism.

Terrorist violence broke out once more in March 1978, on the eve of Israel Prime Minister **Menachem Begin**'s departure for the Camp David talks in the USA. A Palestinian death squad landed from two dinghies on Israel's Mediterranean coast and hijacked two buses filled with tourists north of Tel Aviv. After a nightmare 50-kilometre journey, during which the terrorists shot wildly at everyone they

Olympic Village, Munich 1972
An Arab guerrilla dictates terms to West German officials

passed, they set fire to one of the buses. In what was the worst terrorist attack in Israel's history nearly 40 people (including four terrorists) died and more than 80 were injured. The attack seemed to have been timed to make sure that the problems of the Palestinians would be at the forefront of the talks between Mr Begin and President Carter. Responsibility for the raid was claimed by Al-Fatah, the special terrorist group within the Palestine Liberation Organisation (PLO), commanded by Yasser Arafat.

During the early 1980s, raids by the PLO on targets in Israel continued from their bases in Lebanon. One of the main reasons why Israel invaded that country in 1982 was to destroy these bases and the PLO headquarters in Beirut. The Israelis hoped to drive the PLO out of Lebanon once and for all.

Questions

1. Describe in your own words the methods used by guerrilla groups like the 'Black September' movement.
2. What do such groups hope to achieve by their actions?
3. How successful has Israel been in standing up to the terrorists?
4. Describe what happened either (a) at the Munich Olympics or (b) at Entebbe.
5. Explain why an Al-Fatah death squad attacked Israel in March 1978.
6. What was the reason for the Israeli invasion of Lebanon in 1982?

THE SUPERPOWERS AND THE MIDDLE EAST

The Middle East conflict cannot be looked upon solely as an example of Cold War confrontation between the USA and the Soviet Union – the deep rivalry between the Arabs and the Israelis is the root of the problem. Yet the Middle East is a very important area in the pattern of Superpower confrontation. The USA and the USSR have been deeply involved in the area since 1947 and have carried their own rivalries over into the conflict through their support of Israel and Egypt.

In this section we are interested in answering two important questions, 'Why are the Superpowers interested in this area?' and 'What is the extent of their involvement?'

Superpower Politics

The United States and the Soviet Union first became involved in the Middle East when they co-operated in producing the UN partition plan for the area. As the influence of Britain, which had been very important in the area, declined, the American and Soviet governments tried to increase their influence. Throughout the 1950s they each tried to fill the 'power vacuum' created by Britain's withdrawal from the area in an attempt to increase their prestige and power.

Their first excuse for getting involved came with the non-acceptance of the new state of Israel by the Arab countries in 1948.

In the 1950s the USA tried to keep Soviet influence out of the area by giving financial and military aid to several Arab nations, including Egypt. The West tried to unite the Arab nations in a defensive alliance against the USSR, but the Baghdad Pact, signed by Turkey, Iran, Pakistan, Iraq and Britain in 1955, actually led to increased Soviet involvement in the area in an attempt to undermine the treaty. As the USA increased its delivery of weapons to the pro-Western governments in Jordan, Lebanon and Iraq, the USSR increased its aid to the two Arab states which most objected to American influence in the Middle East: Egypt and Syria. The USSR gave them aid in the form of loans and military experts to train their armed forces.

In spite of their growing dependence on the Superpowers for aid, however, the Middle East nations did not want to be involved in the Cold War rivalry between the USA and the USSR. Several of the Arab countries, including Egypt, accepted aid from the USSR only reluctantly, and Saudi Arabia remained positively hostile towards communist ideas and influence.

In 1958 the Arab states and Israel voted to ask the UN to arrange the withdrawal of foreign troops from the area in an attempt to remove the Cold War influence, and for a time the influence of the USA and the USSR declined.

'Black Gold'

In the 1960s and 1970s the West's interest in the Middle East increased because of oil. The industrial countries of Europe and North America became very dependent on Middle Eastern oil as a source of power for industry and transport, and were concerned that there should be no outbreaks of war which might interrupt vital supplies. In the early 1960s, the USA invested heavily in the Arab countries of Egypt, Iran, Saudi Arabia and Jordan as well as in Israel. To counter increasing American influence the USSR gave aid to Egypt, Syria and Iraq.

Throughout the 1970s and the 1980s the USA and the Soviet Union have continued to be involved in the conflict between Israel and its Arab neighbours in several ways. Politically, the USA is still a major supporter of Israel, although in recent years American governments have followed a more 'even-handed' policy in the Middle East. This means that they have attempted to work closely both with the Israeli and Arab governments in their attempts to find a solution to the area's problems. Arab leaders such as Mr Mubarak of Egypt have visited the White House to discuss how to bring the conflict between Israel and the Arab countries to an end. The USA has also supported efforts by the Saudi government to produce a peace plan.

The Soviet Union also remains politically involved, mainly through its support of Syria which has become the main Soviet client state in the area. Militarily, both countries are involved in the supply of weapons and the training of troops. During the war in Lebanon, the USA became directly involved for a time when US marines formed part of the multinational peacekeeping force. US navy ships also bombarded Druze positions in the Chouf mountains which were firing on the American marines' positions.

1. How did the Superpowers first become involved in the problems of the Middle East?
2. Explain the meaning of the phrase 'power vacuum'.
3. How successful was the Baghdad Pact?
4. Why did oil become an important factor in the Middle East situation in the 1960s and 1970s?
5. Explain the meaning of the phrase 'even-handed policy'.
6. Describe the extent to which the Superpowers have been involved in this area in the 1980s.

THE SEARCH FOR PEACE

Attempts to find a lasting peaceful solution to the problems of conflict in the Middle East have so far been faltering and largely unsuccessful. Several attempts have been made through the United Nations and by the USA.

A promising attempt to bring the Arab nations and Israel together was the UN-sponsored Peace Conference on the Middle East, set up in Geneva after the 1973 war, chaired by both the USA and the Soviet Union. Unfortunately the conference met for only two days before being temporarily adjourned because Israel was about to hold general elections. The conference has never met since. After the adjournment the then US Secretary of State, **Henry Kissinger**, tried to persuade the different sides to reach agreement by his 'shuttle diplomacy': a series of step by step meetings with the leaders of Israel, Egypt and Syria. By the time Kissinger was succeeded as Secretary of State by Cyrus Vance in 1976, he had done a lot of travelling and talking but a permanent peace settlement still seemed far away.

Resolution 242

A very important factor in the search for peace is Resolution 242, adopted by the UN Security Council in November 1967 after the Six-Day War. This Resolution, which was accepted by all the states concerned in the conflict with the exception of Syria, says that states which captured territory in war cannot be allowed to keep that territory permanently. It also emphasises the need to work for a just and lasting peace along the following guidelines:

● withdrawal of Israeli armed forces from territory occupied in the 1967 war;
● an end to the state of war and respect for and recognition of the sovereignty, territorial rights and political independence of every state in the area and their right to live in peace within secure and recognised boundaries free from threats or acts of force;
● a settlement of the refugee problem.

Unfortunately, although Resolution 242 was accepted by the most important Middle East countries and appeared to be the first step on the path to peace, the countries differed widely in their interpretation of it. The Arab states said that it meant withdrawal by Israel from all occupied territory before peace negotiations could even start. Israel claimed that this withdrawal should come as a result of the negotiations. Resolution 242 was allowed to gather dust.

Recent Peace Proposals

Several attempts have been made in recent years to find a lasting peaceful solution to the conflict in the Middle East (see Table 5). The most important of these was the Camp David Agreement. Following talks at Camp David in the USA between President Carter, Menachem Begin of Israel and Anwar Sadat of Egypt, a peace treaty between Egypt and Israel was signed in Washington in March 1979. It was agreed that the state of war between the two countries was over, that Israel would withdraw its forces from the Sinai peninsula over a three-year period (this was completed by April 1982) and that Egypt and Israel would begin talks aimed at setting up a 'self-governing authority' for the Palestinians of the West Bank and Gaza.

The PLO and most Arab governments condemned this treaty and President Sadat became hated in some parts of the Arab world. In October 1981 he was assassinated in Cairo and was succeeded by Hosni Mubarak, who assured Israel that he would continue the peace negotiations begun by his predecessor. Progress towards Palestinian self-government was limited, however, and ground to a halt in 1982.

In August 1981 a new peace plan was put forward by King Fahd of Saudi Arabia. It included acceptance of the Palestinians' right to establish an independent state in the West Bank with East Jerusalem as its capital. This plan differed from earlier Arab proposals in recognising the right of all states in the area, including Israel, to exist.

Following the Israeli invasion of Lebanon, President Reagan put forward another peace plan in September 1982. It was designed to give each side in the Arab–Israeli conflict what it most required, on condition that it accepted the right of the other side to receive its requirement. The Palestinians would be given the West Bank and Gaza as a homeland 'in association with Jordan' and there would be no further Israeli settlements built there. In return, Israel's security would be guaranteed by the United States. Israel rejected the plan because it would lead to the setting up of an independent Palestinian state which would threaten its security.

When President Sadat made his 'Sacred Mission' to Israel in November 1977, hopes were high that real progress towards a settlement of the Middle East conflict would be made. Events since then, particularly the reaction of the Arab world to the Camp David agreement, the assassination of Sadat and the conflict in Lebanon, have dashed these hopes. The Middle East is likely to remain at the centre of world attention as an area of conflict for many years to come. Solution of the major problem – the fate of the Palestinians – is no nearer now than it was before 1977.

Questions

1. What attempts were made to find a solution to the Arab–Israeli conflict before 1977?
2. How successful were these attempts?
3. Describe the plan for peace contained in UN Resolution 242.
4. What was agreed at Camp David?
5. How did the 1981 Saudi peace plan differ from previous Arab proposals?
6. Outline the main proposals in the 1982 Reagan peace plan.
7. Why has little progress been made towards a lasting solution during the last few years?

The Gulf War

After several months of border clashes, Iraq and Iran – traditional enemies with deep-rooted ethnic and ideological differences – went to war with each other in September 1980. The war was launched by Iraqi President **Saddam Hussein** in an attempt to topple the **Ayatollah Khomeini**, who in turn pledged to fight until 'the government of heathens in Iraq topples'.

The war had important world-wide implications beyond the worry about yet another dispute in an area of political and military instability. The Gulf states supply around 40 per cent of the West's oil and any interruption of supplies from the two warring countries and the surrounding states (particularly Saudi Arabia and Kuwait) would cause severe economic and industrial problems. The area is also strategically important to the United States and the Soviet Union.

After eight years of fighting which cost more than 2 million lives and an estimated $1 billion a month for each side, a position of stalemate seemed to have been reached. Iran appeared to be stronger in terms of military equipment than Iraq, but Iraq had more support from other Arab countries. France also gave strong support to Iraq in the form of arms supplies, including the latest Super Etendard jet fighters equipped with Exocet missiles. China also supplied Iraq with military equipment. The conflict became increasingly intense in the late 1980s. It was further complicated by the Iranian forces attacking neutral ships in the Gulf, especially in the Strait of Hormuz. In 1986–7 the USA, Britain and a number of other countries sent

naval vessels into the area to protect oil tankers and keep the international shipping lanes open. In 1988, following a number of incidents involving Iranian and US forces, an American missile-carrying destroyer the *USS Vincennes* shot down an Iran Air airbus carrying 290 passengers. This incident led to the Ayatollah Khomeini calling for an all-out war against the USA and its allies.

A second complication was the fate of a number of British hostages who, although captured in Lebanon, appeared to be held by groups controlled by Iran. These hostages, including Terry Waite who had been acting as a negotiator in attempts to free the other hostages, found themselves at the centre of the crisis which developed in 1988.

Crude oil supply lines

Afghanistan: great power interest and involvement

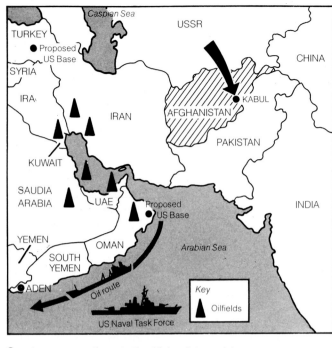

USSR

1. Afghanistan is a border neighbour.
2. The USSR had supported the Government of Afghanistan before 1979 and supported the new Government led by Babrak Karmal.
3. Afghanistan is close to huge Middle East oil supplies for the USA and the West.
4. The USSR was afraid that a revolution in Afghanistan might lead to a Muslim, Islamic Revolution similar to the one which changed Iran's Government. Islamic revolutionary ideas might even spread to the USSR's Muslim population of roughly 40 million.

USA

1. Afghanistan is a neighbour of Iran, with whom the USA had close links before the removal of the Shah in the Islamic Revolution.
2. Afghanistan is close to the Middle East oilfields which supply some of the USA's oil needs.
3. The USA fears an increase in Soviet power in the Middle East.
4. The USA was afraid of Soviet advance towards the Arabian sea for southern 'warm water' ports for the Soviet navy.

China

1. Afghanistan is a border neighbour.
2. China had been supplying military aid to Pakistan, Afghanistan's neighbour.
3. Chinese advisers had been working in Pakistan.
4. China was afraid that its own large neighbour, the USSR, was advancing its power and influence in areas close to China.

Great power reactions to the Afghanistan crisis

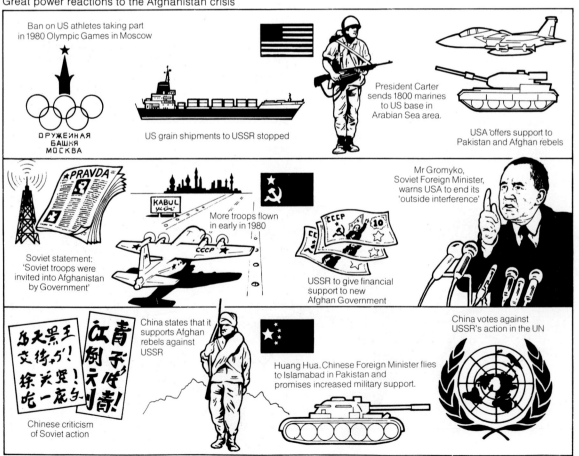

Afghanistan

The Soviet military intervention in Afghanistan in 1979 led to indirect confrontation not only between the USA and the Soviet Union, but also between China and the Soviet Union. The reasons why these three great powers are interested in this area and the ways in which they reacted to the crisis are shown in the diagrams.

Since they first arrived in Afghanistan, the Soviet troops have met with fierce opposition from the Mujahedin guerrillas whose activities were the main reason for the Soviet intervention in the first place. By 1984 a stalemate had developed. The Soviet Union had a force of over 100 000 troops in the country: enough to control the main cities but not the wide areas of countryside.

Soviet supply convoys were frequently attacked by the Afghan rebels and the Soviets retaliated by burning fields and villages and shooting villagers. The guerrillas also successfully attacked the oil and electricity supply lines to the capital city, Kabul. An estimated 20 000 Soviet troops and 50 000 Mujahedin tribesmen have died during the hostilities. By 1985, the USA was giving £150 million a year to the rebels, through Pakistan, but this is not as much as the Mujahedin would like.

In May 1988 the Soviet Union began withdrawing its 115 000 troops from a struggle which had lasted 8½ years and cost almost 15 000 Soviet soldiers their lives. During that time, almost 1 million Afghans were thought to have died and more than 3 million refugees fled to Pakistan and Iran. 'The Soviet Union's Vietnam' at last seemed to be over as part of Mr Gorbachev's new approach to international relations.

Questions

1. Why have these three major powers been involved in the Afghanistan crisis?
2. Who are the Mujahedin?
3. Explain the phrase 'the Soviet Union's Vietnam'.

Africa: Continent in Crisis

THE RISE OF BLACK NATIONALISM

The demands for the removal of white colonial rule, which still dominated most of the continent of Africa in the 1950s, increased during the 1960s. By the late 1970s the 'winds of change' had swept over the continent and only a few white minority govern-ments retained power. While some of the change-over to black nationalist governments was peaceful, in other cases there were violent conflicts before the colonial powers left. In North Africa, the French fought a bitter eight-year war until 1962 to try to keep Algeria under French rule. Britain was involved in a war in Kenya until it gained independence. It also arranged a settlement to end the civil war in Rhodesia, which became the independent Zimbabwe. Belgium hurriedly left the Belgian Congo area to its own future and the violent civil war which followed claimed the lives of thousands, including that of the then Secretary-General of the United Nations, Dag Hammarskjold, who died in a plane crash while on a UN Congo peace mission in 1961. Portugal later gave up its hold on Mozambique and Angola.

Why is there crisis in Africa? One of the most serious problems in Africa in the 1980s is poverty: caused by natural disasters, such as drought, and by non-natural disasters, such as war and vast foreign debts, over £100 000 million in 1988.

The governments of some recently independent states, such as Zimbabwe, face difficulties in trying to solve such problems.

In some cases, e.g. in Angola, Ethiopia and the Sahara, the problems are increased by internal rebellions, border disputes and guerrilla raids.

Many African countries are also facing the problem of how to cope with increasing involvement of the Superpowers and their allies in African disputes. Lastly, there is the problem of apartheid (separate development) in South Africa.

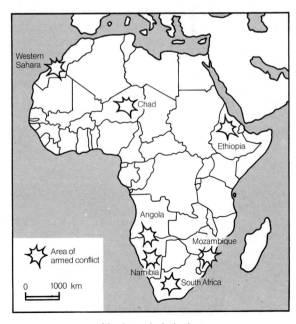

Africa's armed clashes

Drought, war, too many people

POVERTY

In the early 1980s drought, wars, debts and poor farming caused serious food shortages in many areas of Africa. A UN survey estimates that in about 20 African countries, such as Ethiopia, Chad, Mali, Upper Volta, Uganda and Lesotho, over 20 million people are facing starvation. Indeed, about 200 million, half of Africa's total population, eat less than a 'survival' diet. In the last 20 years there has been little increase in food production, and Africa has become a net importer of food. During this time, however, population has increased steadily, so that many Africans, especially children, suffer serious malnutrition and ill-health. In 1984–5 about half a million people died in a famine in Ethiopia.

Questions

1. Why is there crisis in many parts of Africa?
2. Describe the size of the 'poverty problem' in Africa.
3. Why has famine been widespread in Africa in the 1980s?

SUPERPOWER INVOLVEMENT IN AFRICA

The peaceful settlement of disputes in Africa is made more difficult by the involvement of both the USA and the USSR.

The USA and several West European countries have major trade and aid links with African countries. They also supply military weapons. For example, the USA has supplied weapons and tanks to both Somalia and Ethiopia in their war in the 'Horn of Africa'. France still has military bases in Ivory Coast, Senegal and Gabon, and has given aid to Chad. Indeed, in 1978 French troops were involved in conflicts in Africa to support pro-Western governments in Mauritania, Chad and Zaire. In 1983 about 3000 French troops and military equipment were flown to Chad to fight on the government side against Libyan-backed guerrillas. American transport planes were used to ferry Moroccan troops to Zaire to replace French and Belgian units fighting pro-communist guerrillas in southern Zaire. British and American companies have big trade deals in Nigeria. For example, the USA buys 47 per cent of Nigeria's oil and sells goods and services worth $1000 million a year to Nigeria. Many British and American multinational companies are involved in South Africa, e.g. Ford, Dunlop, Plessey and Leyland. This trade with South Africa is important to Britain and the USA but makes them unpopular with black nationalist governments in Africa. Britain and the USA are interested in a peaceful settlement to the demands for black majority rule in southern Africa.

After Vietnam, the USA is unwilling to get involved again in major overseas conflicts. Congress refused to give President **Ford** additional funds to counter Soviet aid in Angola, and in 1978 President Carter refused to give military aid to Somalia although the USSR aided Ethiopia. Some Americans consider that Soviet aid and weapons are helping the USSR to establish its influence in Africa and think the USA should be doing more to counter it. However, in the early 1980s the USA did give aid to several countries, and aimed to achieve the withdrawal of Cuban forces from Angola.

The USSR sees its role in Africa as helping to overthrow the colonial powers, aiding black nationalist liberation movements, supporting sympathetic governments and aiding anti-West forces. It has supplied aid to both Angola and Mozambique, and military equipment (aircraft, tanks, guns, missiles) to Somalia and Ethiopia. The massive aid given by the USSR is accompanied only by a few Soviet advisers. The main aid in manpower is provided by Cuban troops, instructors and technicians. Cuban forces in Africa now number about 35 000 (about a quarter of Cuba's armed forces). At present Cubans are involved in training and advising armed forces in Angola, Guinea, Libya, Ethiopia, Uganda, Tanzania and Mozambique.

Many African countries accept Soviet aid, though they would not necessarily support direct Soviet influence in their countries. They are, however, suspicious of Western aims in southern Africa where the several Western countries such as the UK and the USA have strong economic links with white-ruled South Africa. A war in southern Africa could

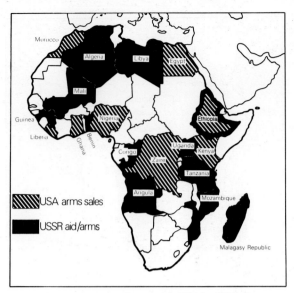

Superpower involvement in Africa, 1976–8

involve many African countries, and ultimately raise the danger of an international conflict involving the Superpowers themselves.

Questions

1. Why is the USA interested in what happens in Africa?
2. What are the aims of the Soviet Union in getting involved in Africa?
3. In what ways are each of the Superpowers involved in Africa?

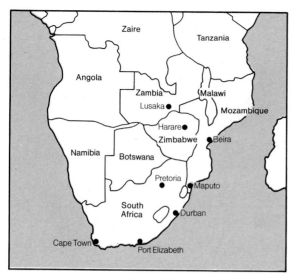

Southern Africa

CHANGE IN SOUTHERN AFRICA

In 1975 Portugal's decision to leave its colonies of Mozambique, Angola and Guinea-Bissau created a new situation in Southern Africa. Portugal had been spending nearly half of its income fighting wars against black nationalist movements in these areas. Its control over Mozambique and Angola had helped protect powerful white-ruled South Africa from much of the effects of change in the continent. However, the establishment of black communist governments in Mozambique in 1975, and in Angola after a savage civil war, meant that Ian Smith's illegal white government in Rhodesia and Vorster's white minority government in South Africa became much more closely involved in armed struggles with black liberation movements.

By 1980 Rhodesia had become the independent black majority state of Zimbabwe. Thus it seemed that the 'winds of change' had become storm clouds over southern Africa, as South Africa confronted black guerrilla armies which had bases in the black nationalist countries to the north.

By the mid-1980s, however, the picture had changed yet again. South Africa, using its considerable military and economic power, was gradually able to force its neighbouring black nationalist states – Angola, Mozambique, Zimbabwe and Botswana – to stop providing bases for anti-South African groups. At the same time, within South Africa, there was increasing unrest, rioting and killing as black South Africans demanded an end to the strict apartheid laws.

Namibia

Namibia, formerly South-West Africa, is controlled by South Africa, despite objections by the United Nations and the International Court of Justice. The United Nations' view is that South Africa has no legal right to occupy Namibia and should allow the territory to have its independence. By the mid-1980s, however, several UN missions to South Africa had failed to produce any agreement for South African withdrawal.

There are several reasons why South Africa has not left Namibia. Firstly, Namibian independence would produce yet another black majority government on South Africa's borders, and South Africa wishes to delay this for as long as possible. Also, there are important mineral deposits (uranium, diamonds, copper) in Namibia and most of the mining contracts are under South African control. Many Western countries, including Britain, obtain uranium for nuclear power from Namibian mines. Most of the land in Namibia is owned by the South Africa-supporting white minority.

Within Namibia, the black liberation group SWAPO (South West Africa People's Organisation), led by Sam Nujoma, has been fighting a civil war against South African occupation. However, South Africa has powerful military forces in Namibia, and many of the SWAPO forces have had to move over the border to safer bases in Angola.

Questions

1. Why was Portugal's decision to give up its African colonies an important one for southern Africa?
2. In what ways is South Africa involved in Namibia?
3. Why has South Africa been able to dominate its neighbouring black nationalist countries?
4. What agreements was South Africa trying to gain in the early 1980s with (a) Angola and (b) Mozambique?

Angola and the 'Cold War'

In 1976 the civil war in Angola ended when the communist MPLA (Popular Front for the Liberation of Angola) defeated its rivals UNITA (Total Independence for Angola) and formed a new government. The United States and South Africa had supported UNITA, while the USSR and Cuba supported the new government.

By 1980, however, despite the presence of 20 000 Cuban troops and advisers and millions of pounds of Soviet aid, Angola was in difficulties. SWAPO guerrillas from Namibia had several camps and training areas in the south and South African military units made devastating raids into Angola to destroy these bases. Also, the rebel group UNITA re-appeared in some strength and by 1984 was able, with South African support, to make raids into northern Angola. This aided the South African plan, partly shared by the USA, that in return for South African forces leaving Angola and Namibia, Cuban troops should leave Angola. By the mid-1980s Angola was being forced to consider this plan.

Mozambique

In Mozambique the communist government of Zamora Machel faced considerable problems. After independence from Portugal in 1975, ANC (African National Congress) refugees from South Africa settled there. These black South African nationalists, whose political party is banned in South Africa, were frequently attacked by South African forces. These military raids, and a prolonged drought in 1983, forced the Mozambique government in early 1984 to agree with the South African government not to harbour ANC refugees in return for economic aid. In the late 1980s, Mozambique's problems increased considerably with the death of President Mackel in a plane crash in South Africa in 1986 and the savage attacks of the South African backed Renamo guerrilla groups.

Zimbabwe

In 1977 Britain and the United States put forward a plan for a settlement of the civil war in Rhodesia. It included the following.
(a) A move from white to black rule in 1978, supervised by a British 'governor'.
(b) 'One person, one vote'. Adults of all races to have the right to vote.
(c) The Rhodesian army and guerrilla armies to be disbanded and replaced by a UN force.
(d) A new army for Zimbabwe (the African name for Rhodesia).
(e) Britain/USA to provide about £862 million to help develop Zimbabwe.

In the election held in 1979 the two main contestants were Robert Mugabe and Joshua Nkomo, both former guerrilla leaders in the seven-year war to remove Ian Smith's white minority government in Rhodesia (now Zimbabwe). Mr Mugabe's ZANU Party won 57 of the 80 seats for black MPs in the Zimbabwe Parliament. Mr Nkomo, although given a position in the Cabinet, criticised the new leader for massacres in the province of Matabeleland. In 1982 Mr Nkomo was dismissed, claiming Zimbabwe was becoming a one-party state.

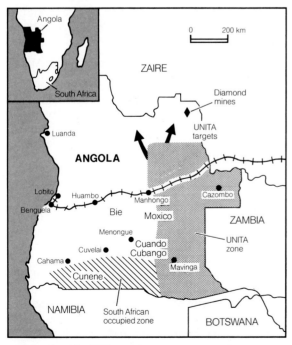

Angola 1984 (*Guardian Weekly*, 22 Jan. 1984)

Robert Mugabe

Zimbabwe's problems were further increased when, in 1983, South Africa for a time cut off fuel supplies on the overland railway line to Zimbabwe causing serious fuel shortages. Also, the USA halved its $70-million-a-year aid to Zimbabwe because of its criticisms of the USA at UN meetings.

South Africa

South Africa is one of the wealthiest countries in Africa, with huge mineral resources (gold, diamonds), developed industries and prosperous agriculture. These resources, plus well-armed military forces, give South Africa a dominant role in Southern Africa in the 1980s. Indeed, South Africa influences areas beyond its own borders. Despite this power and influence, however, South Africa still faces a number of problems.

1. *Neighbouring countries.* By the mid-1980s South Africa, by means of devastating military raids, had forced Mozambique and Angola to have talks about their relations on South Africa's terms, and to reduce anti-South African guerrilla groups on their land.

2. *Namibia.* This area, formerly South-West Africa, was once a German colony and was handed over to South African administration by the League of Nations after the First World War. When the United Nations was set up, South Africa would not recognise UN authority over Namibia and continued to rule the area and exploit its mineral wealth. The United Nations set a limit for South African rule to end by 1978, and accepted, along with the Organisation of African Unity, that SWAPO (South-West African People's Organisation) was the true

representative of the Namibian people. SWAPO guerrillas had been fighting a civil war in Namibia against South Africa since 1959.

3. *Isolation from the international community.* Although South Africa is a member of the United Nations, it is much criticised by many other countries. South Africa left the Commonwealth in 1961. The UN Security Council passed a ban on arms sales to South Africa in 1963. Many countries refuse to take part in sporting events with South Africa because they object to its policy of **apartheid**. In July 1976 several African nations withdrew from the Montreal Olympic Games because a New Zealand rugby team had toured South Africa, while the 1986 Commonwealth Games in Edinburgh were threatened by withdrawals because English and Welsh rugby teams toured South Africa.

In 1983, however, South Africa was offering large prize money to world sports personalities in an effort to get international recognition. Golf stars such as Jack Nicklaus, Lee Trevino, Seve Ballasteros and Greg Norman played for prize money of over $1 million, a world record. In 1984 President Botha travelled to several European countries, including Britain.

4. *Racial tension* in South Africa due to the inequalities of the apartheid system.

APARTHEID

'There are those in the world outside who believe they can bring South Africa to its knees with a mandatory arms boycott. I tell them – they have another guess coming.'

(John Vorster, former Prime Minister of South Africa speaking in a Transvaal town in 1963.)

This defiant speech was made in reply to the UN Security Council ban on arms sales to South Africa, which was imposed because of the hostility of many countries to South Africa's sysem of apartheid. Apartheid ('apartness') became an official policy after 1948 when the Nationalist Party came to power. It involves the separation of people according to their colour. South Africa's population (1983) is classified thus: whites (British and Dutch settlers and European immigrants 5 million; Bantu (Africans of various tribes) 22 million; coloureds (mixed race) 2.8 million; Asians (mostly Indian) 900 000.

To encourage the separate development of the Bantu population, designated areas or 'homelands' with their own form of government have been set up by the South African government since 1976.

There is little chance, however, that the homelands or **Bantustans** could survive as truly inde-

South Africa's Prime Minister, P. W. Botha

pendent areas since they are poverty stricken. poor in mineral and agricultural resources, and dependent on South African government finance. There is high unemployment in the Bantustans so many people leave to get jobs in white-owned factories and farms outside.

In practice, separate development is not equal development and the apartheid laws discriminate against non-whites, as the chart below indicates.

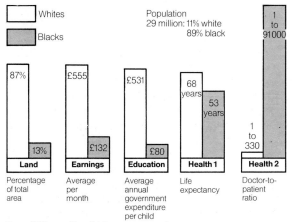

Source: SA Survey of Race Relations

Comparison of conditions for black and white South Africans (*Sunday Standard*, 29 May 1983)

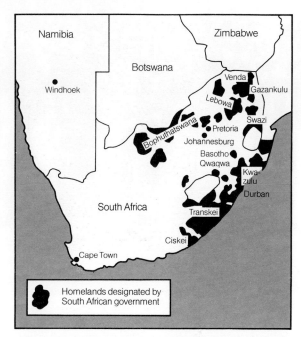

Homelands designated by South African government

There is discrimination in the laws, which force all black South Africans to carry reference books. Failure to produce this book at any time can lead to imprisonment. There is discrimination against black people in transport, job opportunities, education, housing and many other public facilities. Despite recent minor changes such as more non-whites being allowed into skilled jobs, more consultation with non-white leaders and some multi-racial sporting events, the basic economic and political power is still in the control of white South Africans.

In 1960 a protest march in Sharpeville against the apartheid laws led to the shooting and killing of 69 black people. By 1976 much greater opposition and protest arose in the Johannesburg township of Soweto, which has a population of about one million black people. Weeks of rioting by young black people demanding equal education opportunities with white children ended with a death-toll of over 600. These riots, together with the activities of the secret police and the deaths of several black prisoners, including Steve Biko in 1977, have greatly increased the tensions in South Africa's urban areas.

The tensions were not reduced when, in 1984, white South Africans voted for a new Constitution which gave coloureds and Indians limited power, but which totally excluded South Africa's black majority. In 1984–5 over 700 black Africans died in widespread rioting and clashes with the police. In the absence of the imprisoned Nelson Mandela, leader of the black African National Congress Party (ANC), black protest groups formed the United Democratic Front led by Bishop Desmond Tutu and Rev. Allan Boesak.

Soweto riots

Questions

1. What is 'separate development' in South Africa?
2. In what ways is South Africa becoming more isolated from other countries in the world?
3. In what ways is South Africa trying to overcome its isolation?
4. What events have increased racial tension recently in South Africa?

Conflict in Other Parts of Africa

Several of the conflicts in other parts of Africa in the 1980s involved not only government forces against rebels, but also the Superpowers and their allies.

CONFLICT IN THE HORN

In North-East Africa, 'the Horn', Ethiopia is at war on two fronts: with Eritrean guerrillas in the north who want independence, and with Somali forces in the south who claim the Ogaden region of Ethiopia.

The communist government of Ethiopia, which came to power in 1974 with the defeat of Emperor Haile Selassie, ended American aid and sent home 4000 American advisers and technicians. Ethiopia then got aid from the Soviet Union and Cuba. Soviet military equipment and technicians and about 8000 Cuban advisers have been helping the Ethiopian government on a large scale since 1977. In the meantime, the USA has supplied aid and military

equipment to Somalia which conducted a border war in the south against Ethiopia.

Why are the Superpowers Involved?

(1) The USSR wants a seaport base for its navy ships in this area which would give the Soviet fleet supervision of shipping between Indian Ocean and Mediterranean Sea.

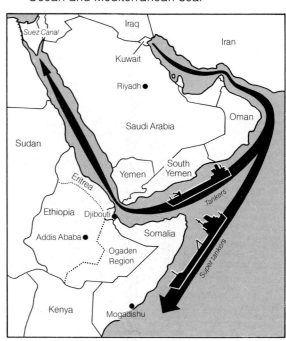

The position of Ethiopia and oil routes in the Horn of Africa

(2) The USSR would like a port in the area to add to its network of navy facilities in South Yemen.
(3) The USA and Western countries are concerned about the possible threat to oil supplies (see map).
(4) The USA is building a huge naval base (cost $150 million) on the island of Diego Garcia in the Indian Ocean, which would give it a supervision of shipping in Red Sea and Indian Ocean.

Despite this involvement, in 1983 during a severe drought affecting over a million people in northern Ethiopia with severe famine, Western governments were not keen to give famine aid to an ally of the Soviet Union.

CHAD

Chad, in North Africa, gained its independence from France in 1960. Since then there has been almost continuous civil war between government forces and guerrillas who control northern Chad. During the 1980s this conflict grew in importance as other countries, including the superpowers, became involved. The Chad government, led by President Habre, is supported by France, Zaire and the USA. The Muslim guerrillas, led by Goukouni Oueddei, are supported by Libyan troops and military equipment supplied by the Soviet Union. Meanwhile, Libya and the USA are in direct dispute over the claim by Colonel **Gadafy** of Libya that the Gulf of Sirte in the Mediterranean is part of Libyan territory.

SAHARA

In Western Sahara, Algerian-backed Polisario guerrillas are fighting against Morocco for independence for the former Spanish Sahara. The civil war has been fought since 1976. French aircraft have made air strikes against guerrilla positions and, in 1982, the USA gave Morocco $30 million military aid in the form of tanks and planes. Morocco has committed about 100 000 troops to try to gain possession of the oil-rich 'useful triangle'.

Questions

1. In what ways is the Soviet Union involved in Ethiopia?
2. What aid has the Chad government been given by France and the USA?
3. What is the dispute concerning the 'useful triangle' in Sahara?

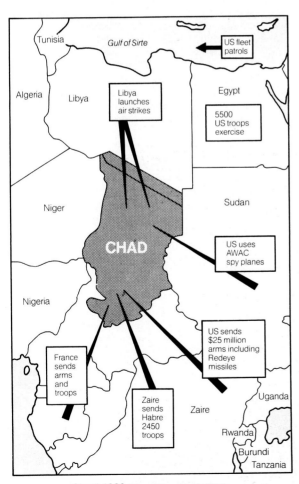

Chad 1983 (*New African*, Sept. 1983)

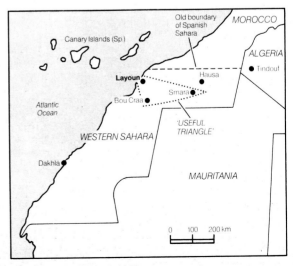

Western Sahara 1983 (*The Economist*, 11 June 1983)

Central America

Who's Who in Central America

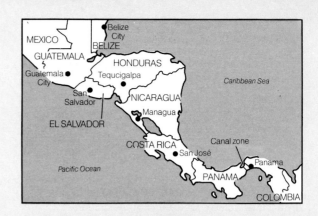

GUATEMALA

POLITICS Ruled by military dictators since US-assisted coup overthrew the democratic government of Jacobo Arbenz in 1954. Most recent coup ousted General Efrain Rios Montt, a born-again Christian considered too liberal by the country's oligarchy. Current leader is Brigadier Oscar Mejia Victores – a hard-line anti-communist.

THE WAR Scattered guerrilla forces have fought from mountain strongholds since late 1950s; peasant support and government repression have accelerated since late 1970s. The army is the largest and most sophisticated in Central America, trained in counter-insurgency techniques by US advisers. Recent military aid will help General Mejia escalate the army's campaign against the guerrillas.

HUMAN RIGHTS More than 100 000 civilians have been murdered by government forces in the last decade. Rule of law non-existent. Church workers estimate up to 1 million internal refugees and 100 000 more in Mexico.

EL SALVADOR

POLITICS 1982 elections vaulted right-winger Major Robert D'Abuisson into power with Alvarado Magana as figurehead president. The main opposition force, the *Democratic Revolutionary Front* (FDR), boycotted the elections because of death threats to its leadership by right-wing groups. Guerrilla forces have proposed direct negotiations with the US and Salvadoran governments to achieve a political solution. In 1984, José Duarte was elected President.

THE WAR Guerrilla forces were formed in the early 1970s. *Farabundo Marti National Liberation Front* (FMLN) is a tightly-organised fighting force of an estimated 10 000. Government troops armed, trained and advised by the US, which has poured almost a billion dollars into the country in the last four years.

HUMAN RIGHTS Atrocities, deaths and 'disappearances' by right-wing death squads and army make El Salvador a human rights nightmare. Civilian killings continue at 400–500 a month. After years of delay, five government troops were imprisoned for the murders of four US nuns.

HONDURAS

POLITICS President Roberto Suazo Cordova elected in 1981 after 18 years of military dictatorship. Real power is still vested in the army led by General Gustavo Alvarez, a hardline right-winger. Power behind the throne is US Ambassador, John Negroponte, who oversees the US military build-up.

THE WAR Main base of US action against the Sandinistas and Salvadoran guerrillas. Air strips, radar stations and new troop training facilities are being built. There are more than 300 US military advisers and technicians, 125 Green Berets and 150 CIA agents in the country. *Contras* operate freely inside Honduras.

HUMAN RIGHTS 'Human rights are an invention to protect terrorists' says army leader General Alvarez. Violations by armed forces have increased since 1982 with outspoken government opponents targeted for murder.

NICARAGUA

POLITICS The 1979 revolution led by *Frente Sandinista* (FSLN) replaced the Somoza family dictatorship. Power now rests in the hands of the nine-member National Directorate of the FSLN. Attempts to initiate local involvement through neighbourhood committees, co-operatives and trade unions have been made. Elections are scheduled for 1985.

THE WAR Prime target of US-backed war efforts in the region. Over 6000 counter-revolutionaries, trained and outfitted by the CIA and led by ex-Somocista national guardsmen, make forays from their bases in Honduras. 150 covert CIA agents are involved – the largest CIA operation since Vietnam. Fighting has not undermined popular support for the Sandinistas.

HUMAN RIGHTS Sandinistas have admitted 'errors' in their early dealings with the Miskito Indians but stand by their right to relocate 8000 Indians from the border war zone. Political parties permitted; few cases of torture, 'disappearances' or political murder; press censorship is still in operation.

(*New Internationalist*, December 1983)

REGION OF UNREST

In Central America there are about 25 million people, mainly Spanish-speaking descendants of local Indians, Spanish settlers and black plantation workers. A major cause of unrest in the area is that most of the countries suffer serious poverty and within many of the countries there are great differences between rich and poor. For example, in El Salvador, Guatemala and Honduras about three per cent of the population have 50 per cent of the income and own 60 per cent of the land. These inequalities are further increased by rising unemployment and landlessness, as peasants are moved from their land, which is then taken over by large, private companies.

In many of these countries this poverty has led, in the past as at present, to civil unrest and revolution. Civil wars and political violence have been common for many years as poverty-stricken peasants try to remove wealthy dictators in their countries.

By the 1980s there was increasing unrest. The success of left-wing revolutions in Cuba in 1959 and in Nicaragua in 1979 in overthrowing unpopular dictators encouraged left-wing guerrillas in other Central American countries such as El Salvador.

Tension in the area increased in the early 1980s when President Reagan ordered greatly increased military aid to America's allies: El Salvador, Guatemala, Honduras and Panama. Israel also supplied military equipment to some of these countries, while Argentinian military instructors trained Honduran troops. With economic and military aid to Nicaragua from the Soviet Union and Cuba being increased, there was a serious threat of more

Civilians leave their village after intense fighting between army and guerrillas in Usulatan Province, El Salvador

Table 6 Money and People in Central America

	Population 1981 (millions)	GNP per capita 1981	Debt service as percentage of export earnings	Major exports	Infant mortality (per thousand)	Literacy	Life expectancy
Guatemala	7.4	$1140	7.9	coffee cotton sugar	66.5	58	58
El Salvador	5.0	$ 650	5.5	coffee cotton sugar	42.6	70	59
Nicaragua	2.8	$ 860	9.3	coffee cotton sugar	93.7	88	57
Honduras	3.8	$ 600	18.8	bananas coffee beef	87.0	60	56
Panama	1.9	$1910	36.6	bananas sugar shrimp	24.9	88	70
Costa Rica	2.3	$1430	29.8	coffee bananas cocoa	17.9	90	70
Belize	0.13	$1080	N/A	sugar citrus bananas	40.0	80	60

New Internationalist, December 1983

widespread war in the area. Indeed, in 1983 there were clashes between Nicaragua and Honduras along their border area.

The main immediate result of the increase in violence in the area is that many thousands of civilians are killed and many become refugees.

As revolutions spread across the borders of the countries – 'La revolucion no tiene fronteras' – so the violent activities of government troops, anti-government guerrillas and 'death squads' increases. In El Salvador, for example, about 300 people a month died violently in this small country during 1981 and 1982. There has been a long-running civil war between US-supported El Salvador government troops and their opponents, the left-wing Farabundo Marti National Liberation Front.

Questions

1. Describe the civil war in El Salvador.
2. What poverty problems are common to many Central American countries?
3. What is the effect on civilians of the wars in Central America?

The Human Cost In Central America

POVERTY AND WAR

There are two million war refugees and displaced people from Guatemala, El Salvador and Nicaragua: that is, 1 in 14 of the population. Continual civil war has made poverty worse: agricultural wages in El Salvador have fallen to a third of their value in 1971. Oxfam staff report:

'The women point out pictures of their loved ones and tell us of imprisonment, death and dawn swoops. Arele's husband disappeared a year ago. He was a carpenter. He left at 8.00 am to pick some wood and has never returned. She has no idea whether he is alive or dead. She has four children. She is in tears.'

– El Salvador, 1983

'We're always frightened. We can't tell you how many times we've been chased by 30, 45 and more soldiers yelling at us from a distance, "stay, don't run, we're friends"; and when they get close, they start firing and they laugh when they see that the women and little children run in terror and the children cry. In February a group of 25 to 30 soldiers machine-gunned, chopped with machetes and decapitated 17 women; amongst them 4 children of 8 months old, a 4 year old and a 7 year old.'

– Villagers, Guatemala, 1983

'Martin, the co-ordinator of the coffee-pickers union, told us how 64 coffee pickers had been kidnapped in November and December last year and taken to Honduras. Nothing has been heard of them since. While explaining this, he told us that his wife, Francisca, and three children aged 6, 8 and 10 had also been kidnapped last December, and that he had received no news of them since. One of the coffee pickers escaped and reported that those who did not agree to join the "contras" were killed.'

– Nicaragua, 1983

(contras are the anti-government forces attacking from Honduras)

(*Bother*, publ. Oxfam, February 1984)

The body count

The most conservative estimate of the human cost of the Central American conflict – the dead, the 'disappeared', the displaced and refugees – is over 2 million lives: 10 per cent of the population of Guatemala, El Salvador, Nicaragua and Honduras. In the first six months of this year, over 600 Nicaraguan civilians were killed 'accidentally' in clashes between rebels and army units.

In all, more than 60 000 are dead as a direct result of the conflict. In Guatemala alone, 27 000 innocent peasants have lost their lives, believed killed by government security forces; at least 15 000 were killed in the first year of Rios Montt's presidency. According to the Catholic church in El Salvador, there were 249 political murders over a six-day period in January this year.

Thousands more have simply 'disappeared' since 1980; in El Salvador, church and human rights groups put the number at over 3000.

The United Nations High Commission for Refugees estimates that the region has more than 315 000 refugees. Another 250 000 Salvadoran refugees are believed to be in the US. Refugee camps in southern Mexico house over 100 000 Guatemalans – mainly Indians fleeing government action in the highland provinces. Honduras and Costa Rica shelter a growing number.

But the most staggering figure is that for displaced people – refugees in their own homeland – estimated at between 1.7 million and 1.8 million, with a million in Guatemala alone.

With the abandonment of rural areas and flight into the towns, food supply systems are breaking down.

(Lisa Nelson, *South*, September 1983)

Once More onto the Beach

War games in Honduras, war jitters in Nicaragua

As 24 landing craft surged into the shallows off the white sandy beaches, carrying hundreds of US marines in tropical camouflage gear, Harrier jump jets streaked overhead. A six-ship task force was anchored two miles out to sea, while clattering Cobra helicopter gunships provided cover. After landing, the troops pressed forward through swampy terrain. In about two hours they had seized their first objective, an airport 12 miles inland.

Less than four weeks after the invasion of Grenada, US soldiers once again had launched an amphibious assault in the hemisphere. But this time no one shot back. The landing at Puerto Castilla on Honduras' northern coast marked the beginning of a seven-day training mission with 700 Honduran troops. It was part of a series of joint military exercises involving the US and its staunchly anti-communist ally. Though billed as routine, Big Pine II, as the exercises are called, reflected a major build-up of US military might aimed largely at intimidating Honduras' southern neighbour, Marxist-led Nicaragua.

(*Time*, 28 November 1983)

SUPERPOWER INTEREST AND INVOLVEMENT

The United States

The United States has been involved with Central American countries for over a hundred years. There are several reasons for this.

Geographically, Central America is very close to the United States and there have been close trading links for many years. The area is sometimes referred to as 'America's backyard', and many US industrial firms have interests there. Historically, the United States has felt free to invade several of the countries in Central America and the Caribbean area during this century. Thus the US helps its allies to put down left-wing revolutions, while supporting anti-government guerrilla forces in countries it is opposed to. In 1983, for example, US troops invaded the island of Grenada and overthrew a government to which the American government was hostile.

Economically, the USA is involved in Central America in several ways: American companies make up 80 per cent of all foreign firms in Central America; and over 1000 companies in Central America are owned by US multinational companies. The USA is also the main trading partner for much of Central America.

Politically, America's interest in Central America is to try to keep in power governments which meet with America's approval. Thus, in the 1980s, the right-wing governments of Honduras, Guatemala and El Salvador received US aid, despite world-wide concern about the violation of human rights in these countries. On the other hand, the US strongly opposes the communist government in Cuba, and has cut off aid to the left-wing government in Nicaragua. America believes that if one country in the area becomes communist, then others will 'topple' too. This is the Domino Theory.

AID AS A WEAPON

The US has been pouring massive amounts of aid into the region since 1980 in a desperate attempt to shore up beleaguered regimes in El Salvador, Honduras and Guatemala. Military aid to Honduras jumped 650 per cent from 1980–83 while economic aid to Guatemala rose by over 500 per cent in the same period. Soviet and Eastern Bloc aid is increasing in Nicaragua. Moscow has supplied obsolete trucks and other weapons to the Sandinistas. But the amount is only a fraction of the US effort. Without US dollars in hard-hit treasuries countries like El Salvador would be unable to survive the onslaught of guerrilla forces.

(*New Internationalist*, December 1983)

In 1984, the Kissinger Commission, set up by the US government to report on affairs in Central America, stated that 'Central America critically involves our own security interests. What happens on our doorstep calls to our conscience.' The report recommended donating $400 million dollars' aid to Central America in 1984, in addition to $477 million dollars already allocated. The report further suggested a spending of $8000 million dollars by America in the area between 1985 and 1990.

The Domino Theory: America's view of the crisis in Central America

US aid to Central America
(*New Internationalist*, Dec. 1983)

US AID ($ millions)

☐ Military

■ Economic

* The annual cost of the US convert war against Nicaragua was estimated at $30 to $50 million for 1983. The CIA wants $80 million for 1984 to support 12000 to 15000 *Contras*.

The USSR

The influence of the Soviet Union was increased by the success of the communist revolution in Cuba. The USSR supports guerrilla movements of 'oppressed peoples' against their governments. Thus, the USSR gives aid in trade, finance and military equipment to Cuba and Nicaragua. Also, Cuba itself supplies many advisers to several countries in Central America and the Caribbean area. In Nicaragua about 3000 Cuban advisers help in education, health and military training. Cuba has close trading links with the USSR, and about one-third of Nicaragua's aid is from the Soviet Union and East European countries. The USSR has promised about $500 million aid over several years, and 1000 Nicaraguan students attend technical colleges in the USSR.

Questions

1. For what reasons is the USA involved in Central America?
2. What is meant by the 'Domino Theory' in Central America?
3. In what ways is the USA involved in Central America?
4. What are the aims of the USSR in Central America?

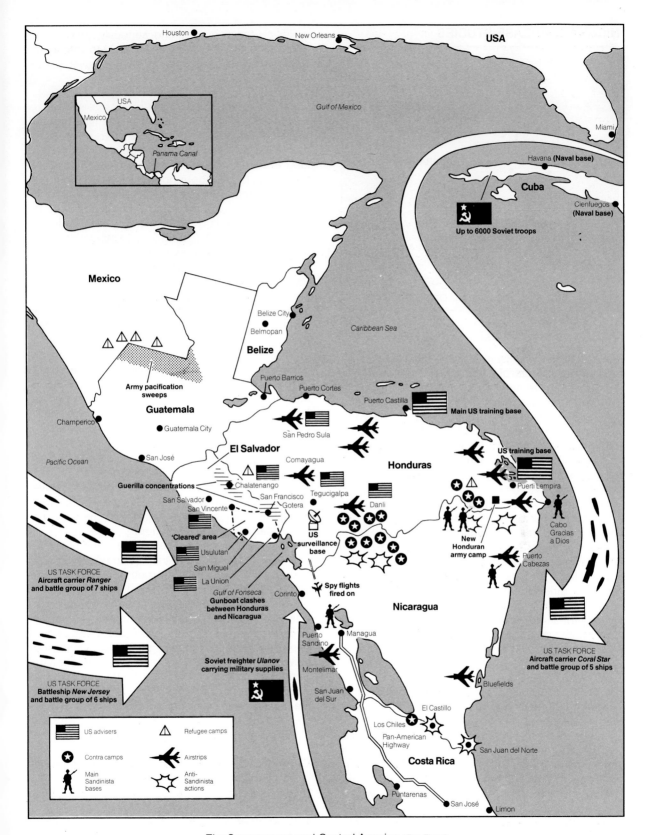

The Superpowers and Central America (*The Times*)

NICARAGUA: CASE STUDIES

A Government Official

José Napoles works in a government office in Nicaragua's capital city, Managua. He supports the Sandinista government which came to power in 1979 with the overthrow of the US-supported dictatorship of President Somoza. José knows the present communist government, led by Daniel Ortega, is putting forward reforms to help overcome poverty. There are health and education programmes, and José has been involved in the organisation of a literacy programme. Illiteracy went down from 50 per cent in 1980 to 11 per cent in 1984.

In 1983 75 per cent of industry and 80 per cent of agriculture were still owned by private citizens. There is a shortage of money, made worse by fears of invasion after US troops invaded Grenada in the Caribbean in 1983 and overthrew a left-wing government. Since the USA objected to the Nicaraguan government being in power and cut off aid, some money for social reform has been diverted to build up Nicaragua's military strength.

A City Youth

Philipe Gonzales is 17 years old and also lives in Managua. He sees much poverty around him in the city where about half the population live at subsistence level. Philipe has recently attended classes to learn to read. Previously he had no chance to attend school. After the US invasion of Grenada in 1983, he and many other civilians were given basic military training. He hopes to join the army, which has about 50 000 troops. His hero is Augustino Caesar Sandino, a Nicaraguan who led his 'Sandinistas' in battles against a US invasion in the 1920s.

Philipe takes his training seriously, just as he does the fact that in 1985 he was able to vote in an election in Nicaragua open to all those over 16.

A 'Contra'

Enrico Salazar was an officer in the Nicaraguan army of President Somoza before it was defeated in the 1979 revolution. When the government forces lost, Enrico and several other officers fled from Nicaragua to neighbouring Honduras. In Honduras he and other ex-Nicaraguan officers who had supported the former right-wing government in Nicaragua joined up to form the 'Contras'. Their aim is to overthrow the left-wing Sandinista government which they claim is communist.

There are about 5000 Contras; they do their training in Honduras with American instructors. Most of their weapons, ammunition, food and clothing is supplied by the United States. Enrico has already been on several raids with the Contras into Nicaragua, to attack Nicaraguan villages. Indeed, on one occasion they stayed at a temporary camp in northern Nicaragua for two weeks and recruited to the Contras some Miskito Indians who lived in that area. The Miskitos were angry with the Nicaraguan government which wanted to move them from their lands near the Honduras border.

A Peasant Farmer

Antonio Orosco and his brother, Francisco, have only recently learned to read. They grow tomatoes, melons and maize on land given to them by the government after the revolution.

Antonio and Francisco are farmers and proud of it. They are also proud of their country's revolution and more than a little worried that the distant fighting on the border with neighbouring Honduras will bring the killing, the fear and the hunger that was so much part of their lives only five years ago.

'Before the revolution,' says Antonio, stopping to sweep the horizon with his right hand, 'all this land served one man, a millionaire. We were farmers without land. Now it is serving 50 families. Before, everything went to the rich. Now we are masters of the land, we are no longer hungry.'

Questions

1. Why was there concern in Nicaragua over the US invasion of Grenada in 1983?
2. Who are the Sandinistas?
3. Why do the Contras attack Nicaragua?
4. In what ways have the lives of some peasant farmers in Nicaragua changed in recent years?

4. Tension in the Communist World

International relations in the period since 1945 have come to be dominated by the struggle between the communist and non-communist blocs. However, within the communist world there are strains and tensions which have had an effect on the relations between the USA and the USSR. Two such examples of internal communist conflict can be seen in the relations between the USSR and East Europe and between the USSR and China.

Eastern Europe

The map below shows those countries which make up Eastern Europe. Like the countries of Western Europe, each country is quite different from any other: in language, nationality, history and culture.

However, they all have one thing in common which distinguishes them from the countries of Western Europe: they all have communist governments, and for more than 30 years have lived as part of a communist system. If a young East German boy goes on holiday to Zakopane in Poland and meets a young Czech girl they will understand each other's way of life well enough despite the difference between their past histories.

But it is wrong to think of these East European countries forming one united bloc. East Germany, Poland, Czechoslovakia, Hungary, Bulgaria and Romania are all linked to some degree with the Soviet Union. Yugoslavia and Albania, although also communist, are independent of the Soviet Union.

BACKGROUND

To see how these countries became communist we must go back to the end of the Second World War. As the Soviet armies drove their way through Eastern Europe towards Germany they occupied those countries which they freed from Hitler's control. Once under Soviet control **Stalin**, the Soviet leader, was determined that their new governments would be friendly towards the Soviet Union. This

Eastern Europe

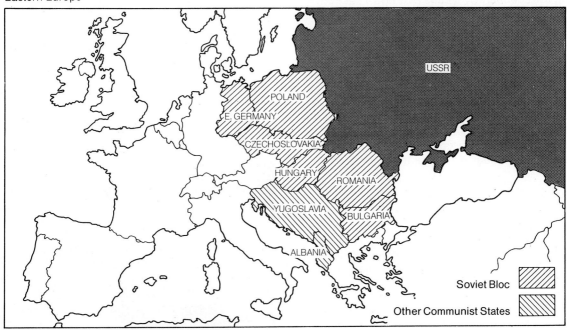

meant that in practice they would be communist governments headed by people appointed by the USSR. Those leaders who either were not communist or had opposed Stalin were forced to flee abroad or face imprisonment.

By 1948, when a Stalinist government had been imposed in Czechoslovakia, the pattern was complete: Stalin had Eastern Europe in a rigid grip. An **Iron Curtain** had fallen across Europe dividing East from West. The East European countries became known as 'satellite' states because of their dependence upon the Soviet Union. Within each East European country there was a tightening of control over all aspects of life: non-communist parties were suppressed; political opposition was destroyed and the economies were organised along Soviet lines. The East European countries were tied economically to the USSR through the Council for Mutal Economic Assistance (**Comecon**) set up in 1948, and militarily through the Warsaw Pact of 1955.

TITOISM

The one exception to this overall control was Yugoslavia, where communism had been set up without the help of the Soviet armies because of the success of the anti-Nazi partisans. The Yugoslav leader, **Tito**, was initially willing to model his country on Stalin's USSR: by making it a one-party state where political opposition was not allowed; by nationalising all farms and industry; and by planning the economy by means of a Five Year Plan.

But by 1948 Tito began to put into practice his own version of Yugoslav communism. In his own words, 'The Yugoslav brand of communism ... was not imported ready-made from Moscow.' In Yugoslavia communism became known as 'Titoism' and showed the other East European countries that there were roads to communism other than the Stalinist one. Titoism was bitterly attacked by the Soviet Union. Yugoslavia, however, managed to remain outside Soviet control and follow its own line, as it does today even after the death in 1980 of Tito himself.

EASTERN EUROPE TODAY

Today, although still under Soviet control, the East European countries have a little more freedom and independence than they had under Stalin. We can see how events have developed in East Europe by examining three East European countries.

Hungary

The Hungarian leader, János Kádár, held the post of First Secretary of the Communist Party from 1956 to 1988. During this period, a number of bold economic reforms have been introduced which have given Hungary a great improvement in living standards. These reforms have allowed factory managers to produce what they think best and to sell their products in a competitive market as they would in a capitalist country, although the factories themselves remain state owned. These developments have become known as '**goulash communism**', and with them has come increased trade with the West. However, economic reforms have not been matched by political reforms and criticism of the communist system is still not permitted.

Kádár became leader after a series of events which were to shake the Soviet grip on Eastern Europe. Stalin died in 1953 and **Nikita Khrushchev**, the man who eventually replaced him as Soviet leader, made an historic speech in 1956 denouncing Stalin — a man who up to that time had been treated like a god. This speech reflected the more liberal attitude which was already affecting Eastern Europe.

In Hungary a number of unpopular political changes led to open revolt in Budapest during the last week of October 1956. The former Prime Minister Nagy was re-instated as the Hungarian leader as a result and announced the abolition of the one-party system. Political prisoners were released and members of the secret police were attacked and killed. When Nagy announced that Hungary would withdraw from the Warsaw Pact this proved too much for Khrushchev and a Soviet army was sent to restore 'order' in Hungary — at an eventual cost of 30 000 Hungarian and 7 000 Rus-

Prague, 1968: a Czechoslovakian protester confronts a Soviet tank

sian lives. By 4 November the rebel government was crushed and a 'loyal' regime under Kádár put in its place.

Czechoslovakia

Gustav Husák was First Secretary of the Czechoslovak Communist Party from 1969 till 1987. In the year he came to power a young Czech student named Jan Palach committed suicide, by publicly burning himself, as a protest to the world about what had happened to his country. This came at the end of a period known as the 'Prague Spring' – a series of events which was to shake Soviet control of Eastern Europe as much as the Hungarian uprising had.

During the 1950s and early 1960s, Czechoslovakia had been rigidly ruled. In 1967 a new leader called Alexander Dubček took over and began a programme which led to major economic reform. It was announced that political opposition to the government would be allowed. Greater freedom of speech was allowed and the press and TV began to flourish as though awakening from a long winter. A new spirit of hope began to sweep Czechoslovakia – it was called the 'Prague Spring'.

Once more this proved too much for the USSR. Despite the promises of the Czech leadership that they had no desire to leave the Warsaw Pact, Brezhnev, the Soviet leader, was frightened lest these ideas might spill over from Czechoslovakia into other East European countries and even into the USSR itself. In August 1968 Soviet and Warsaw Pact troops invaded Czechoslovakia, entered Prague and brought an end to this experiment of 'socialism with a human face'.

Dubček was forced to agree to Soviet occupation and was eventually replaced in 1969 by Gustav Husák who has since then tried to restore 'normality' in Czechoslovakia. There are still those in Czechoslovakia who support the ideas of the 'Prague Spring', in particular a group of dissidents called the Charter 77 Group who have published a programme in defence of human rights.

The world-wide condemnation of Soviet action in Czechoslovakia came from both communist and non-communist sources but once again the Soviets had shown that Eastern Europe was an area where they decided how far and how fast reform could go. Brezhnev later defended his actions by claiming that when there was a threat to the development of communism within Eastern Europe it was the duty of other communist countries to stop that threat. This was to become known as the 'Brezhnev Doctrine' and was seen as a clear warning to other East European countries.

Poland

The Polish leader, General Jaruzelski, is head of a military council which has governed Poland since 13 December 1981, when the Polish army declared a 'state of war' in Poland and put the country under martial law. The imposition of martial law brought to a head a series of dramatic events which had threatened to shake Soviet control over Eastern Europe as much as events had in Hungary in 1956, and Czechoslovakia in 1968.

With more than 35 million people, Poland is the largest of the East European countries. This, plus a long history of national struggle dating back many centuries, has given the Poles a determination to keep themselves independent of the USSR as much as possible. Polish nationalism has been shown in a number of ways. Polish agriculture differs from that of much of the Soviet bloc, in that much of the farming land in Poland is still divided into small private farms. The Polish Roman Catholic Church, despite official discouragement, has become a major force in the country and a focus for Polish nationalism. The strength of the Church was given a great boost in 1978 with the election of a Polish cardinal as Pope John Paul II.

In politics Poland has also followed its own line since becoming part of the Soviet bloc. On several occasions riots and political disturbances in Poland have led to a change of government. The major causes were economic: the disturbances of 1956, 1970 and 1976 were sparked off by government attempts to increase food prices. These demonstrations over price rises showed a deep-rooted discontent with the overall economic and political system in Poland. This was to become clear in the events which took place during 1980 and 1981.

In July 1980 the Party Secretary, Edward Gierek, proposed to increase meat prices. This led to a series of strikes which were to build up to a general strike centring on the Lenin shipyard in Gdansk. From this strike emerged the figure of **Lech Walesa** who was to become the leader of the Polish workers. Walesa forced the government to agree to the setting up of 'free trade unions' which were to be independent of the Communist Party. These free trade unions were grouped together under the banner of 'Solidarity' and quickly grew to have over 10 million members. No other communist government in Eastern Europe recognised trade unions which were not controlled by the Party. As Solidarity grew in strength it became clear that it was more than a trade union and was becoming a political force for democratic change in Poland. It also became clear that Poland was moving to a position in which the Party was sharing power with the people through Solidarity.

During 1980–1 the Polish economy, which was already in a weak state, became weaker still. There were also a number of political changes in government leaders culminating in General Jaruselski becoming Party Secretary in October 1981.

The USSR, along with other East European countries, viewed these developments with alarm. They were especially concerned at the possible spread of the 'Polish contagion' throughout Eastern Europe and even into the Soviet Union itself. However, despite various military exercises near the Polish border, no armed intervention took place and Poland was left to solve its own problems – as long as there was not a total collapse of control by the Party.

Eventually the crisis came to a climax in December 1981 when the Polish army imposed martial law. Solidarity was suspended and later banned. Its leaders, including Walesa, were detained and the Polish Communist Party was purged of those who had argued for reform. Martial law was lifted in December 1982 but by that time the Solidarity experiment was over. The memory of Solidarity was revived in 1983 when Lech Walesa was awarded the Nobel Peace Prize and its spirit will undoubtedly live on in the minds of the Polish people. Equally, the fear of Solidarity will remain with the governments of Eastern Europe and the Soviet Union.

Krakow, Poland: a Solidarity demonstration

Bulgaria, Romania and Albania

Elsewhere in Eastern Europe we find countries with varying degrees of dependence upon the USSR.

Of all the East European countries Bulgaria, along with East Germany, has the closest relations with the Soviet Union. Bulgaria's economy is very much linked to that of the USSR and in foreign policy it has always supported its Soviet ally.

Under President Ceaucescu, Romania has established a very hard-line political system in which little opposition to the Communist Party is allowed. However in foreign policy Romania has followed a very independent line. Although a member of Comecon and the Warsaw Pact, Romania has defied the USSR in maintaining good relations with China, in building close economic contacts with the West and in criticising Soviet intervention in Afghanistan. Above all, Romania is the only member of the Warsaw Pact to refuse to allow the stationing of Soviet troops on its territory.

Albania was led by Enver Hoxha from the end of the Second World War till his death in 1985. Under Hoxha, Albania became the most isolated of the East European states breaking with the Soviet Union in 1960 and with China in 1977. Under Hoxha's successor, Ramiz Alia, there are small signs of an end to Albania's international isolation.

Since coming to power in 1985 Mikhail Gorbachev has introduced major social, political and economic reforms in the USSR under the policies of **glasnost** and **perestroika**. These are having an impact upon Eastern Europe as the leaders of these countries begin to adapt to changes within the Soviet Union itself.

Questions

1. Explain how the countries of Eastern Europe came to be under Soviet control after 1945.
2. Explain the terms 'Iron Curtain' and 'satellite countries'.
3. What is the importance of Comecon and the Warsaw Pact in binding the countries of Eastern Europe to the Soviet Union?
4. What is Titoism and why did Yugoslavia manage to remain outside Russian control?
5. Describe in your own words the events in Hungary in 1956 and in Czechoslovakia in 1968.
6. What was the 'Brezhnev Doctrine'?
7. Describe in your own words the events in Poland during 1980–1, and explain why the Soviet Union was so concerned about these.
8. Briefly outline the relationship between the USSR and
   (a) Bulgaria, (b) Romania, (c) Albania.

Sino–Soviet Dispute

The Soviet leading clique have not shown one bit of good faith about improving Chinese-Soviet relations. Indeed they have whipped up one wave of anti-China feeling after another.

Chairman Hua in *New China News Agency*, August 1977

A departure from general laws of socialism, including proletarian internationalism could lead other parties into the grave consequences seen in China – the Chinese people's socialist gains have been gravely endangered.

Mr Brezhnev, 1977

China must develop the most advanced weapons in the world to deal with a surprise attack by Russia – China's most dangerous enemy.

Chinese Army newspaper

Russia has massed a million troops along the Chinese border posing a serious threat to China.

Chinese *Red Flag Journal*, July 1977

Modernisation of the Army is essential to take care of the Northern Bear.

Chinese People's Daily, 1977

. . . Reckless and provocative actions by the Chinese Authorities . . .

Soviet note, 1969

When you dance with a bear keep your axe handy.
(A Chinese warning to the USA about having disarmament talks with USSR.)

Chinese Foreign Minister, Ch'iao Kuan Hua

The Soviet Union is more ferocious, more reckless, and more treacherous than the United States.

Chinese People's Daily, 1977

Thirty Soviet troops crossed the Ussuri River frontier by boat and opened fire on Chinese inhabitants. The USSR admitted the crossing but denied injuring anyone.

News flash, 1978

His speeches are demagogic and hypocritical. He is undermining communist unity with fanatical stubbornness.

Soviet press comment on Chairman Hua's visit to Eastern Europe, 1978

These statements suggest that China and the USSR, the two great communist powers, are bitter enemies, confronting each other poised for war. Indeed, in recent years there has been conflict, though on a very limited scale.

Border Conflicts

NEWS FLASH 1969 'Chinese troops killed three Soviet border guards near the junction of the Amur River and Ussuri River, on the China–Soviet disputed border area. In reply to this, the USSR has moved more troops into the border area.'

NEWS FLASH 1974 'A serious dispute has arisen between the two major powers over a Soviet helicopter which was forced to land on the Chinese side of the border.'

In the 1974 incident the Chinese accused the USSR of spying activities over Chinese territory. The USSR denied this entirely, stating that the helicopter crew

Sino–Soviet border clashes

had lost its way. The crew were later paraded through towns in northern China and were not returned to the Soviet Union until after a year in captivity.

Soviet frontier troops and vehicles are confronted by a Chinese border patrol

YEARS OF CO-OPERATION

Although China and the USSR have had disputes over border areas, the main feature of their relations from 1949 until about 1960 was co-operation. First, when China became a communist country in 1949, there was widespread poverty, transport was in chaos, and industry and agriculture had been seriously affected by the Revolution. China turned to its large communist neighbour for financial aid and trade to build up economic strength. Second, as the Soviet Union was a communist country, it could serve as a model for China's own efforts to build a communist state. Third, the USA was a threat to both the USSR and China, indeed the latter's government was not recognised by the USA as the legitimate government of China. During these years, China co-operated with the Soviet Union and accepted it as 'leader of the socialist camp'.

YEARS OF DISPUTE

After 1957 the close co-operation between China and the USSR began to show signs of stress. First, the 'Great Leap Forward', started in China to improve industrial and agricultural output rapidly, was criticised in 1958 by Soviet advisers in China. They warned that the pace was too fast to be successful and were then themselves criticised by the Chinese. Second, there arose differences about how to interpret the works of **Marx** and **Lenin**. When the Russian leader Khrushchev made a verbal attack on Stalin and stated that war with the West

was not inevitable and that a move from capitalism to communism could be peaceful, this view of communist ideology was severely criticised by the Chinese. Third, there was little respect between the two leaders **Mao Zedong** and Khrushchev. Mao had adapted Marxist ideology to the Chinese situation and felt that Khrushchev was not a true communist. Khrushchev's visit to the West was seen as proof of this. Fourth, as China's feeling of independence of the Soviet Union grew, it felt increasingly that China, and not the USSR, was the true leader of the communist world. In 1961 China gave aid to Albania, a European country which the USSR considered to be in the Soviet area of influence.

After 1960 the dispute became quite open, with China taking a more independent line in its view of world affairs, e.g. aid to Albania and criticism of Khrushchev's visit to the USA. China also launched a bitter propaganda attack on the USSR over its withdrawal during the Cuba crisis in 1962, and the US/USSR Test Ban Treaty. The Soviets, for their part, continued to refuse to share their atomic secrets with China, and criticised the Chinese 'Cultural Revolution' of the late 1960s, during which Mao encouraged mass criticism of ideas that were not revolutionary in China, nor indeed in the USSR.

YEARS OF CO-OPERATION AGAIN?

During the 1980s these two great powers, although still criticising each other, have been less hostile in their comments and actions. The Soviet Union, feeling increasingly surrounded and threatened by other powers such as the USA, NATO and China, and concerned about growing Chinese trade links with the USA, was looking for ways to improve Sino-Soviet relations. Also, the USSR was counting the cost of having to keep over 500 000 Soviet troops and military equipment guarding its 7200-kilometre border with China.

On the other side, China still criticised the USSR for its 'imperialism' in Afghanistan, and its close links with China's South-East Asia neighbour, Vietnam. However, China was unable to 'modernise' its army and industry as quickly as expected and in 1982 agreed to 'talks about talks' with the USSR.

THE SINO–SOVIET DISPUTE IN RECENT YEARS

The Border

During the 1970s and 1980s, China has continued to complain to the USSR about where exactly their border should be, and about the large number of military forces which the Soviet Union has placed

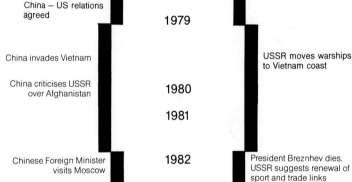

Sino-Soviet Relations Since 1949

CHINA	Year	USSR
China/USSR Aid Treaty signed	1949	Soviet advisers in Chinese Army
China declares 'Leader of the Socialist World'	1958	
Chinese **cadres** criticise Soviet advisers		Soviet advisers criticise 'Great Leap Forward'. USSR refuses to share atom secrets
	1960	
China denies that USSR leads Communist World		Withdrawal of Soviet aid and advisers from China
China claims part of USSR		USSR signs a Nuclear Test Ban Treaty with USA
China explodes atom bomb	1969	
Soviet troops killed in border clashes		USSR moves more troops to border area
Pres. Nixon visits China China enters UN.		Soviet helicopter pilots held on Chinese side of border.
Mao dies	1976	USSR accuses China of 'provocative policies'
New leader Hua criticises USSR policy		
Chairman Hua visits Yugoslavia, Rumania and Iran.	1978	USSR signs friendship treaty with Vietnam
China – US relations agreed	1979	
China invades Vietnam		USSR moves warships to Vietnam coast
China criticises USSR over Afghanistan	1980	
	1981	
Chinese Foreign Minister visits Moscow	1982	President Breznhev dies. USSR suggests renewal of sport and trade links with China
	1983	
Meeting in Beijing of Soviet Deputy Minister and Chinese officials		President Andropov calls for improved Sino-Soviet relations
	1984	USSR- China talks in Moscow
Chinese Deputy Premier meets Mr Gorbachev in Moscow	1985	
Sino-Soviet trade of £2000 million	1987	
	1988	Gorbachev proposes a Soviet-Chinese summit

on its side of the border. The issue has been given much publicity in China, with China claiming parts of the 7200-kilometre border which had been 'forced' from it by Russia in nineteenth-century treaties. Under the new Chinese leaders, who do not entirely share Mao's hatred of the USSR, some meetings were held with Soviet diplomats in 1982 about river rights in the disputed zone. Although little agreement was reached, the talks did help to reduce tension and allow China to concentrate its resources on improving its economic power. China is also intent on modernising the outdated equipment of the Chinese Army and Air Force. In the border areas Chinese forces are confronted by much better-equipped Soviet forces whose numbers could be further increased by troops drawn from the Warsaw Pact forces.

Foreign Policy

Since Mao's death in September 1976, the new leaders of China have continued the independent line in foreign relations.

In keeping with Mao's aim of industrial development and military improvements and expansion, the new leaders such as **Deng Xiaoping** are keen to 'modernise'. Unlike Mao, however, they are prepared to trade with the 'capitalist West' to speed up the modernisation. As early as 1977, a major Chinese trade delegation visited Britain to tour industrial companies such as Hawker Siddley, Rolls-Royce and British Steel. China has already bought 34 Trident airliners and shown interest in Harrier jump jets. Anti-tank missiles have been bought from France and anti-tank helicopters from West Germany. In 1984 China agreed to buy 30 satellite earth stations from Canada, at a cost of £10 million, to set up a telecommunications network in China.

Since 1971, when China entered the United Nations, it has criticised the USSR several times, especially in 1980 over Soviet action in Afghanistan. By 1983, When China was admitted to the Nuclear Power Commission, Chinese missiles, both land and submarine, had a range of about 3200 kilometres. By then China had the third biggest submarine fleet in the world, and was on equal terms with the USA, the USSR, Britain and France in that it had submarines capable of firing long-range nuclear missiles.

China also has been involved in African affairs: in 1975 the Tan-Zam Railway was completed by Chinese engineers; in 1978 Chinese officials, concerned about possible increase in Soviet influence, visited Zaire in Central Africa. China's view, however, is that Soviet involvement in Africa could be as disastrous as US involvement was in Vietnam. In 1982 Premier **Zhao** visited ten African countries, calling for unity by Third World countries.

The USA

China's relations with the USA have taken a new turn recently. From accusing the USA of being a 'paper tiger' and 'imperialist power' China now has trade links with the USA. In 1978 an American firm arranged to buy Chinese oil, and in 1983 two large American oil companies, Texaco and Chevron, signed agreements to drill for oil in Chinese off-shore waters. Also in 1983 the US firm Honeywell Controls gained an order to install computers in 14 Chinese universities, while another US firm, ITT, signed a £300-million deal to update China's telephone and telecommunications systems. Indeed by 1984 there were over 120 American firms based in Peking. US leaders such as President Nixon and President Reagan have visited China, as did over 150 000 American tourists in 1983. In 1984 the USA agreed to sell anti-tank missiles and air defence missiles to China.

China wishes to expand its industry and agriculture independently of the USSR but to do so needs trade. By trading with the USA, China can build its economic and military power while at the same time asserting its independence of the USSR. China also sees its relations with the USA as a counterbalance

Premier Zhao visits the USA, 1984

to the threat from the USSR, and has publicly warned the USA to be careful in its relations with the USSR over detente. China fears that the USA, by discussing disarmament and arms reduction with the USSR, will be caught off its guard by 'the northern bear', and indeed has encouraged the USA to strengthen its Pacific Fleet against possible Soviet attack.

SOUTH-EAST ASIA

In South-East Asia, China's policy has also been influenced by its relations with the Soviet Union. For example in 1977, when Vietnam complained about the small amount of aid it received from the USSR, China immediately offered to help. The following year, however, the USSR and Vietnam signed a long-term friendship agreement and there were skirmishes on the China/Vietnam border. In 1979 Chinese troops actually invaded Vietnam for about two weeks before retreating. By 1983, however, Vietnam was offering 'to restore good neighbourly relations' with China by suggesting a border cease-fire, despite further border skirmishes in that year.

In 1977 the Vietnam–Cambodia War put a strain on Sino–Soviet relations since the USSR supported Vietnam and China supported Cambodia (now Kampuchea). In 1978 China signed a treaty with Japan and in 1983 China and Japan issued a joint statement stating their concern over the number of Soviet SS-20 missiles in the area.

At Mao's funeral in 1976, the Premier of China, Hua Guofeng, declared that American and Soviet imperialism were equally bad, and that China's growing independence of the USSR might lead, despite continuing difficulties over the border and ideological differences, to a steadier relationship with both the USA and the USSR.

In 1988, Mr Gorbachev called for a Summit meeting between China and the Soviet Union. At the same time, Vietnam suggested it might be agreeable to the withdrawal of its troops from Kampuchea. This could improve relations between Vietnam and China.

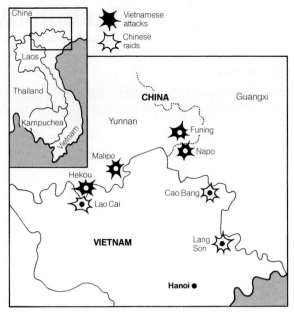

(*Newsweek*, 2 May 1983)

Questions

1. For what main reasons did the USSR and China quarrel?
2. Why is China more tolerant towards the USA now than previously?
3. What signs are there that USSR/China relations may improve again?

5. Flashpoint Confrontation

Introduction

So far we have concentrated on the main areas of confrontation between the Superpowers by looking at the most important events in their relations which have taken place since the end of the Second World War. In this chapter we turn our attention to the possible dangers which the world would face if the United States and the Soviet Union reached the stage of fighting each other directly in a 'hot war'.

Nuclear War

Hiroshima

August the 6th 1945, 8.15 a.m. The streets are full of people; people going to work, people going to school. It is a lovely summer morning: sunshine and blue sky. Blue sky stands for happiness in Japan. The air-raid sirens sound. No one pays attention. There's only a single enemy aircraft in the sky.

The aircraft flies across the city. Above the centre, something falls. It's hard to see – the bomb is very small; two kilograms in weight, a little larger than a tennis ball in size.

It falls for 10 or 15 seconds, it falls and falls. Then there is a sudden searing flash of light, brighter and hotter than a thousand suns. Those who were looking directly at it had their eyes burnt in their sockets. They never looked again on people or things.

In the street below there was a business man walking to his work; a lady, as elegant as she was beautiful; a brilliant student, leader of the class; a little girl, laughing as she ran.

And in a moment they were gone. They vanished from the earth. They were utterly consumed by the furnace of the flash. There were no ashes even on the pavement, nothing but their black shadows on the stones. Scores of thousands more, sheltered by walls or buildings from the flash, were driven mad by an intolerable thirst that followed from the heat. They ran in frenzied hordes towards the seven rivers of the delta on which Hiroshima is built.

They fought like maniacs to reach the water. If they succeeded, they stooped to drink the poisoned stream, and in a month they, too, were dead. Then came the blast, thousands of miles an hour. Buildings in all directions for kilometres, flattened to the ground. Lorries, cars, milk-carts, human beings, babies' prams, picked up and hurled like lethal projectiles hundreds of metres through the air.

Then the fireball touched the earth, and scores of conflagrations, fanned by hurricane winds, joined in a fire-storm. And many thousands more, trapped by walls of flame that leaped higher than the highest tower in the town, in swift or in longer agony, were burnt to death. Then all went black as night.

The mushroom cloud rose 12 000 metres. It blotted out the sun. It dropped its poison dust, its fallout, on everything that still remained not lethal in Hiroshima. And death by radio-active sickness from the fallout was the fate of those who had survived the flash, the river, the blast, the fire-storm.

These words were written by Philip Noel-Baker, one of the people who helped to draw up the United Nations Charter.

'A Nuclear Midget'

The Science Editor of *The Times* said:

'On that fatal morning 240 000 people died within an hour. Today in Hiroshima, many young people who were only embryos in their mothers' womb when the bomb fell, show the fatal seeds of leukemia. Let's remember that the Hiroshima bomb was a nuclear midget. Many of the present weapons are a hundred times as powerful, and some a thousand times. The stockpiles of the world, if they were used, would serve to exterminate mankind, three or four times over.'

The diagram on page 67 shows the effect that a 20-megatonne nuclear bomb would have on Scotland. (The Soviet Union has recently tested a 57-megatonne bomb.) The imaginary target shown is the important petrochemicals complex at Grangemouth. Other potential targets in Scotland include the naval dockyard at Rosyth, the US submarine base in the Holy Loch, the RAF stations at Leuchars and Lossiemouth, as well as the major cities.

The destruction which would result from such an

August, 1945: Hiroshima a few days after the bombing

attack is clearly shown. But as Philip Noel-Baker's description of Hiroshima suggests, some of the most terrible results of nuclear attack are not immediately visible. A nuclear war could affect human life in five different ways.

(a) Those close to the area where the bomb falls are immediately killed or terribly maimed by the blast and the fireball.

(b) Even more serious are the effects of the nuclear radiation which is released when the bomb explodes. Skin diseases, cancers, diseases of the blood such as leukemia and internal haemorrhages can affect those who survive the

The effects of a 20-megatonne bomb on
a target such as Grangemouth

1. 0–7 km: houses totally destroyed, streets impassable
2. 7–10 km: houses irreparably damaged, streets blocked until cleared with mechanical aids
3. 10–25 km: houses severely to moderately damaged, progress in street made difficult by debris
4. 25–40 km: houses lightly damaged. streets open but some glass and tile debris

immediate effects. Death from these diseases can occur many years later.

(c) The long-term effects of radiation are perhaps the most unpredictable and horrible effects of nuclear war. These can lead to terrible deformities in generations who weren't even born when the bomb fell.

(d) Most difficult to assess are the psychological effects on a nation which is on the receiving end of a nuclear attack. The Japanese people have been so deeply affected that they have built a museum of war which contains deformed human foetuses preserved in chemicals to encourage people to devote their lives to peace, not war.

(e) Recently scientists have shown that there may be another effect of nuclear war, which could be the most devastating of all. A nuclear explosion sends enormous amounts of dust into the atmosphere. As this settled over the

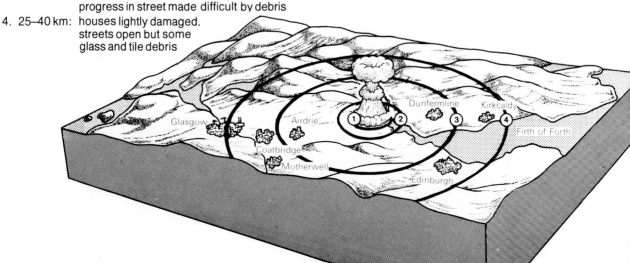

area of the attack, it would block out the sun, leave the area in permanent darkness and plunge the survivors into a 'nuclear winter'. A full-scale nuclear war could bring about temporary ice-age conditions over at least half the world. If this lasted long enough, the lack of sunlight could kill off plant life and threaten the very survival of the human race.

Questions

1. How many people died immediately as a result of the Hiroshima bomb?
2. Why will we never be able to estimate the total effect of the bomb?
3. Explain why the possible targets mentioned might be attacked. (Can you think of other possible targets in your area?)
4. List the five dangers to human beings which result from a nuclear explosion.

Nuclear Warfare Today

The bomb which was dropped on Hiroshima and caused such damage is now, in today's nuclear world, like the old musket was to the machine gun.

The Hiroshima atomic bomb was equal to the explosive strength of 20 000 tonnes of TNT. Today's nuclear weapons are equal to one million tonnes of TNT. This means that today's bombs are 5000 times more powerful than the Hiroshima bomb.

The Hiroshima bomb was dropped from an aeroplane; the nuclear weapons of today are mostly delivered by ballistic missiles.

Today's weapons are therefore much more destructive and much more sophisticated than the original nuclear weapons.

THE JARGON OF NUCLEAR WARFARE

Nuclear warfare has developed a special vocabulary of its own. Some of these special terms are given here to help you understand some of the new weapons systems in use today.

ABM	Anti-Ballistic Missile: fires nuclear warheads at incoming enemy missiles – a defensive weapon
IRBM	Intermediate-Range Ballistic Missile: range of up to 6500 km
ICBM	Intercontinental Ballistic Missile: range of over 6500 km
MRV	Multiple Re-entry Vehicle: missile with several nuclear warheads
MIRV	Multiple Independently-targeted Re-entry Vehicle: missile with several nuclear warheads which are independently aimed at different targets
SLBM	Submarine-launched Ballistic Missile
Kilotonne	a nuclear bomb with a destructive power equal to 1000 tonnes of TNT
Megatonne	a nuclear bomb with a destructive power equal to 1 million tonnes of TNT
Deterrence	the theory that possession of nuclear weapons prevents (or deters) an enemy from attacking
Overkill	the ability through possession of a vast amount of nuclear weapons to destroy an enemy many times over
Tactical nuclear war	a limited war which would use small-scale (tactical) nuclear missiles with a range of about 160 km. This would be a war limited to one specific area such as Europe or the Middle East
Strategic nuclear war	a major nuclear war which would use large-scale intercontinental (strategic) nuclear weapons. This would be a global war.

SOME MODERN NUCLEAR WEAPONS

The Polaris submarine In the Holy Loch near Dunoon there is a rather unusual submarine base which is home for British and American Polaris submarines. These submarines can stay underwater for up to three months at a time and carry 16 ballistic missiles, each of which is fitted with three 200-kilotonne MRV warheads with a range of 3000 kilometres. (Remember the damage done to Hiroshima was by a 20-kilotonne bomb dropped from an aeroplane.) These submarines patrol the seabed and are virtually undetectable and virtually invulnerable. If Britain or the USA were to be attacked by the Soviet Union and all their land-based nuclear missiles were destroyed before they could be launched, then the Polaris submarines at sea could launch a large enough attack in retaliation to inflict major damage upon the Soviet Union. It is therefore a major deterrent to nuclear attack. It is planned to replace Polaris with the Trident submarine which has 24 ballistic missiles, each with 17 MIRV warheads with a range of 11 000 kilometres.

The cruise missile In November 1983, despite a massive protest movement, the first of a new type of missile arrived at Greenham Common in England. This was the ground-launched cruise missile and was the first of 160 which were to be deployed in the United Kingdom as part of a NATO plan agreed in 1979 to strengthen Western Europe's nuclear defences. As part of the agreement West Germany, Italy, Belgium and the Netherlands were also to deploy cruise missiles, whilst West Germany was also to deploy Pershing missiles. These intermediate-range missiles were in reply to the deployment of mobile SS-20 missiles by the USSR in Eastern Europe.

The cruise missile is an American missile which can be launched from land, ship or plane and is therefore highly mobile in terms of launching. Those deployed in Europe will all be ground-launched. The missile can fly at 900 kilometres per hour about 20 metres above the ground. This enables it to slip under radar control to deliver 200-kilotonne nuclear warheads with amazing accuracy: to within 10 metres of their targets.

The cruise missile shown in the diagram would operate as follows:
(1) A cruise missile fitted with a nuclear warhead is fired from a submarine and flies low above the sea to avoid radar screens. The missile is guided by computer instructions which are checked by the missile's own altimeter.
(2) The missile now enters enemy territory flying at 900 kilometres per hour and below 30 metres. It is guided by computer from special maps produced from satellite air photographs.
(3) The cut-away shows the map split into 10-metre squares which identify contours in the land as well as high buildings.
    The missile can 'read' the ground using laser beams or radar altimeter and feed the information back to the computer to alter course if necessary.
(4) The final approach to target which is a rocket base. The missile is exceptionally accurate: to within 10 metres over 3000 kilometres. It could hit 'not just a given house, but a given room in the house', says one RAF expert.

How the cruise missile works

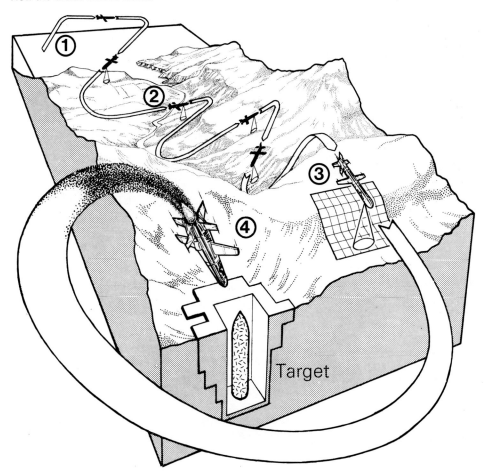

Target

Penetrates walls of buildings and armour of tanks. Leaves buildings intact for future use. Kills people.

Leaves little radioactive fallout so forces can enter a bombed area almost immediately.

Can be made small and fired with pinpoint accuracy.

BUT—death from neutron streams can be slow and painful, taking days or weeks.

The neutron bomb A nuclear explosion causes blast, heat and radioactive fallout. A neutron bomb takes this energy and converts it into instant, high-energy radiation. A small neutron warhead would cause a blast and fireball effect over only 250 metres while releasing a stream of lethal radiation which would affect the cells of living organisms over a distance of about 2.5 square kilometres. Unlike conventional nuclear explosions, this radiation does not result in lasting contaminating radio-activity and the site could be occupied within a few days. This weapon, which seems to come from the pages of science-fiction, 'can penetrate tanks and weapons without destroying their fabric, while striking at human beings and other living organisms'. It raises the possibility of fighting a limited nuclear war largely confined to tank forces, not necessarily involving the massive destruction of civilians, as a limited conventional nuclear war would.

Submarine-launched ballistic missiles, cruise missiles, neutron bombs: these are but three of the weapons systems in today's nuclear arsenal. There are many more, and recent reports suggest a new type of defence system may be on the horizon: ray weapons based on laser beams which can destroy enemy missiles. All this suggests that the arms race is continuing as quickly as ever and that the pattern of warfare is continually changing.

Questions

1. In what ways are today's nuclear weapons a greater threat than those of the early years of nuclear warfare?
2. Explain how the Polaris submarine can be described as a deterrent.
3. How does the neutron bomb differ from a conventional nuclear weapon?

The Nuclear World

NUCLEAR FUTURE?

As tensions mount in South Europe, Albanian warplanes drop nuclear bombs on Naples. Tel Aviv is destroyed by a nuclear attack from an unidentified country; Egyptian atomic bombs devastate London and Washington; China, the Soviet Union and Britain are drawn into war. Soon mushroom clouds cover nearly the entire planet.

This view of the end of the world, from Nevil Shute's book *On the Beach*, seemed almost science-fiction when written in the early 1950s. At that time only three countries (USA, USSR and Britain) had atomic weapons. Even up to 1964, by which time France and China had exploded nuclear devices, there was still the feeling that the spread of nuclear weapons, while a serious problem, would be controlled as part of arms control agreements. However, in recent years the number of countries possessing the potential to make nuclear weapons has increased considerably and the possibility that 'mushroom clouds cover nearly the entire planet' has moved dangerously nearer.

Nuclear Proliferation

The increased demands for advances in military technology and energy production by many countries have encouraged the development of further forms of nuclear power. Plutonium, for example, is not found in nature but can be produced as a by-product in conventional nuclear breeder reactors. Countries developing nuclear energy for peaceful purposes could turn out nuclear weapons by means of plutonium, a valuable source of energy but also the explosive heart of many nuclear weapons. The problem now is that nuclear energy and weapons **proliferation** are closely linked (see Nuclear World map).

It is estimated that there are now over 50 countries producing some plutonium from a total of over 400 reactors, and that this number of reactors could be trebled by the end of the century. Some countries, however, such as Canada, Sweden, Switzerland, West Germany and Japan can all produce

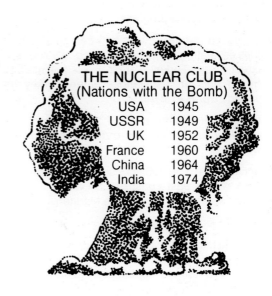

THE NUCLEAR CLUB (Nations with the Bomb)	
USA	1945
USSR	1949
UK	1952
France	1960
China	1964
India	1974

plutonium but do not make bombs. In 1977 President Carter stated that America would not use a plutonium-based energy policy at home, hoping other countries would follow that lead. Despite this, West Germany has sold plutonium processing equipment to Brazil, a deal worth $10 billion and France has sold similar equipment to Pakistan.

The nuclear world

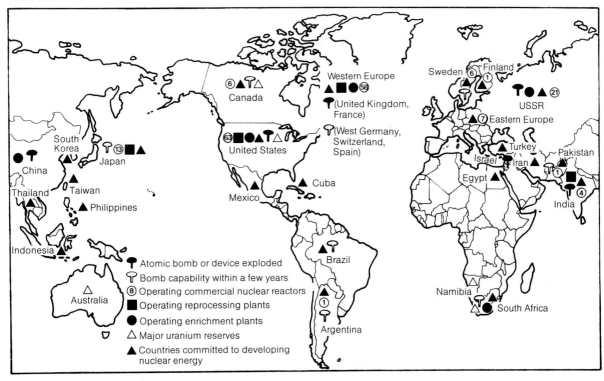

As more and more countries gain nuclear capability so the dangers increase:

- increased danger of war between small countries escalating to nuclear war, e.g. US troops in Greece and Turkey were put on full alert to guard nuclear installations when Turkey invaded Cyprus in 1974;

- the problem facing a commander in battle to decide when to give the order to use nuclear weapons;

- accidents, e.g. in 1963 US submarine *Thresher* sank off the east coast of USA and in 1968 a Soviet submarine sank in the Mediterranean;

- Nuclear leaks: radiation;

- political terrorists might be encouraged to make or capture small plutonium bombs as threats. The 1972 'Black September' Group at the Munich Olympics, and the 1977 Baader Meinhoff Group in Germany have proved their determination.

Questions

1. Why does Nevil Shute's description not look so much like science-fiction now?
2. Why are some countries prepared to sell plutonium-making equipment to other countries?
3. What is meant by 'nuclear proliferation'?

The Arms Race

In the heart of the Pentagon, a heavy oaken door leads to the supersecret National Military Command Centre. No one gets through the door without presenting a color-coded Joint Chiefs of Staff identification badge, which armed guards scrutinize under ultraviolet light. In one section of the two-storey centre, shifts of officers and men from all four of the armed services maintain a round-the-clock vigil. A red telephone links them directly to the White House, a beige phone can instantly reach any US military commander anywhere in the world. Mounted on one wall are half a dozen computer-fed display screens (each 2 m by 2.5 m) which flash the status of US forces. Last week, at the press of a button, the screens gave this picture of some of the US strategic strength on station: 1054 nuclear-tipped intercontinental missiles, most of them sited in concrete-reinforced underground silos scattered across the Great Plains; 21 nuclear powered submarines gliding stealthily through the world's oceans, their 336 slender missiles within range of Soviet targets; 90 B-52 bombers ready to take the air on 15 minutes' alert; six aircraft carrier task groups deployed in the world's oceans; five combat-ready divisions positioned in Germany from the Rhine to the East–West frontier.

These are just a part of the forces in the American military arsenal – unquestionably the most powerful in the nation's history.

The arms race is the struggle between the USA and the USSR for military superiority in the world. Just as the Americans have advanced systems of security and weapons, so too the Soviets develop their systems of security and weapons. Both countries possess vast numbers of strategic bombers, intercontinental missiles and seacraft such as submarines and cruisers. All of these are capable of delivering nuclear attacks. The race has produced so many weapons that there is now 'overkill' capacity. The Soviet Union has the capacity to destroy every major American city 20 times over, while the USA has the capacity to destroy every major Soviet city 50 times over.

'We shall be confronted with the need to answer this challenge in order to ensure the security of the Soviet people, their allies and friends. In the final analysis, this would raise the arms race to an even more dangerous level.'

(*President Brezhnev of the Soviet Union, referring to America's neutron bomb – Tass News Agency Report, 1977*)

'If the Soviets continue to increase the size and effectiveness of their strategic forces, this country, beyond question, will respond to ensure that our forces continue to provide a deterrence that is credible.'

(*US Secretary of Defense, Harold Brown, 1977*)

These statements by leading figures in both the USA and Soviet Union indicate that the arms race is likely to continue despite Strategic Arms Limitation Talks (**SALT**). The struggle for military supremacy between the USA and the USSR is not new, however, and there are a number of reasons why the race has persisted for some time:

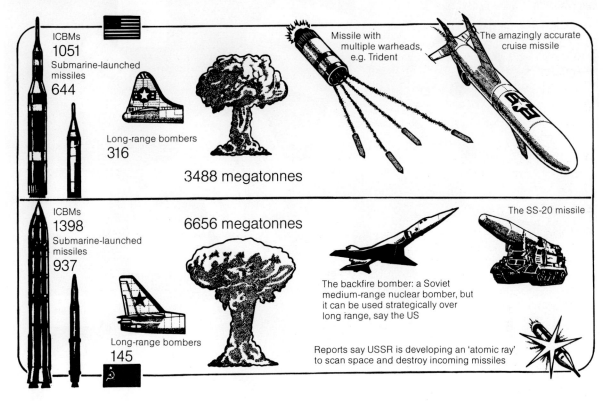

ICBMs
1051
Submarine-launched missiles
644

Long-range bombers
316

3488 megatonnes

Missile with multiple warheads, e.g. Trident

The amazingly accurate cruise missile

ICBMs
1398
Submarine-launched missiles
937

6656 megatonnes

Long-range bombers
145

The SS-20 missile

The backfire bomber: a Soviet medium-range nuclear bomber, but it can be used strategically over long range, say the US

Reports say USSR is developing an 'atomic ray' to scan space and destroy incoming missiles

● fear that one side might launch a sudden attack on the other (Americans still remember the sudden Japanese attack on Pearl Harbor);

● fear that allies (e.g. members of NATO or Warsaw Pact) might lack support in time of crisis;

● fear that one side might take advantage of its superiority to increase its influence in other parts of the world, e.g. development of US and Soviet fleets;

● fear that other countries might turn to the stronger one for help.

THE ARMS BUILD-UP

The build-up in arms is particularly marked in nuclear weapons. One of the difficulties in calculating in whose favour the 'balance' is tipped is that there are various ways of measuring the build-up: (a) by delivery vehicles (missiles, planes) – the USSR has a 20 per cent lead; (b) by number of warheads – the USA has double the amount of the USSR. Other factors such as accuracy, command efficiency, readiness and reliability must also be included.

The Future Balance

The future balance is already see-sawing perilously. The USA has developed the cruise missile, the neutron bomb and anti-satellite weapons, while the USSR is reported to have the 'atom ray' and also a 'hunter killer' satellite which could track and destroy orbiting US spacecraft.

To add to the *Star Wars* qualities of possible future arms, both the USA and the USSR are developing lasers which can vaporise metal. Although biological warfare – the dropping of germs on enemy targets – was banned by the Geneva Convention in 1971, both sides are developing chemical warfare weapons, such as nerve gases which can paralyse or kill.

In electronic warfare there have also been advances. The Americans are reputed to have used 'electronic battlefield' experiments during the Vietnam War, while the USSR has used electronic warfare techniques to 'jam' NATO naval manoeuvres in the North Atlantic area.

Both countries have spent much money on weather research, where there are possibilities of altering weather patterns by seeding rainclouds to produce flooding or drought as required.

Towards Star Wars? (*The Observer*, 22 Jan. 1984)

In 1984 President Reagan proposed a *Star Wars* defence system (**Strategic Defence Initiative: SDI**) to defend the USA against missile attack. The system would use laser-equipped statellites which could destroy enemy missiles and satellites in space. Despite strong objections from the USSR, part of the Star Wars system was given a trial run in 1985 when an anti-satellite weapon (ASAT), fired from a fighter jet aircraft, successfully destroyed a US space satellite over the Pacific Ocean.

By the late 1980s, despite continuing Soviet objections to SDI, and the signing of the 1988 Moscow Treaty reducing intermediate nuclear weapons, President Reagan showed no sign of abandoning the SDI programme.

Questions

1. What security checks are there at the American National Military Command Centre?
2. What is 'overkill'?
3. Why do both countries continue the arms race when they already possess overkill?
4. What weapons could be in the arms race in the future?

6. Reducing Confrontation

Cold War or Co-existence?

In the four decades that have passed since the emergence of the USA and USSR as the leading world Superpowers, a relationship of confrontation and hostility has developed between them. The USA and USSR represent opposing values and beliefs and as a result their economic and political systems are in conflict – the conflict of capitalism and communism. As leaders of two opposing ideologies, they are in conflict throughout the world for influence. Their global interests are so wide and varied that they have been rivals in most areas of the world. However, they have been rivals in a nuclear age, and the development of nuclear weapons has led to a situation where these competing Superpowers know that they cannot make war on each other without destroying themselves and most of the rest of the world. They are, as a result, enemies who are forced to 'co-exist' through a common need for survival. The history of the Superpowers' relations since the end of the Second World War is like that of a roller-coaster, of ups and downs between open hostility and closer co-operation, between Cold War and co-existence.

COLD WAR

The war-time alliance between the USA and the USSR soon faded as the Soviet Union began to take control of the countries of Eastern Europe in order to increase its security. The language of the Cold War began when Winston Churchill spoke in 1946 of 'an iron curtain' falling across Europe. In 1947 the US President, Truman, pledged the USA to 'support free peoples who are resisting attempted subju-gation by armed minorities or by outside pressures'. This was directed against the Soviet Union and became known as the Truman Doctrine or the policy of 'containment' – i.e. the USA would act throughout the world to contain the spread of communism.

In 1948 the first head-to-head confrontation between the Superpowers took place over the city of Berlin. The USA and the USSR entered a period of intense rivalry and hostility but were kept in check by fear of nuclear war. Throughout the 1950s and 1960s the Cold War was fought in Korea, Europe and Vietnam. The most critical moment came in 1962, when the Cuban missile crisis threatened to turn the Cold War into a very hot nuclear war.

CO-EXISTENCE

The Cuban Crisis brought home the narrow line between Cold War and nuclear war. However, even before this there were signs that the Superpowers were willing to work towards a closer understanding. **Khrushchev**, the Soviet leader, had spoken in 1955 of the need for the USA and USSR 'to exist together on the one planet'. The recognition of the dangers of their rivalry and the attempts to work in closer co-operation became known as **peaceful co-existence**. The Superpowers would still compete but would take steps to ensure that this competition did not lead to the danger of war. In 1955 the first post-war summit meeting took place between the leaders of the USA and the USSR. In 1959 Khrushchev visited the USA. Following the Cuban crisis, the USA and the USSR agreed to set up a 'hot line' telephone link by which the leaders of the two countries could contact each other immediately during any future crisis.

Detente

During the 1960s the term peaceful co-existence came to be replaced by that of detente. This French word has no direct translation into English but it has come to mean 'the relaxation of international tension'. In practice this relaxing of tension took two forms during the 1960s and 1970s:
(a) the relaxing of military tension through arms control, and
(b) the relaxing of political tension through economic, social and cultural co-operation.

ARMS CONTROL

A number of arms agreements and talks have been initiated since the 1960s. Some of these have been multilateral in that they have involved a large number of countries, others have been bilateral in that they have involved only the two superpowers.

1963 the Partial Test Ban Treaty: following the near disaster over Cuba, the USA, the USSR and the UK agreed to stop testing nuclear weapons in the atmosphere and to conduct such tests only underground.

1967 the Outer Space Treaty: this treaty, signed by over 60 countries, banned the sending of nuclear weapons into outer space or into earth's orbit.

1968 the Nuclear Non-Proliferation Treaty: this treaty has been signed by over 90 countries all agreeing to limit the spread of nuclear weapons by refusing to exchange nuclear knowledge or equipment.

1971 the Seabed Pact: this treaty has been signed by over 40 countries agreeing not to place nuclear weapons on the seabed beyond a country's 20-kilometre limit.

1972 the Biological Warfare Treaty: this treaty has been signed by over 30 countries and bans the production and storing of biological weapons. It also ordered their destruction and is thus an example of disarmament as opposed to arms control.

1972 SALT 1 (Strategic Arms Limitation Treaty): this agreement followed a number of years of discussion between the USA and the USSR on controlling the arms race in long-range nuclear missiles. The agreement led to a limit on the number of ICBMs, SLBMs and ABMs held by each side.

1979 SALT 2: this treaty extended strategic arms limitation between the Superpowers by placing fresh ceilings on the number of strategic missiles held by the USA and USSR.

1981 Talks were begun in Geneva to limit the number and type of missiles in Europe. These became known as the **INF** talks (**Intermediate-range Nuclear Forces**).

1982 Talks were begun in Geneva to reduce the number of long-range missiles held by the Superpowers. These became known as the **START** talks (**Strategic Arms Reduction Talks**).

1988 INF Treaty: this treaty banned the deployment of intermediate-range nuclear weapons within Europe.

This impressive list of treaties and agreements hides the harsh reality that the arms race has, however, become greater than ever. Talks have either broken down or treaties have been neglected. The 1963 Test Ban Treaty was not signed by China or France who have continued to test nuclear weapons in the atmosphere. The Non-Proliferation Treaty has not been signed by a number of countries who are on the verge of becoming nuclear powers. Major powers such as the USA, the USSR and France have been dealing with countries like Brazil, Argentina and South Africa in material for nuclear energy which can be used in the production of nuclear weapons. SALT 2 was never ratified by the US Senate. The USA and the USSR have continued to spend ever-increasing amounts on nuclear weapons. New nuclear weapons systems are being developed, with space being the next possible area for the arms race.

Steps towards arms control

THE RELAXING OF POLITICAL TENSION

The second form of detente has involved a series of efforts to relax political tension through greater co-operation in a number of areas. It was hoped that the more the two powers co-operated across a wide front of problems, the more they would have in common and the more they would understand and trust each other. This led to a succession of summit meetings between the two countries' leaders. During times of crisis, such as the Middle East war of 1973, the Superpowers were in contact with each other to reduce the risk of being dragged into direct confrontation. Trade agreements were reached – this led in particular to the sale of wheat and Western technology to the USSR. There was more cultural and social contact through sport, music, ballet and theatre and through increased tourism to the USSR and other East European countries.

The high point of detente was reached in 1975, when two events seemed to highlight the relaxation of rivalry and hostility. In July a Soviet Soyuz spacecraft linked up with an American Apollo spacecraft and the crews shook hands 140 miles out in space as a gesture of co-operation. In the same year a major international conference was held at Helsinki at which 35 nations, including the USA and the USSR, signed an agreement that recognised Europe's post-war frontiers and stressed the importance of increased contact between East and West.

DETENTE CRUMBLES

Events have since threatened to bring to a halt this progress in reducing international tension. Both sides had in a sense differing ideas on what detente meant and how it should work. The USA saw detente as providing a number of incentives for the USSR, such as trade, in return for which the USSR would behave internationally in a way more acceptable to the USA. The USSR, on the other hand, did not accept that detente should end East–West struggle for influence throughout the world. Rather, they saw it as setting certain limits within which the two Superpowers could reasonably compete. The USSR saw President Carter's criticisms of their abuse of human rights as breaking the spirit of detente. The USA saw Soviet involvement in Angola, Ethiopia and South Yemen as the furthering of Soviet influence at the expense of detente.

Despite the signing of SALT 2 in June 1979, Superpower detente was dealt a further and crucial blow with Soviet intervention in Afghanistan later that year. The USA withdrew from the SALT 2 agreement, organised an international boycott of the 1980 Moscow Olympics and restricted sales of technology and grain to the USSR. After Afghanistan, relations between the USA and USSR continued to worsen. President **Ronald Reagan**, arguing that the USSR had used detente to move ahead in the arms race, began a major re-armament programme in the USA. In speeches Reagan openly voiced harsh criticisms of the USSR, describing the Soviet Union in 1983 as 'the focus of evil in the

Apollo/Soyuz link up

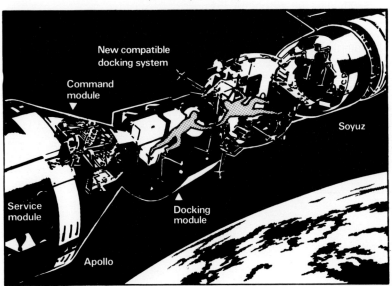

New compatible docking system

Command module

Service module

Apollo

Docking module

Soyuz

modern world'. The decision of the USA and its NATO allies to go ahead with the deployment of cruise and Pershing missiles in Western Europe in 1983 led to the USSR walking out of the INF talks in Geneva. Since the START talks had also been suspended, the USA and USSR found themselves for the first time in 14 years in a situation where they were not involved in arms control talks of any kind. When the Soviet leader **Yuri Andropov** died in 1984, to be succeeded by **Konstantin Chernenko**, relations between the Superpowers seemed to have broken down so far that a second Cold War had begun.

A RENEWAL OF PEACEFUL CO-EXISTENCE

The coming to power in 1985 of the new Soviet leader Mikhail Gorbachev seems to have opened up a new chapter in Superpower relations. Gorbachev has introduced into the Soviet Union a series of social, political and economic reforms aimed at opening up Soviet society and restructuring its economy. He also indicated to Western leaders that he would be willing to enter into serious negotiations aimed at reducing the arms race. Despite the hostility he had earlier shown towards the Soviet Union, President Reagan responded to this and the two leaders met in an international summit in Geneva in 1985. This has been followed by further summits in Reykjavik, the capital of Iceland, in Washington and in Moscow. The most important result of these summits has been the INF Treaty which banned the deployment in Europe of such intermediate-range nuclear missiles as Cruise, Pershing and the Soviet SS.20. The summits have also seen talks on reducing the number of strategic nuclear missiles held by the Superpowers. However, President Reagan's commitment to SDI (Strategic Defence Initiative) or 'Star Wars' has been a block to progress on this. Above all the summits have opened up a renewed era of coexistence between the Superpowers and the prospects of a second Cold War in the 1980s have diminished.

Questions

1. Why have the USA and the USSR become major rivals in the world today?
2. Explain what is meant by saying that the USA and the USSR are 'enemies who are forced to co-exist'.
3. Explain what is meant by the term 'Cold War' and list three examples of the Cold War during the period 1946 to 1962.
4. What is meant by the term 'peaceful co-existence' and what part did the Cuban crisis play in bringing this about?
5. Explain what is meant by the term 'detente'.
6. List the main (a) multilateral and (b) bilateral arms treaties/talks in the period since 1963.
7. Explain why these treaties/talks have failed to halt the arms race.
8. What other evidence was there of detente in Superpower relations during the early 1970s?
9. In what ways did the USA and the USSR view detente differently and what results did this have?
10. What evidence was there of a breakdown in detente since 1979 and in what ways have Superpower relations improved since 1985?
11. Using the information in the text and information from the TV/newspapers, write your views on whether relations between the USA and USSR, at the time of your writing, are those of Cold War or those of co-existence.

PART 2

Co-operation in Europe

1. Conflict to Co-operation

The EEC: the Beginnings

POST-WAR EUROPE

The photograph on this page shows the condition of Europe in 1945 after six years of devastating war and destruction. Twenty-five million people had been made refugees because they had been driven out of their own country or because their homes had been destroyed by bombing. Industry and agriculture were in ruins. Factories had been destroyed and farmland was devastated by years of fighting. Roads, railways and bridges had been destroyed. Europe was in a mess. It was time to pick up the pieces and try to restore normal life.

Often after a major war or catastrophe, when things are at their worst, people start thinking and talking of a new order of society to prevent such disasters happening again. On a world scale, politicians were planning for this through the United Nations. Within Europe, politicians began to talk about a new European unity to replace the old pre-war divisions. During the first 45 years of the twentieth century, Europe had undergone two major wars. Millions had been killed. This was not to be allowed to happen again.

The people of Europe would have to forget old national hatreds and work together to prevent another war. Europe would have to be restored economically so that people could enjoy prosperity again.

Winston Churchill, the wartime leader of Britain, summed up this mood in a speech in 1946:

'What is the sovereign remedy? It is to recreate the European family . . . and to provide it with a structure under which it can dwell in peace, safety and freedom. We must build a kind of United States of Europe.'

Europe in ruins: Hanover, 1945

THE BEGINNINGS OF CO-OPERATION

By 1946 it was becoming clear that if there were to be a United States of Europe it would not apply to the whole of Europe, for soon after the war a major new division began to appear – the division of Europe into East and West, communist and non-communist. This was to give the countries of Western Europe their first push into co-operation – a military one which found its shape in NATO. It was also the threat from communism that gave them their first experience in economic co-operation. Economic recovery was very slow in Western Europe and the USA began to fear that the people might turn to communism as a way out of their difficulties. Acting under the orders of the American Secretary of State, the nations of Western Europe drew up a kind of shopping list of aid that they required. This 'Marshall Plan' gave out millions of dollars of aid and acted like a blood transfusion to the sick economies of Western Europe.

The nations of Western Europe had co-operated in this scheme and this led some statesmen to believe that the path to European unity would not come from some dramatic political event – the countries of Europe were too concerned with their own freedom of action for that – but rather could come from binding their countries in an ever-increasing number of economic organisations. The path to political unity would result from the experience and benefits of economic co-operation.

Such ideas led to Europe's first successful project in economic co-operation. This came from a plan proposed by a Frenchman, **Robert Schuman**. He pointed out that European recovery was being held back by the problems of its coal and steel industries. Europe's reserves of coal and iron ore lay in different countries. Tariffs had to be paid on the import of these basic raw materials. Schuman proposed that the countries of Western Europe should pool their resources in coal and steel and that a joint authority, which would be separate from their national governments, should run them. France, West Germany, Italy, Holland, Belgium and Luxembourg all agreed to co-operate in the scheme and so, in 1952, these six countries set up the European Coal and Steel Community (**ECSC**).

This soon proved to be very successful. It was led by another Frenchman, Jean Monnet, and the member countries began to see the benefits of co-operation. The output of steel greatly increased and this helped all other types of industry. The creation of the ECSC coincided with the start of a decline in coal mining as new fuels began to compete. The ECSC was able to help those who began to suffer from this decline. Redundant Belgian miners were given grants to help them move to another area for work or retrain for new employment. Undoubtedly, the success of the ECSC encouraged the leaders of the six member countries to consider the possibility of further economic co-operation.

Questions

1. Describe the condition of Europe in 1945 after the Second World War.
2. In what way is Churchill's speech typical of the mood of politicians in Europe in the years immediately after 1945?
3. Why do you think it proved more difficult to set up a 'kind of United States of Europe' at once?
4. What was the Marshall Plan and what lessons did economic co-operation like this have for Europeans like Robert Schuman?
5. Describe in your own words the ideas behind the European Coal and Steel Community and explain how it paved the way for closer European unity.

Towards European Unity

The Treaty of Rome, which established the European Economic Community, was signed by six countries on 25 March 1957, and came into force on 1 January 1958. The six countries which took this historic step towards European unity were France, Belgium, Holland, West Germany, Luxembourg and Italy. By signing the treaty 'The Six' agreed to the following.

(1) Free trade within the EEC between member countries. This included the gradual removal of customs duties and tariffs.
(2) A common customs barrier by all member-countries against all non-member countries.
(3) Free movement of citizens and workers of member countries from one part of the EEC to another.
(4) A Common Agricultural Policy (**CAP**): a plan to encourage the development and improvement of farming in all parts of the Community.
(5) Political unity. In the long term it is hoped there will be political unity through the European Parliament.
(6) A European Social Fund: money to be made available to areas in the EEC which have serious problems, e.g. high unemployment, poor housing.
(7) A European Investment Bank: to provide money for huge projects, for example in industry, which a single country would be unable to afford.

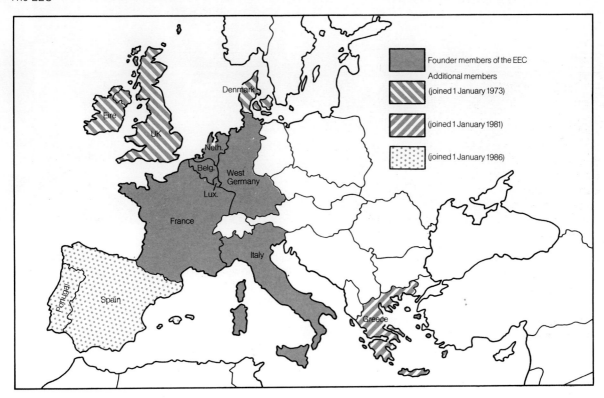

Founder members of the EEC

Additional members

(joined 1 January 1973)

(joined 1 January 1981)

(joined 1 January 1986)

A number of European countries, including Britain, chose not to join the EEC in 1958. The communist countries in Eastern Europe refused to recognise the EEC; under the leadership of the Soviet Union, they had already set up their own version of the EEC, known as Comecon (Council for Mutual Economic Assistance). A number of countries in southern Europe, such as Spain and Portugal, were unable to join because they were not democratic countries. Others, such as Greece and Turkey, were not economically strong enough to become full and equal partners in the new Community. In northern Europe, the Scandinavian countries, with their superior living standards, had already made an unsuccessful attempt at European integration and felt no great urgency to join the EEC.

One of the most significant omissions from 'The Six' was Britain. It could have become a member of the Community in 1958 but for a number of reasons preferred to remain outside. Many British people did not think of themselves as part of Europe, since Britain is separate from the mainland of Europe. Britain had closer connections and trade links with Commonwealth countries such as Australia and New Zealand and did not wish to alter those. Many people in Britain were also afraid of the possible effect on the British Parliament and its decisions if there was a large European Parliament making decisions too. In the 1950s there still remained the idea that Britain was a major world power and should remain independent rather than join in such a close group as the EEC. Finally, Britain's farmers were afraid that cheaper European food would flood into Britain and that they would lose their subsidies from the British government.

Trade with the rest of Europe was nevertheless important for Britain and, in 1959, it helped in the setting up of a new association – the European Free Trade Association (**EFTA**) – along with Norway, Sweden, Denmark, Austria, Portugal and Switzerland. (Finland became an associate member in 1961 and Iceland a full member in 1970.) This association required fewer obligations than the Rome Treaty: the EFTA countries agreed to dismantle the barriers to trade on industrial goods among themselves but each retained its own tariffs and commercial policies towards the rest of the world. For these countries this was a suitable

Ministers of 'The Six' sign the Treaty of Rome, 1957

compromise because it provided a measure of economic co-operation without the full political co-operation required by the EEC.

A CHANGE OF MIND

By the early 1960s, however, the attitudes of several of the countries which had stayed outside the EEC in 1958 had changed. EFTA did not prove to be the success its members had hoped for: the total population of the EFTA countries amounted to only about half the population of the EEC, and there was thus less scope for trade. Besides, EFTA contained none of the economic giants of Europe. Britain's attitude towards the EEC was influenced by its changing position as a world economic and political power. Trade with the Commonwealth was being hit by higher transport costs and many Commonwealth countries were seeking trade with other countries, e.g. Australia began trading increasingly with the USA. Britain also began to realise that it could not match the rise in world power of the USA and the Soviet Union, and began to see Europe as an alternative to relying on the USA.

But perhaps the most important reason for the growing opinion within some of the EFTA countries that they should join the EEC was the success of the Community. There was considerable evidence that the EEC countries were growing wealthier at a faster rate than those countries outside the EEC.

As a result of all these factors, Britain and several other European countries which remained outside the EEC began to consider seriously a belated application for membership in the early 1960s.

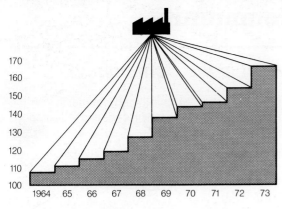

170
160
150
140
130
120
110
100
1964 65 66 67 68 69 70 71 72 73

Industrial production index of the EEC

'The Six' become Twelve

The following table shows the attempts by several countries to become members of the EEC.

1961 Britain (under a Conservative government), Denmark, Norway and Eire applied to join the EEC but were turned down by France, led by General de Gaulle, who was afraid that the entry of these other countries might lead to the loss of French power within the Community.

1967 Britain (under a Labour government), Denmark, Norway and Eire again applied to join, but were once again rejected as a result of French opposition.

NON!

JOHN BULL

1970–3 Negotiations between the EEC and the four applicant countries were renewed in 1970. These negotiations covered many important points, including the contributions of the applicant countries to the EEC budget, agricultural and fishing policies. After long discussions, Britain, Denmark and Eire signed the Accession Treaty and became members of the EEC on 1 January 1973. Norway stayed out of the EEC as the result of a referendum, in which the people voted against joining.

Even after joining the EEC in 1973, the British government had second thoughts about the terms and conditions of membership which it had secured. On 5 June 1975 the Labour government held a referendum to find out whether or not the British people wanted to continue membership of the Community. This is how the voters of Britain decided:

YES   17 378 581 (67.2%)
NO   8 470 073 (32.8%)

The Prime Minister, Harold Wilson, summed up the result as follows:

'It means that 14 years of argument are over . . . those who have had reservations about Britain's commitment should work wholeheartedly with our partners in Europe.'

1981 Greece was admitted as the tenth member of the Community after several years of negotiation.

1986 Spain and Portugal were admitted after eight years of negotiation.

The EEC now has twelve members. Has it reached full membership or will it continue to grow? Norway and Turkey are the most likely future members. Or will the Community break up? Disagreements between member-countries, particularly over budget contributions, fishing rights and the CAP, show that there are still many arguments between them about Community policies.

Questions

1. Outline briefly the main points contained in the Treaty of Rome.
2. Explain why some European countries did not join the EEC in 1958.
3. What is EFTA?
4. Why did the British government change its mind about EEC entry in the 1960s?
5. Make a list of the attempts made by Britain to join the EEC.
6. What was the decision of the British people in the 1975 Referendum on EEC membership?

2. European Community

Aims

Like the United Nations, the European Community is part of an attempt to co-operate to build a just, peaceful and prosperous world. With only ten member nations and 268 million inhabitants the EEC is much smaller than the UN, but through association and trade agreements it is linked with more than half the countries in the world.

The countries of the EEC together have a higher population than that of either the USA or the Soviet Union. It is the world's largest trader, the major importer of goods from the less developed countries and a leading world producer of farm products. The community is not a Superpower, but its economic strength gives it great world influence.

For centuries the countries which now make up the European Community fought each other. Twice these quarrels became world wars in which more than 40 million people died. It is vital to prevent that happening again.

In the 1920s and 1930s many countries suffered high unemployment and tried to survive the economic crisis by putting up tariff barriers against other countries. The result was that conditions got worse and unemployment became even more widespread. The European Community is designed to stop such harmful policies and to encourage the member-nations to solve their problems together.

Individually, Britain and other European countries are small by comparison with the United States, the USSR or China. But if the countries of Europe act together they can have more real influence for prosperity and peace, and can help the world's poor more effectively.

The Community's essential aim, as laid down in the Rome Treaty, is the constant improvement of its peoples' living and working conditions.

Questions

1. Which countries are members of the European Community?
2. List four important aims of the European Community.

What is the Community?

The twelve countries have joined together to form the European Community, which contains three important organisations:

The European Economic Community (EEC)
The European Coal and Steel Community (ECSC)
The European Atomic Energy Community (EURATOM)

The EEC aims to remove the economic barriers between its member-states and integrate their economic policies. This is the organisation on which we shall concentrate since it is the one which has the most influence on our daily lives.

The ECSC, formed in 1952, paved the way for economic unity by placing its six founder members' coal and steel industries in a single 'common market'.

EURATOM's main purpose is to develop the peaceful uses of nuclear energy in the Community.

These three organisations share the same four institutions which have the job of running the Community and making the important decisions for the member nations. These four institutions are:

The Commission
The European Parliament
The Council of Ministers
The Court of Justice

Questions

1. Which three organisations make up the European Community?
2. Briefly describe the purpose of each of these three organisations.

THE COUNCIL OF MINISTERS

The most important decisions are made by the Council of Ministers, whose job it is to decide on proposals made to it by the Commission. The Council consists of ten ministers, each representing one of the member-governments. The actual ministers who attend depends on the particular subject being discussed. Usually the Foreign Ministers of each member-government attend, but if the subject being debated is one which is closely concerned with the work covered by another minister it is usual for that person to attend. The twelve ministers with

EEC headquarters: the Berlaymont Buildings in Brussels

responsibility for industry, for example, would attend if the matter being discussed was one which could have an important effect on industrial policy in the Community. Similarly, the ministers for agriculture, fisheries, environment, finance and so on would be called upon to give their expert opinions and advice on days when topics closely related to their areas of responsibility were being discussed.

Voting in the Council is rare: most decisions are reached after a period of discussion and compromise. When voting does take place, a system of weighted votes is used, which gives greater influence to the member-nations with larger populations. At present, the number of votes is as follows:

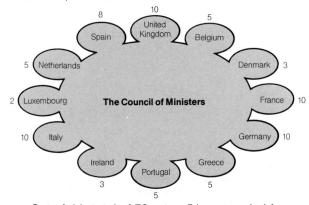

Out of this total of 76 votes, 54 are needed for a majority. If any member-nation feels that the decision taken is not in the interests of its own people, it may use a veto to stop the proposal being passed.

Questions

1. Describe the membership of the Council of Ministers.
2. What is the Council's main job?
3. How are decisions reached in the Council?
4. Explain the voting system in the Council.

THE COMMISSION

The Commission, together with the Council, is involved in the day-to-day decision-making process of the Community. The Commission makes policy proposals, which it sends to the Council of Ministers, after consulting a wide range of experts and interested people and organisations.

The Commission has 17 members as follows:

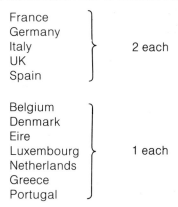

France	
Germany	
Italy	2 each
UK	
Spain	
Belgium	
Denmark	
Eire	
Luxembourg	1 each
Netherlands	
Greece	
Portugal	

These members are appointed jointly by their member-governments for a four-year renewable term of office. Once appointed, the 17 Commissioners are not national representatives, but Community statesmen, pledged to act independently in the interest of the Community as a whole. They must think and act as Europeans.

Each Commissioner is responsible for a particular area of Community policy such as agriculture, transport, the environment and so on. Regular discussions are held between each Commissioner's department and interested groups such as trade unions and other pressure groups. Following these discussions, the Commissioner produces draft proposals designed to improve the quality of life of the people of the Community. This draft proposal is then discussed by all 17 Commissioners who decide on the final proposal to go to the Council of Ministers. The Commission reaches its decisions by simple majority vote if necessary, and is answerable to the European Parliament which can dismiss it on a two-thirds vote of no confidence.

Questions

1. Describe the membership of the Commission.
2. Explain the job of a Commissioner.
3. Write a short description of the European Commission.

THE EUROPEAN PARLIAMENT

The European Parliament consists of the 514 representatives of the people of the twelve member-nations. The seats are distributed as shown below.

Each Member of the European Parliament (MEP) provides a direct link between his or her constituents and the European Community. The eight Scottish constituencies are shown in the map below.

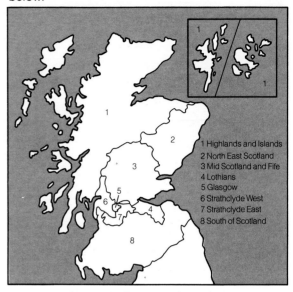

1 Highlands and Islands
2 North East Scotland
3 Mid Scotland and Fife
4 Lothians
5 Glasgow
6 Strathclyde West
7 Strathclyde East
8 South of Scotland

Scotland's Euro-constituencies

The representatives are elected for a period of five years. Some of those elected may also be full members of their national parliaments, although they need not be so.

Parliament's headquarters are at present in Luxembourg, where about half of its week-long, monthly sittings are held. The others take place in Strasbourg. Its job is to debate in public any issue of interest to the Community. Parliament's formal powers are limited but real: it has the right to be

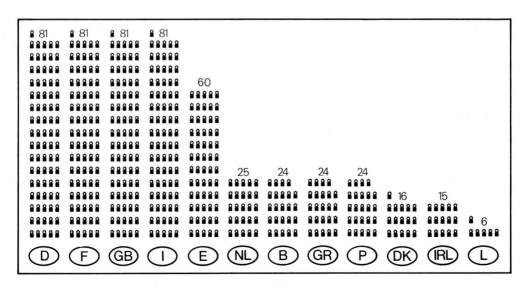

Europe from left to right (*The Economist*, 23 June 1984)

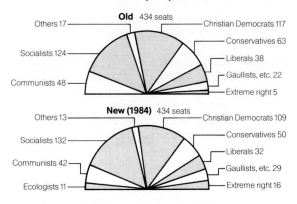

Seats in the European parliament:

Old 434 seats

Others 17
Socialists 124
Communists 48

Christian Democrats 117
Conservatives 63
Liberals 38
Gaullists, etc. 22
Extreme right 5

New (1984) 434 seats

Others 13
Socialists 132
Communists 42
Ecologists 11

Christian Democrats 109
Conservatives 50
Liberals 32
Gaullists, etc. 29
Extreme right 16

Questions

1. Describe the membership of the European Parliament.
2. What is the Parliament's job?
3. How has Parliament's role in the Community changed in recent years?
4. Describe the political groups in the Parliament.

consulted on important items of Community legislation, has growing powers over the Community budget, and can dismiss the Commission, over which it exercises general supervision, by a vote of censure. Parliament's role in the Community today depends as much on informal agreements as on formal powers. New procedures for closer links with the Council of Ministers, for example, and new responsibilities have added to Parliament's influence in the Community in recent years.

It is likely that the importance of the European Parliament will increase in the future. With directly elected MEPs, conscious of their duties and responsibilities to the people of Europe, the Parliament may well become the most important of the four institutions responsible for running the Community.

Members of the Parliament take their seats in the House according to their political ideas and convictions rather than nationality. They have formed six European political groups, each of which usually speaks and votes together.

The European Parliament has 15 specialised committees, each dealing with particular areas of the Community's activities, as shown below.

European Parliamentary Committees

THE COURT OF JUSTICE

The European Court of Justice is a supreme court of ten independent judges, assisted by four advocates-general, all appointed jointly by the member-states for renewable six-year terms. Their decisions are taken by a simple majority vote.

The Court is the final arbiter on all legal questions relating to Community laws and treaties. It deals with several kinds of dispute:

Member-State v Member-State
Member-State v Community Institution
Community v Firms, Individuals or
Institution Community Officials

It can also hear appeals from member-states, from the Commission, from the Council or from any individual, on all of whom its decisions are binding.

For example, if the government of one member-nation thinks that the government of another member-nation is taking steps which break a Community agreement, the former may complain to the Court. The Court will listen to evidence from all those involved then, guided by the laws of the Community, decide how the problem should be resolved.

In 1976 a total of 132 cases were brought before the Court, including six actions taken by the Commission against member-states for failing to meet a Community obligation, four actions taken by member-states against the Commission, and 22 actions taken by individuals against the Council of Ministers and the Commission.

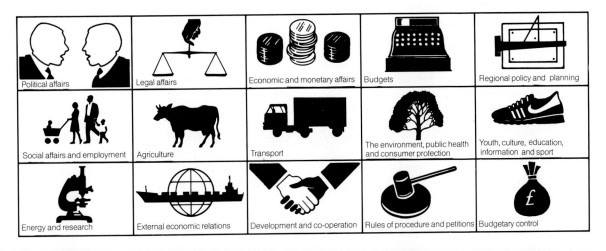

Political affairs	Legal affairs	Economic and monetary affairs	Budgets	Regional policy and planning
Social affairs and employment	Agriculture	Transport	The environment, public health and consumer protection	Youth, culture, education, information and sport
Energy and research	External economic relations	Development and co-operation	Rules of procedure and petitions	Budgetary control

One of the cases dealt with in 1976 shows how the Court can help an ordinary person. In 1970 an air hostess, Mlle Defrenne, who worked for the Belgian airline Sabena, began a battle in the Belgian courts for equal pay with male cabin staff. Her case was dismissed but she appealed on the grounds that Article 119 of the Treaty of Rome (which establishes the principle that men and women should receive equal pay for equal work) had formed part of Belgian law since Belgium signed the Treaty in 1957. The European Court ruled that Article 119 did apply to the member-states, and Mlle Defrenne was awarded equal pay with male cabin stewards.

Questions

1. Describe the membership of the Court of Justice.
2. What kinds of disputes are dealt with by the Court?

How a Community decision is made

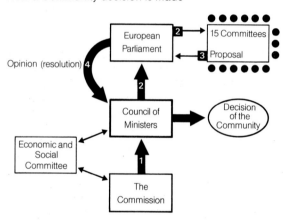

Stage 1 The proposed change or new law is prepared by the Commission, often after consultation with the relevant Parliamentary committee, and is sent to the Council of Ministers for their consideration.

Stage 2 The Council sends the proposal on to Parliament for its opinion, where it is considered by one of the 15 specialised committees. At this stage the Commission is also closely involved. The Commission officials, and often the commissioner responsible for the topic being considered, have to explain and defend their proposal before the committee.

Stage 3 The Parliamentary committee's final report is debated in a full session of Parliament, where further changes and amendments to the original proposal may be made. The debate ends with a vote.

Stage 4 The opinion (or 'resolution') of Parliament is then sent to the Council of Ministers. Meanwhile, the Commission will have altered and amended its original proposal to take account of the findings of the Parliamentary committee. After a further period of discussion the Council makes and announces its final decision.

In addition to the four main Community institutions there are more than 70 consultative bodies to aid the Community's work. One of the most important is the Economic and Social Committee, a 156–member body, representing employers' organisations, trade unions and other interests, including consumers, in equal numbers. Twenty-four seats each are alloted to Britain, France, Germany and Italy, twelve each to Belgium, Greece and the Netherlands, nine each to Denmark and Ireland, and six to Luxembourg. The Commission and the Council must consult the Economic and Social Committee on all major proposals, and it may also give advice on its own initiative.

What does the Community do?

Most of us take for granted the fact that we live in the British Isles and the fact that the British government in London takes decisions and makes laws which affect our lives in many different ways. But few people ever stop to think about what Britain's membership of the European Community means for them. To many people the Common Market is remote, with its headquarters 'somewhere on the continent', whose only effect on ordinary people is to be seen in rising prices in the shops. Yet the whole purpose of having a European Community in the first place is to bring benefits to the lives of its ordinary citizens. The actions and decisions of institutions like the European Parliament and Council of Ministers have a very direct effect on the lives of Europe's people.

The policies of the EEC which affect us may be arranged in four main groups:

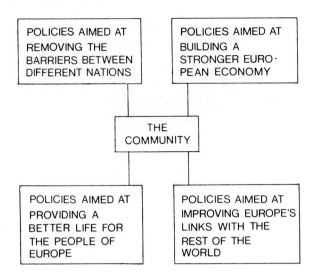

POLICIES AIMED AT REMOVING THE BARRIERS BETWEEN DIFFERENT NATIONS	POLICIES AIMED AT BUILDING A STRONGER EURO-PEAN ECONOMY
	THE COMMUNITY	
POLICIES AIMED AT PROVIDING A BETTER LIFE FOR THE PEOPLE OF EUROPE	POLICIES AIMED AT IMPROVING EUROPE'S LINKS WITH THE REST OF THE WORLD

Question

1. What are the main aims of the Community's policies?

REMOVING THE BARRIERS

Trade Barriers

From the very beginning it was realised that if the Community was to develop and gain in strength, it was necessary to integrate the economies of the member-nations to form a common market where people, goods, ideas and money could move without being unnecessarily hindered. It was hoped that this would allow wealth to be more evenly shared throughout the Community and that this economic solidarity would be the foundation-stone of eventual political solidarity. This would, in turn, remove the possibility of further conflict between the nations of Europe.

Starting in 1953 with coal and steel (the most important raw materials of war), the member-countries have gradually removed most of the national barriers to trade between them. Most of this process was completed by July 1977, when Britain, Eire and Denmark completed their **transitional period** and became fully integrated. This means that, except for a few non-industrial products, all goods traded between all the Community members are free of customs duties and other export and import duties. Manufacturers now have a much larger market in Europe – but they must also be able to compete with foreign manufacturers throughout the Common Market. One of the main benefits to consumers is that they now have a much wider range of goods at lower prices to choose from.

In addition to removing the barriers to trade within the Community, the member-nations have also replaced their different national **tariffs** on imports from the rest of the world with a **common external tariff**. This means that countries outside the EEC still have to pay tariffs on the goods they send to the Community, but the tariffs are now at the same rates for all the member-countries. As with the removal of internal barriers, this simplification has led to increased trade and a greater choice of goods for the Community's people.

Apart from tariffs, many other obstacles to Community trade have been tackled. The countries of Western Europe have, naturally, over the years developed different trade policies, tax systems, technical standards and health and safety rules, some of which can obstruct trade. The Community has investigated these problems and, in some cases, has taken action aimed at reducing their effects. For example, all members have adopted a value-added-tax system in place of turnover or purchase taxes, and it is hoped that in the future the rates of VAT will be the same throughout the Community.

Britain's trade with the Community

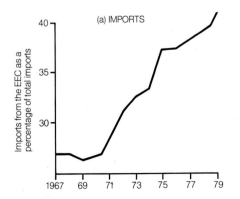

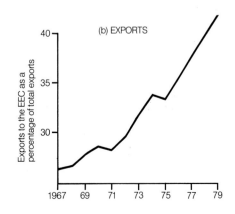

As the barriers have fallen, trade has increased, both within the Community and between the Community and the rest of the world.

But in spite of these improvements some problems still remain. Travellers, for example, still have to face customs formalities when travelling within the Community. And these customs laws still have loopholes which are exploited by large multinational companies. Decision-making can be slow and cumbersome and there is no machinery for the settlement of disputes about Community customs regulations.

Other Barriers

Money To allow goods to be traded easily throughout the EEC, the methods of paying for these goods must also be simplified. Money for investment must be allowed to move to those parts of the Community where it is most productive and/or most needed. Many of the restrictions have now been removed and it is much easier for people to transfer investments and money to other member-countries, but there is still a lot of progress to be made in this area.

An important long-term aim of the Community is that all the member-countries should link their different currencies to a European Monetary Union, in which each country would use the same 'Euro-currency'. As a first step towards this aim, the idea of a European Monetary System (EMS) was put forward in 1978. This would reduce fluctuations between the currencies of member countries.

Disagreement among the member-nations about this scheme centred on whether there should be a large transfer of resources from the richer to the poorer countries of the EEC (including the UK) built into the system when it officially started on 1 January 1979.

People The Community believes that its people must be at least as free to travel as money and goods. Citizens of any member-country are now able to go to any other member-country to get a job. They need no work permit, only a passport or identity card. Their wages, working conditions, training opportunities, social security, trade union rights and opportunities to buy or rent a house or property must be on equal terms with people in the host country. Almost one and three quarter million Community citizens work in Community countries other than their own, and there are more than four and a half million immigrants from outside the Community. There is even a Community-wide employment service which helps to match job offers with applications.

People can also set up a business, offer services, or practise a profession anywhere in the Community. Banks may open international branches throughout the EEC, and road-transport companies now have more freedom to operate throughout the member-countries. But in many of the professions, qualifications differ from one country to another and the Community is now trying to persuade its member-countries to recognise each other's diplomas and degrees so that doctors, lawyers and engineers, for example, may work in any member-country.

The Community's trade policies

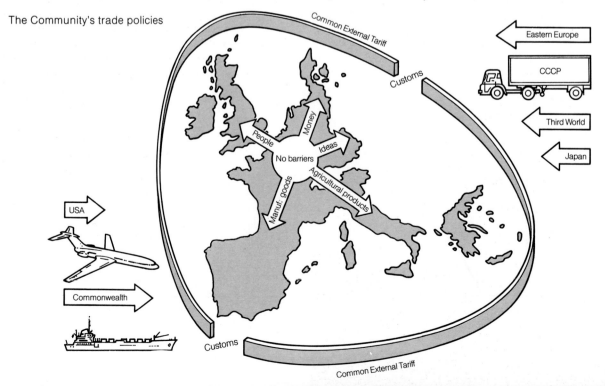

Questions

1. Why is it important that the economies of the EEC member-countries should be integrated?
2. Explain what is meant by the 'common external tariff'.
3. What have been the results of the removal of the trade barriers?
4. Why is it important that there should be fewer barriers to the movement of money for investment within the Community?
5. What is the EMS and why were there disagreements about it during 1978?
6. What laws has the EEC passed to encourage movement of people within the EEC?

BUILDING A STRONGER ECONOMY

In a world of economic problems and dangers, the EEC must take positive steps to make its own economy stronger and more able to resist world fluctuations. The main policies involved are those concerned with agriculture, fishing, industry, transport and energy.

Agriculture

If you go into your local shop or supermarket you will find many products from the farms of other member-countries of the EEC. Butter from France and Germany, bacon from Denmark, cheese from Holland and France, and many different varieties of wine from Italy, France and Germany – these are just a few examples from a whole range of products which have become more widely available in our shops since Britain joined the EEC in 1973. Being able to buy foreign products in our shops is nothing new, of course, but what is new is that it is much

Lorries carrying French UHT milk arriving in Britain

easier for farm products to be sold throughout the Community, thus giving a greater variety to consumers.

Farming is very important to many millions of people throughout the EEC. All of us depend on farmers for the food we eat. Many people also depend on farming for their jobs – nine million at the present moment. The EEC is also the world's largest importer of agricultural products from other countries.

The very important part played by agriculture in the Community can be seen in the figures for the 1984 Community budget in Table 7.

Table 7 Total commitments (1984)

Expenditure	Amount (million ECUs)
Agriculture	17 175
Fisheries	112
Social policy	1 644
Regional policy	1 455
Research, energy, industry and transport	1 750
Development aid	897
Repayments and reserves	1 109
European Commission	804
Other institutions	426
Total	25 362

Before they joined the EEC, each of the member-nations protected their own farmers from foreign competition, mainly by paying them subsidies and by limiting imports from abroad. The first aim of EEC agricultural policy is to remove these barriers to trade in farm produce between member-countries, and in many ways it has succeeded in achieving this. The Common Agricultural Policy (CAP) has been described as the 'engine of the Common Market' and has been a very important instrument of European co-operation and integration. The main aims of the CAP are shown below. (Some of these aims may be conflicting: can you suggest which?)

Aims of the Common Agriculture Policy

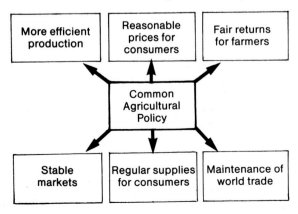

The CAP is based on common **target prices** set each year by the Council of Ministers on proposals from the Commission. These cover items such as grain, fruit and vegetables, beef, wine, poultry, fish, pigmeat, plants, eggs and milk products. The main exceptions are mutton, lamb and potatoes.

The target price is what farmers can expect to get for their products throughout the EEC during the year. The price is designed to represent a fair return. However, if a farmer has to sell below the target price for any reason, the EEC will buy the produce. The price paid by the Community is usually about eight per cent below the target price and is called the intervention price. The produce bought by the Community in this way is stored or sold abroad.

Because the CAP has to operate in a Community whose member-countries use different currencies, the values of which may rise or fall, a special system has been developed so that agricultural goods can cross national frontiers as freely as possible. Farm support prices in each member-state are calculated by using special exchange rates known as 'green' rates, giving each country its own level of support. Britain, for example, has benefited from this system because, in spite of the falling value of the pound in recent years, food prices in Britain have not risen as much as they should. The EEC has in fact been subsidising our food imports by using the more highly valued **green pound** to calculate the levels of subsidies. In West Germany, on the other hand, the green deutschmark keeps farm prices higher than is justified by the true value of the deutschmark.

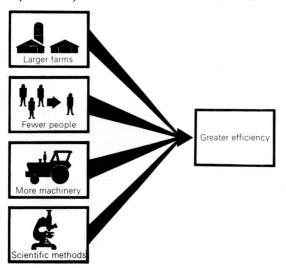

Aims of the EEC's Agricultural Improvement Policy

Unfortunately, the policy does not always work as it is supposed to. When target prices are set too high the result is over-production, leading to surpluses of certain products, e.g. the 'butter mountain' and the 'wine lake'. Many consumer organisations also feel that target prices are set in the interests of producers and that consumers suffer through having to pay higher prices.

The way in which the EEC's agricultural policy has been perhaps most successful so far is in its efforts to improve the efficiency of European farming. This has been done by encouraging an increase in the size of farms, reducing the labour force on the land and encouraging the use of more machinery and scientific farming methods throughout the Community.

Questions

1. How important is agriculture in the European Community?
2. Explain the aims of the CAP.
3. What is meant by (a) target prices and (b) intervention price?
4. In what ways has the CAP not always been a success?
5. What successes has the EEC's agricultural policy had so far?

Fishing

LIke the farming industry, the fishing industry provides us with an important part of our diet, and also gives employment to many people. Until 1983 the member-countries of the EEC were involved in a long-drawn-out dispute about fishing. The problem was that the member-countries could not agree on a policy for the Community which would protect dwindling fish stocks, preserve the livelihood of British fishermen and yet allow access to the fishing grounds around Britain for countries like Denmark and France.

Early in 1983 a Danish fisherman, Kent Kirk, who was also a Member of the European Parliament, challenged a British ban on foreign boats fishing within 20 kilometres of the British coast. He hoped to be arrested, then planned to appeal to the European Court of Justice about Britain's policy. His boat was intercepted by a Royal Navy fisheries protection ship escorted by an RAF Nimrod reconnaisance aircraft, and Kirk was later found guilty of illegal fishing and fined.

On 25 January 1983, only a few days after Kirk's arrest, the member-countries agreed on a Common Fisheries Policy (CFP). The agreement reduced the rights of foreign boats to fish along nearly three-quarters of Britain's coastline. Each country was granted a quota of fish they are allowed to catch, which is to be reviewed each year. A 20-kilometre limit was introduced on nearly all coasts, and a conservation 'box' around the Orkney and Shetland Islands. This agreement will last initially for a period of ten years. It is hoped that the agreement will satisfy the three main difficulties which caused the earlier problems. In 1984 the member-countries agreed their quotas with no repeat of the previous arguments and protests.

Questions

1. Explain why the Community found it so difficult to find a common fisheries policy.
2. Describe the main points in the CFP agreed in 1983.

Industry

Many of the industries of the European Community have gone through a difficult period during the recession of the last few years, and most of the EEC's action in the industrial field has aimed at helping member-countries with their industrial problems. But the Commission has also been trying to remove many of the technical and legal barriers to trade in industrial goods to help strengthen Community industry. The three most important measures taken to increase the industrial strength and unity of the EEC in recent years have been:

(a) helping industries with special problems, e.g. steel, shipbuilding, paper and textiles;
(b) encouraging the development of new high-technology industries such as data processing;
(c) supporting research and development programmes on a Community-wide basis.

The European steel industry in particular has been in need of help in recent years. The low world demand for steel coupled with low prices has led to the Community's steel industry working at only 60 per cent of its capacity, and many workers have been made redundant, especially in Britain. The EEC has helped to relieve part of the problem by preventing steel imports at unreasonably low prices from countries outside the Community, and by setting up a system of minimum prices for steel produced within the EEC. The Commission has also begun to consider long-term proposals for the restructuring of the European steel industry. It plans to reduce the industry's surplus capacity and increase its competitiveness compared with non-member countries by modernising old-fashioned steelworks. In 1980, after several years of voluntary cut-backs, compulsory production quotas were

introduced. Substantial aid has been given to steel workers forced into early retirement or short-time working – £60 million in 1981 alone.

In textiles, the Community has negotiated with developing countries to allow a planned growth of their exports and thus give a breathing space for our domestic industries to adapt. Textiles still account for nearly 10 per cent of all manufacturing jobs in the Community and are vital to the economies of many of its poorer regions. The aim is not to run down European textile production but to establish an industry which is competitive worldwide.

Questions

1. What action is being taken to strengthen industry in the EEC?
2. What measures are being taken to solve the problems in the steel industry?

Transport

A well-developed and integrated system of transport is essential if the EEC is to gain the full benefits of its trade policies. The Community is trying to develop a common policy for road, rail, inland water, sea and air transport in order to remove further barriers to trade. As trade within the EEC increases and the number of people travelling between member-nations grows, the Community hopes that a common system of regulations, such as those governing the maximum distance travelled by juggernauts in a day and the maximum number of hours worked by their drivers, will help, not hinder, development.

Question

1. Why is the development of an efficient and integrated system of transport important to the future of the EEC?

Energy

Even with the recent valuable discoveries of natural gas and oil in the North Sea, the Community is a net importer of energy. The 1973–4 oil crisis, which led to greatly increased prices in Middle East oil, showed the danger of relying too much on outside sources of energy and the urgent need for EEC action.

The ECSC has been tackling the problem of reorganising the coal industry since the mid-1950s, and EURATOM has been concentrating on research and development of nuclear power production in response to the continuing rise in the EEC's energy consumption and the cost of imports. But it was the oil crisis, during which the Community's members at first acted selfishly in their own national interests and only slowly reached agreement on a joint policy towards overseas oil producers, that finally showed the need for a completely new and comprehensive energy policy. In June 1974 the Commission put forward a new plan with the following proposals for 1985.

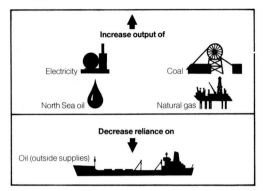

EEC energy policy

Since these proposals were made, the people of the Community have been using less imported oil. While total demand for energy fell by 11.5 per cent between 1979 and 1982, oil consumption fell by 21 per cent. In 1982 oil accounted for 49 per cent of Europe's internal energy consumption, compared with 54.5 per cent in 1979. Over the same period the share of electricity generated by solid fuel and nuclear power rose from 58 to 69 per cent.

While being aware of the potential dangers, the Community has always taken the view that for Europe, which is poor in energy resources, nuclear power will play a vital role in years to come.

Questions

1. What effect did the 1973–4 oil crisis have on EEC energy policy?
2. Describe the EEC's present energy policy.
3. What progress has been made towards meeting the EEC's proposals on energy?
4. Explain the Community's view on nuclear energy.

BUILDING A BETTER LIFE

The European Community is about people – the most basic reason for having a Community at all is the hope that it will help to achieve a better life for everyone who lives or works in it. The responsibilities of the Community in this field are:

- to improve living standards;
- to develop the poorer regions;
- to provide jobs and welfare services;
- to improve education and training;
- to protect consumers;
- to improve the environment.

Living Standards

Between 1958 and 1972 the people of the original six member-nations found they benefited greatly from being in the EEC. Their real wages, reflecting the amount of goods they could buy, increased as shown in Table 8.

Table 8 Percentage increase in real wages, 1958–72

BELGIUM	+ 93
FRANCE	+ 109
W. GERMANY	+ 79
ITALY	+ 121
LUXEMBOURG	+ 75
NETHERLANDS	+ 106

Since 1972 this growth rate has slowed down as the European Community has suffered from the steep rises in world prices for energy and raw materials and the world recession in industrial production and trade. There is hope, however, that when the recession is over the people of the Community can look forward to a return to improving living standards.

Question

1. How have people's living standards been affected by the setting up of the EEC?

Helping the Poorer Regions

A large part of the EEC's effort and money is devoted to helping those areas of the Community which suffer from the problems of high unemployment, poverty and economic decline: areas such as southern Italy, Northern Ireland and Greece. Areas such as these already receive aid from their own national governments, but the EEC provides a very valuable additional source of funds for the poorest areas.

Poorer areas of the EEC

Southern Italy & Sicily	Ireland
Sardinia	Northern Ireland
Brittany	Greece

The European Regional Development Fund is the main instrument used for helping the problem areas. It was set up in 1975 to give grants:

(a) to help investment in industry and services which create new or safeguard existing jobs;
(b) for investment in roads, water-supply and industrial estates linked with safeguarding jobs;
(c) for investment in poorer rural areas.

Applications for grants are made by the national governments. In order to qualify for a grant from the Fund, the project for which aid is requested must be in an area which qualifies for national regional aid (a 'development area' or 'special development area' in the UK) and be supported by national public funds. This makes sure that the areas with the greatest needs are given the highest priority.

The Fund's resources are shared out according to the needs of the problem areas of the different member-nations as shown in the pie chart. Between 1975 and 1983 Britain received a total of £1147 million in grants from the Regional Fund. Some of the most recent schemes which have been assisted are the construction of a new National Exhibition

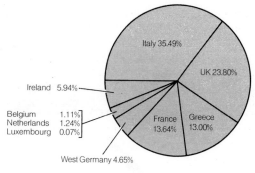

EEC Funds

Centre on the derelict site of the former Queens Dock in Glasgow (£11.3 million), the installation of a new colour light signalling system by British Rail at Dundee (£1.3 million), and the building of an electricity generating station at Lerwick by the North of Scotland Hydro-Electric Board (£5.4 million).

Questions

1. What problems is the EEC Regional Policy designed to remove?
2. List some of the countries which benefit from this policy.
3. In what ways does the Regional Development Fund help the problem areas?

New fling for the Highlands

A European Parliament committee has published a report calling for massive integrated development aid for the Scottish Highlands and Islands and other 'severely disadvantaged regions' in Europe.

The Parliament's influential Agriculture Committee says that the European Community's Common Agricultural Policy (CAP) has not only failed to prevent a serious decline in the population of peripheral rural areas, but has actually encouraged competition, which could be putting farmers in poorer areas out of business.

A high proportion of the population of the Highlands and Islands is employed in agriculture and suffers from low incomes, high unemployment and under-employment,

poor communication and transport links, bad soil and climate and a lack of markets, according to the report, which was compiled by Scots Conservative MEP James Provan.

Emigration from the Highlands is by no means a new phenomenon. In an area covering about 36 000 square kilometres, or about half of Scotland, there are about 323 000 people. The population density of about nine people per square kilometre compares with 67 for Scotland, 244 for Britain and 62 for Basilicata – the most sparsely populated area of Southern Italy.

Increased Community aids to hill farmers, investment in infrastructure projects such as roads, communications and ports, incentives to encourage firms to invest in the area, improved marketing structures, such as co-ops and modernisation of agricultural techniques could all help, according to the committee.

But with parts of the region suffering double the national

average of unemployment, jobs remain a priority. Other sectors such as tourism, forestry and fisheries, are in desperate need of development, if young people are to find employment in Scotland's increasingly elderly society, say the MEPs.

Integrated development programmes, on the lines of those proposed for Mediterranean regions by Commission Vice-President Lorenzo Natali in February, are therefore what the committee has in mind. Their implementation could be the first step towards a European Rural Development Fund, says Mr Provan. The Parliament's Environment Committee has backed the Provan Report, but emphasised the need for aid in sectors other than agriculture, including heavy industry, crafts, forestry, fisheries and tourism. It also welcomed environmental provisions to protect the natural beauty of the Highlands and Islands, included in integrated development plans.

(Europe '83, May 1983)

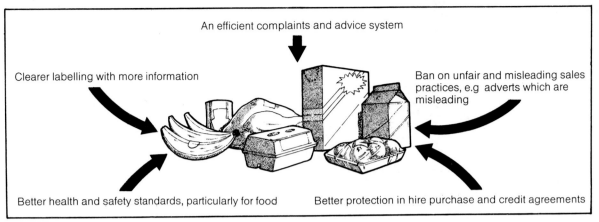

An efficient complaints and advice system

Clearer labelling with more information

Ban on unfair and misleading sales practices, e.g adverts which are misleading

Better health and safety standards, particularly for food

Better protection in hire purchase and credit agreements

How the Community helps consumers

Jobs and Welfare

The EEC actively tries to increase the number of jobs available and improve working conditions. The ECSC has made loans available to help attract new job-creating industry to areas which used to depend on coal and steel. The European Social Fund gives help to projects for training and retraining workers who would otherwise be unable to obtain jobs. Since 1973 Britain has received £732 million from the European Social Fund to retrain workers and to teach job skills to young people.

The member-nations have agreed to Commission proposals to protect workers against mass dismissals.

At present the Community has six priority targets:

- a 40-hour working week for all workers;
- four weeks annual paid holiday for all workers;
- protection against large-scale dismissals;
- progress towards equal pay for men and women;
- more help for migrant, elderly and handicapped workers, and for school-leavers;
- action to reduce the effects of rising prices.

Questions

1. What action has the EEC taken to help workers in Europe?
2. How does the Community intend to help workers in the future?

Education and Training

In addition to its retraining and resettlement programme, the EEC is trying to improve vocational training standards and methods, especially for migrant and handicapped workers and in special areas or industries, including agriculture and road transport. A Vocational Training Centre and a European University Institute are being set up in addition to the existing six 'European schools' where the children of Community employees and some others receive a bilingual 'European' education. The main benefit to Britain so far has been over £2 million received to help in the education of immigrants.

Question

1. Which particular groups of people is EEC educational policy designed to help?

Consumer Protection

The greater variety of products now available throughout the EEC increases the need for better consumer information, protection and representation.

The aim is to ensure that people throughout the Community know exactly what they are buying and how much it costs, and that if they have any complaints these will be listened to and acted upon.

Question

1. How do EEC regulations help to inform and protect consumers?

The Environment

Pollution of the environment and the increasingly rapid use of dwindling supplies of raw materials and natural resources are problems of world-wide importance. The EEC is no exception and must act to tackle these problems. The aims of environmental policy in the EEC are:

Cleaning Brittany beaches

- to prevent, reduce and eliminate pollution;
- to maintain the balance of nature;
- to tap natural resources without causing any unnecessary ecological harm;
- to persuade policy-makers to consider the environment when shaping other plans.

The amount of work to be done is vast, the problems many. The pollution of the Rhine, Lake Zurich and the Mediterranean; the problems of the inner city areas of cities like Glasgow and Liverpool; air pollution in the industrial regions of Europe – all present major challenges to the progress of the Community.

Two of the major problems are oil pollution and the effects of acid rain. There is also concern about the transport and disposal of deadly chemicals such as dioxin.

"Europa ohne Grenzen 1983"

A German cartoonist's comment of the alarming ease with which the deadly dioxin was allowed to cross Community frontiers (Copyright: *EG Magasin*)

OIL POLLUTION

The Commission has sent the Council a proposal for a directive on the drawing-up of contingency plans to combat accidental oil spills at sea.

The danger of accidents is ever-present. A large proportion of Western Europe's oil supply is transported by sea in large tankers some of them carrying over 5000 tonnes. And wider exploitation of the oil from the European continental shelf by means of drilling platforms constitutes a growing potential threat.

According to the figures available, European coastal waters have been affected by about 20 per cent of the accidental spills occurring (32 spills between 1974 and 1981). For example, the Regional Oil-Combating Centre for the Mediterranean in Malta recorded 72 accident alerts in the Mediterranean between 1977 and 1982. In 12 cases where the accidents were followed by an oil spill the latter polluted the sea and the beaches.

(*Europe '83*, October 1983)

ACID RAIN

The Community is rich in forests. They cover one-fifth of its total land surface and provide employment for 1.4 million people. But as European Commission President, Mr Gaston Thorn, noted on a visit to West Germany's Black Forest, many of the trees are dying, struck by a variety of diseases flowing from pollution of the air and soil.

Sulphur dioxide is the main enemy, but this 'acid rain' is only one of several toxic substances that are poisoning the forests. The culprits are mainly heavy industry and energy plants, and their fumes and emission particles are oblivious of national boundaries. The first signs of damage appeared in the mid-1970s, and have been accelerating since.

But the damage is not confined to West Germany. Similar deterioration has been verified in the forests of Scotland, Denmark, France, northern Italy, Greece and the Low Countries. Further afield the forests of Norway and Sweden are also suffering.

In the last few years the Community has adopted several directives designed to limit poisonous emissions from factories and other plants, including limitations on emission of sulphur dioxides and suspended particulates and on lead in air. Other directives are concerned with the sulphur content of certain liquid fuels, pollution from exhaust gases of motor vehicles and the lead content of petrol.

(*European Communities Background Report*)

DEADLY CHEMICALS

Seveso, a village in Italy, has become synonymous with the horrifying chemical accident that occurred in 1976. Waste contaminated by dioxin was shipped to an unknown destination from the area in 41 containers, in an atmosphere of cloak-and-dagger secrecy.

It was eventually found to have been dumped in a building near St Quentin, northern France, and is now to be finally disposed of in Switzerland.

This affair has spotlighted an area of concern of the European Commission – the shipment within the Community of toxic wastes. For those two tonnes from Seveso represent only a small fraction of the 20 or 30 million tonnes of poisonous industrial waste within the Community – and even less of the 150 million tonnes of total industrial waste.

About a million times the amount of poisonous waste from Seveso crosses borders of member-states every year.

(*Europe '83*, June 1983)

Questions

1. What are the aims of EEC environmental policy?
2. Describe some of the environmental problems the EEC must tackle.
3. What is 'acid rain' and what problems does it cause?
4. Explain in your own words what the cartoonist is trying to say.

THE COMMUNITY'S LINKS WITH THE REST OF THE WORLD

Although the European Community is primarily concerned with co-operation and integration *within* the ten member-nations, it recognises that as a leading industrial power and the world's largest trader it has international responsibilities. It is not a Superpower, but its members' combined economic strength gives it great influence.

The Community is pledged to promote world trade, world development and world peace.

The Community in Europe

The EEC is not the only important economic grouping of countries in Europe. The European Free Trade Association, which includes Austria, Finland, Iceland, Norway, Portugal, Sweden and Switzerland, and to which the UK, Eire and Denmark belonged before they joined the EEC, has an industrial free-trade agreement with the EEC. The EEC has also proposed closer economic links with the Comecon countries of Eastern Europe, and there is already close co-operation with Yugoslavia.

There is also hope that the growth of the Community is not yet finished. Membership is open to any democratic European country that is able and willing to join. At present Spain and Portugal are in the process of negotiating entry terms.

Questions

1. What links does the EEC have with other countries in Europe?
2. Which countries are at present negotiating entry to the Community?

The Community and the Third World

The EEC is the **developing countries'** biggest single market, and is also the biggest giver of aid to these countries.

Trade In 1975 total trade between the EEC and the developing countries was worth $115 000 million. The EEC is by far the largest export market for these countries, taking over 32 per cent of their total exports, about twice as much as the USA, and accounting for 44 per cent of the EEC's imports in 1975.

Third World exports to the EEC

32%

Community imports from the Third World

44%

EEC trade with the Third World

Between 1971 and 1975, imports from the **Third World** rose by 24 per cent per year and were the result of a deliberate policy to encourage such trade. The most important agreement between the EEC and the developing nations is the Lomé Convention, which is designed to provide 'a new model for relations between developed and developing states'.

The First Lomé Convention came into force in 1975. It was signed between the EEC's member states and 46 of their former colonies in Africa, the Caribbean and the Pacific for a period of five years. In 1980 Lomé II – a new improved and extended version of the original contract – was signed, this time by the EEC and 57 ACP states. This has now increased to 63 ACP states.

But the Lomé Convention has not always lived up to expectations. The ACP countries still import more from the EEC than they sell to it, giving them a trade deficit. Prices for many of the products of the ACP countries collapsed at the beginning of the 1980s, and many of these countries had financial problems which the EEC was unable to help. EEC food aid to the ACP countries and to Asia and Latin America has also been criticised. The Community has off-loaded farm surpluses, including milk-powder, butter oil and cereals, which has encouraged dependence on imported food in these countries and discouraged food production in the developing world. The world economic recession hit the Third World countries hardest of all. Yet a third Lomé agreement is inevitable in 1985.

Questions

1. What is the Lomé Convention?
2. What are the problems with the Lomé Convention?
3. Why is the EEC vital to the needs of the African, Caribbean and Pacific (ACP) countries?

The Community and the United States

The EEC is the United States' most important trading partner, both for exports and imports. Since the start of the Community in 1958, US exports have increased in all areas.

Over the years the balance of trade has shown a surplus in favour of the US. In 1976 the Community's trade deficit with the US was almost $10 000 million, a figure which caused considerable concern in the Community.

Relations between the Community and the US became strained in 1983 following the introduction of restrictions on the amounts of steel imported by the EEC from the US. The United States imposed similar restrictions on steel imported from the Community.

Questions

1. How important is EEC trade with the US?
2. Why is there cause for concern about trade with the US?
3. What disagreement arose between the US and the EEC in 1983?

CONCLUSION : EUROPEAN UNION?

In the last few pages we have looked at the major policies of the European Community which affect the lives of every one of us. These policies are not static: they must be constantly changing and adapting to take account of new circumstances and new objectives. In 1976 Mr Leo Tindemans, the Belgian Prime Minister, drew up a Report on European Union which seeks ways of gradually changing relations between the member-nations and broadening their collective action. The Report notes that in some fields the Community has far-reaching powers while in others it remains undeveloped. European union requires a common economic and monetary policy, and common policies on industry, agriculture, energy and research. Regional and social policies must reduce inequality and unite the people of Europe. European union must also make itself felt in people's daily lives, helping to protect their rights and improving their conditions. The process will be slow, but, says the Tindemans Report, the price of inaction would be a weakened, divided and increasingly impotent Europe.

Questions

1. What did the Tindemans Report see as the main requirements for European union?
2. If European union is not achieved what is the likely future for Europe?

3. Co-operation in Action

Regional Help for Scotland

There are a variety of funds available under the Community Regional Development Policy. The aim of this policy is to level out the differences in wealth and opportunity between rich and poor regions in the Community. Community policy has not been entirely successful for there is still a tendency for the rich regions to grow richer and for the poor to grow poorer. However, areas like Scotland have received various injections of money from the Community to help create employment over a wide range of projects.

Scotland has received:

● Some £630 million in loans from the European Investment Bank. This has been used to create jobs in the oil, gas, steel and electricity industries. It has been used to finance a new whisky plant and typewriter factory in Glasgow and for an airport and oil tanker harbour in the Shetlands.
● Some £170 million from the Regional Development Fund has been used to fund projects ranging from Pitlochry Festival Theatre to Dundee Airport.
● Some £120 million from European Coal and Steel Community funds has been used in developments at Hunterston and Longannet and to improve miners' houses.

The East Kilbride expressway: a project funded by the EEC

● Some £21 million from the Farm Fund has been used to help agriculture and fishing.
● Money from the Social Fund has been used for training and retraining workers.
● In addition, Glasgow and Edinburgh have received grants under the poverty action programme to help people in areas of multiple deprivation. Details of this type of help can be seen in the following case study of Craigmillar in Edinburgh.

Craigmillar Festival Society

Craigmillar is a large housing scheme on the eastern side of Edinburgh. It is mainly a council-housing area with many of the houses built in the 1930s. It faces many of the problems common to large housing schemes on the outskirts of Scotland's cities and large towns. 'With a population of 25 000 we are equivalent to a town the size of Dumfries – but we had none of the amenities of a town.' This was how Mrs Helen Crummy, founder and secretary of the Craigmillar Festival Society, summed up the area's problem over lack of facilities. In addition to this the area has suffered from high unemployment and many other social problems. As a result it has been described as an area of 'multiple-deprivation'.

In 1964 the residents of the area set up the Craigmillar Festival Society to brighten up the area by running an annual festival of drama, music, art

and sport. Since then the Festival has developed, and now is involved in a whole number of community self-help schemes for children, old people and many others. It has become one of Scotland's best-known and most successful examples of community action.

In 1975 the Festival Society found out about an EEC scheme called 'Pilot Schemes to Combat Poverty' and decided to find out whether Craigmillar could benefit from it.

Although the other organisations who had received help from the scheme had been mainly academic research groups and not community action groups, the Festival Society was successful in its request for help.

The EEC contributed a grant of money once they had approved the Society's plans, on condition that the local authority (Lothian Region) and the central government contributed as well. Once things were settled, the EEC provided 50 per cent; Lothian Region 25 per cent and central government 25 per cent.

In all, the EEC grant amounted to two annual sums of £125 000 and £150 000. How has the money been used?

The grants have largely been used to get a number of important projects off the ground. It has been used as 'seed money' in the Festival's attempts to regenerate Craigmillar by getting the local people themselves involved in self-help schemes. The main theme has been to bring about social improvements through cultural projects.

The money has been used for 22 pilot schemes, among which are:

● creating an Arts Centre in an old church;

● setting up a children's playbus scheme;

● renovating an old cottage in Hawick as a holiday and outdoor centre;

● creating an audio library in the local public library;

● setting up, in conjunction with Lothian Region's Job Creation Programme, a special education unit for children who cannot adapt to normal school life;

● setting up a number of special projects for children in need and a day club for the elderly.

Questions

1. Write a description of Craigmillar and its problems.
2. Describe the part played by the Craigmillar Festival Society in overcoming these problems – you will need to explain the term 'community action'.
3. How has the EEC become involved in Craigmillar?
4. How has Craigmillar benefited from this EEC help?

Migrant Workers in the EEC

A MIGRANT IN MUNICH

The station drew him back to it like a magnet. There he met some of his friends who also worked in Munich. Sometimes, Mustapha just watched the crowds go by. Often he would see other migrant workers at Munich station from his own country, Turkey, or from other countries such as Yugoslavia, Italy, Greece and Spain. These migrant workers had been drawn to Germany, as he had been, in the 1960s and early 1970s, by the prospect of jobs, high wages and good living standards. Like Mustapha, most had to get work permits if they came from countries outside the EEC. In Germany, the total of migrant workers and their families is about four million people. Indeed, Mustapha has heard that in Frankfurt there are more migrant workers than German workers.

Mustapha, like most of the other migrant workers, came originally without his family and managed to get a job, after a few days' training, on the assembly line of the BMW car works in Munich. Although the job itself was not very difficult, he was paid much more than he had earned in his small home town in Turkey. Mustapha, like most of the *gastarbeiters* (guest workers), sent most of his wage back home. He had originally intended to return to Turkey, but since he was getting good pay, he made the decision to renew his work permit and then bring his wife and family to live with him in Munich.

A problem for most 'gastarbeiters' in Germany is that they are unable to speak the German language. Mustapha has learned some German words and phrases but mainly he speaks his native Turkish language, so he finds it difficult to mix with German people. His family also have difficulty with the language. His wife, in particular, has difficulties when shopping as she speaks no German and is able to speak only to other Turkish migrants. At school, his younger son has not been doing too well, despite special German language courses, because he cannot understand some of what he is told. As soon as he comes home from school, he speaks Turkish with his friends and listens to Turkish pop music.

Immigrant worker at BMW carworks, Munich

A much more serious problem for the 'gast-arbeiter' like Mustapha is the increasing unemployment in the 1980s. His elder son, Ali, left school two years ago, but like many other young people in Germany, he cannot get a job, despite having been on a work training scheme. Ali gets frustrated and angry because he cannot get a job, and also because he feels he is not wanted in Germany. He has seen graffiti on walls near his home, saying 'Turks go home', and two of his friends were attacked in a disco one night by a group of German youths.

Mustapha is very concerned about the job prospects for his two sons. He knows there is an unemployment rate of about 14 per cent for migrant workers, and about one-third of young Turkish workers in Germany are unemployed. He has even considered the German government offer of £3000 to return to Turkey with his family because his wife and sons are unsettled. However, the unemployment rates in Turkey are even higher than in West Germany, and at least in Munich he still has his job and a small flat for his family.

As Mustapha sits in Munich station, watching migrants arriving and leaving, he has plenty to think about.

WHO ARE THE MIGRANT WORKERS?

By the mid-1980s there were about six million migrant workers (12 million including families) in the EEC.

There are two main types of migrant worker in the EEC. One group, like Mustapha, come from countries – often less developed countries – outside the EEC. In France, for example, the majority of the four million migrants (including families) come from Africa, especially North Africa. The other group are workers from one EEC country who move to another EEC country to get jobs. An example of this group are the Newcastle bricklayers in the TV fiction serial 'Auf Wiedersehen, Pet', who work on a building site in West Germany.

Migrant Workers' Rights

Many immigrants to EEC countries in the 1960s and 1970s got jobs, brought in their families and settled, often in the poorest areas of European towns and cities. By 1973 some countries, such as West Germany, were beginning to restrict the entry of migrant workers. It was only in 1974 that the European Commission accepted that the EEC should have a responsibility towards these migrants.

As citizens of the EEC, workers from EEC countries who move to other EEC countries have the right:

(1) to work in any member state of their choosing;
(2) to obtain the social security benefits of the country they are staying in;
(3) to move from one country or job to another;
(4) to bring their families to join them;
(5) to send family allowances back home;
(6) to join trade unions.

Workers from countries outside the EEC who move into EEC countries have some of the rights of EEC migrant workers but are more restricted:

(1) they must have a work permit;
(2) they are confined to certain jobs;
(3) they cannot move freely from one country to another.

The Social Fund of the EEC now provides money to help migrants – those who are citizens of the EEC – to train for jobs and to help them and their families to adjust to life in a new country. It also provides money to train welfare workers and teachers who are responsible for special integration courses for migrant workers and their families. These courses include help with problems relating to language, housing, education, welfare benefits and unemployment.

UNEMPLOYMENT IN THE EEC

Unemployment is now one of the most serious problems facing the EEC. The slow-down in economic growth during the 1970s, and the decline in older industries such as coal, steel and textiles, has led to general unemployment, increasing in the EEC from about six million in 1978 to 12 million (about 12 per cent) in 1984.

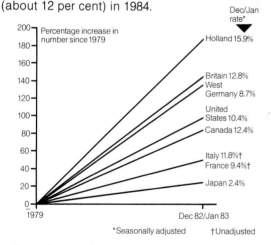

Unemployment in the EEC (*The Economist*, 5 March 1983)

For young workers (under 25 years of age) the unemployment scene was even worse, with about five million young people (25 per cent) unable to get jobs. For them the unemployment rate in 1983 ranged from 15 per cent in West Germany to 28 per cent in Britain and over 30 per cent in the Netherlands.

With increasing unemployment, there are increasing difficulties for migrant workers, not only in trying to get jobs. Some EEC countries put tough restrictions and even bans on further recruitment of migrant workers. West Germany, with over 300 000 migrant workers jobless, and France have offered money to migrant families to leave.

Percentage of (employable) under-25s unemployed

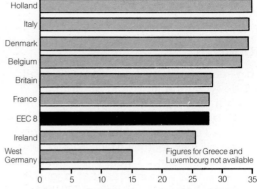

Young on the dole (*The Economist*, 30 April 1983)

A further problem for migrant workers, especially those from outside the EEC, is that, as unemployment rises, there is sometimes a rise in anti-immigrant attitudes. For example, in Britain race relations groups complain of increasing violence and attacks on Indians and Pakistanis. In West Germany the Turks have become the subject of racist jeers and complaints. In France in 1983 several Algerians were killed in incidents involving French youths. In the same year in the town of Dreux, near Paris, an anti-immigrant National Front candidate won the local election in the town, which has a large number of immigrants.

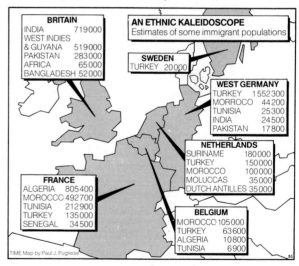

Questions

1. From which countries do migrant workers come to (a) Germany and (b) France?
2. What problems can face migrant workers in another country?
3. What rights does a migrant worker who is already an EEC citizen have?

Long-distance Road Transport

EURODRIVER

The big refrigerated truck, loaded with meat, moved slowly off the ferry boat at Stranraer. It had been a fairly quiet crossing from Larne in Ireland. Bob Smith, the driver, and his co-driver Tam Kyle had managed to get some rest before continuing on their journey which was to take them from Ballymena in Northern Ireland to Paris. Rest periods were important on a journey of this length, particularly driving a £20 000, 30 tonne juggernaut capable of speeds of 110 kilometres per hour. Bob's route took him from Stranraer along the A75 road to Gretna. This was one of the worst parts of the journey, since it was a narrow single-lane each way road with many twists and turns, which made him thankful for the truck's 12 gears. This 160-kilometre stretch of road, 'the goat track' as Bob called it, was being used by an increasing number of juggernauts which transport millions of tonnes of goods between Ireland and the Continent. Improvements are planned for this part of the 'Euroroute' over a period of five years, at a cost of about £18.5 million. In 1979 the Newton Stewart by-pass section, including a bridge over the River Cree, was completed. In 1984, with the help of an EEC grant, a start was made to by-passes for Creetown and Gatehouse. Bob was thankful that these other traffic bottlenecks would be removed. After Gretna there was motorway driving south through England via Birmingham and London to Dover.

At Dover all permits and documents relating to the driver, the lorry and the load were checked by customs officials. Bob's lorry carried a TIR (Transport International Routier) disc on it, so customs officials did not need to check the load as this had been done when the lorry was loaded in Northern Ireland. The load would not need to be opened until it reached its destination.

After the ferry journey, the two men arrived at Calais. Before they could leave for Paris, another check was carried out by customs officials. The permit has to be stamped on entering another EEC country. As well as knowing about which documents are required for signing, Bob also has to know about continental driving laws and vehicle regulations for each country he enters. He must also be aware of differing traffic conditions, traffic signals and road signs. Under EEC laws the road traffic regulations are gradually

Trucks waiting to board the ferry at Dover

being brought into a common system. Britain's distances should all have been given in kilometres by 1980, but many road signs are still given in miles only.

Just before they drove out of Calais, Bob checked with the French police that the road to Paris was clear. He had been warned that French farmers were stopping foreign trucks as a protest against imported meat. Indeed, in one incident in 1984, two truck drivers whom Bob knew had their truck stopped by a barricade of farm tractors on the autoroute north of Paris. Angry French farmers made them open the truck doors and then poured diesel oil over the meat, ruining the £50 000 load. The Calais police told Bob there had been no incidents in the past few days and that he could continue his journey to Paris.

Road signs showing distances in miles and kilometres

104

HOW EEC TRANSPORT LAWS AFFECT LORRY DRIVERS

Permits (to carry goods across frontiers) are issued by the EEC in limited numbers to each member country of the EEC and each member country then issues them to its road hauliers who wish to transport goods across that country's borders.

Drivers' Hours In 1977 the EEC Council of Ministers agreed on regulations concerning the working hours and conditions of road transport drivers of lorries over 3.5 tonnes gross weight.

The main points of the regulation are:

(a) two drivers are required for distances exceeding 450 kilometres;
(b) no period of continuous driving shall exceed four hours;
(c) daily driving time shall not exceed nine hours;
(d) a driver must have at least a 30-minute break between driving periods.

Tachograph A further regulation by the EEC makes it compulsory for all lorries over six tonnes and all buses carrying more than nine passengers in EEC countries to have a tachograph fitted. This is a combination of speedometer and clock which keeps a note of the driver's hours at the wheel, the number of kilometres covered, and even the length of the rest period. This was made compulsory from January 1982 in all EEC countries. Britain and Ireland were slow to carry out this rule; many drivers and owners objected because they believed tachographs would restrict overtime earnings and increase costs, and that this 'spy in the cab' would take away drivers' freedom. The EEC Commission, however, argue that the tachograph will improve drivers' conditions and improve safety. In Germany the number of commercial vehicle accidents has declined since tachographs were fitted.

CHANNEL CROSSING

It may be that in the near future thousands of truck drivers, car drivers, and bus parties of holiday-makers may not need to wait at ferry ports to cross the Channel. Recently, British, French, Dutch and German firms have expressed new interest in the old idea of a bridge/tunnel/rail link between Britain and France. In 1985, a group of British and French firms put forward a £20 000 million twin rail tunnel plan. In 1987 work began on the 50 km Eurotunnel, with a completion date of 1993.

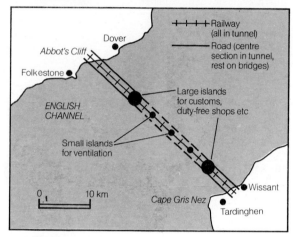

The Channel 'brunnel' (*The Economist*, 30 Jan. 1982)

Questions

1. List some of the documents a British lorry driver might have to show to French customs officials.
2. In what ways did French farmers protest against imports of foreign meat to France?
3. What are the arguments in favour of fitting tachographs to heavy lorries and buses?
4. By what methods in the future might trucks cross the Channel from Britain to France?

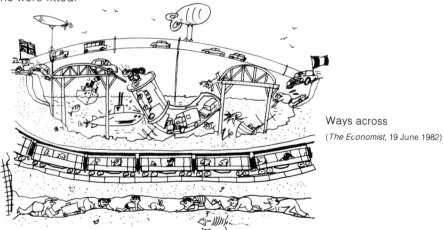

Ways across
(*The Economist*, 19 June 1982)

4. Problems and Achievements: a Summary

Achievements

1 Membership
In over 25 years since the EEC was set up, no full member-country has left. Other countries, e.g. Turkey, wish to join. Norway may also apply for membership, after previously voting against joining.

2 Trade
Customs union has worked. Trade barriers have been removed within the EEC and internal trade has increased. The aim is a single market by 1992. There are also trade agreements with over 50 countries outside the EEC.

3 Agriculture
The Common Agricultural Policy (CAP) has kept some security of food supplies to EEC members, while world supplies varied. Also CAP subsidies have prevented many farmers losing their jobs and farms.

4 Regional policy
Money from the EEC's Regional Fund has helped projects in poorer areas. Over eight years to 1984, Scotland got a total of £338 million. In 1983, £83 million was allocated to Scotland, including £1.2 million to Sinclair Research in Dundee for a micro TV project.

5 Political union
The European Parliament has been in existence for 25 years. Direct elections to the European Parliament were held in 1979 and in 1984. In Britain, the Labour Party has ended its threat to seek to leave the EEC. Over 60% of the European electorate voted in the 1984 election.

6 Budget
The sum of £14.5 billion was allocated for 1984 to help Europe's industry, agriculture and social conditions. There was an increased budget to tackle economic recession.

PROBLEMS

1 Membership
Some members are not keen on increasing the membership. For example, France and Italy fear extra competition in Mediterranean foods, fruit and wine if Spain and Portugal join. Their provisional membership date of 1986 may be delayed. West Germany and Britain fear that extra members may add to financial problems in the EEC.

2 Trade
There have been trade disputes between member-states. In 1984 French farmers temporarily prevented British and Belgian meat and Italian wine being delivered in France.

3 Agriculture
Problems have arisen over the large amount of subsidies given to farmers by the EEC. The CAP funds take about 75 per cent of EEC money. There are large amounts of unwanted food surpluses, e.g. butter mountains, wine lakes and powdered milk hills. There are disputes between farmers of different countries over imports, e.g. British dairy farmers urged the government to ban French UHT (ultra heat treated) long-life milk from Britain.

4 Regional policy
There is a serious imbalance between rich and poor regions within the EEC. Some areas, such as Scotland, have suffered serious problems of high unemployment as industries such as steel, coal and textiles run into economic difficulties.

5 Political union
The European Parliament still has no fixed base but moves expensively between Strasbourg, Brussels and Luxembourg. There are different forms of electoral systems for the European Parliament in various countries. Some people feel that they are too remote from their Euro MP in a constituency of about 500 000 people. Only 32% of Britain's electorate bothered to vote in the 1984 election.

6 Budget
There is concern in the 1980s that the EEC budget spending is going beyond EEC income. Only two countries, Britain and West Germany, are net-contributors to the EEC funds. In 1984 Britain claimed it was paying in too much and threatened to refuse to pay EEC budget income if it did not get some money refunded. About 75 per cent of the whole budget of the EEC goes to the Agriculture Fund.

7 Language

Ten different countries send representatives to Parliament and other meetings to discuss problems. There is continuous translation of speeches in Parliament in all EEC member languages. A European driving licence in several languages will be available from 1986. A new European passport is available.

7 Language

The wide variety of languages within the EEC can make communication difficult. The EEC spends about £40 million a year on paper and printing costs for books, pamphlets and magazines in seven different languages. Translation of EEC documents involves 40 per cent of Commission staff.

8 Decision-making

Decision-making offers all members a chance to make their views known at a wide variety of committee meetings. EEC ministers for fishing reached a decision on 1984 fishing quotas in one day.

8 Decision-making

'Europe is in a state of crisis – paralysed by its inability to make decisions.' (Gaston Thorn, President of the European Commission 1983.) The EEC has failed to reach decisions on several critical issues such as the EEC's financial crisis and rising unemployment. A summit meeting in Athens in 1983 attended by the EEC heads of government failed to reach any decision.

9 Fishing

EEC Fishing Policy agreement was reached in 1983, after years of disagreement and hostility. Members' fishing protected from outside competition. Fishing agreements were signed with Norway, the USSR and Greenland.

9 Fishing

British and Danish fishermen blame the EEC for loss of jobs in the fishing industry, and for allowing non-member Norway to have herring quotas in EEC waters.

10 World trade

The EEC forms a major world trading power. The EEC has close trade links with the USA but opposed the US ban on supplies to the Soviet gas pipeline construction in 1982, and opposed the US ban on European special steel in 1983. There was an agreement with Japan on the level of imports of Japanese video tape recorders in 1984. The EEC also has trade links with COMECON (East European countries) and with Third World countries.

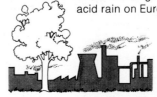

10 World trade

There have been disputes in the EEC over the continued import of New Zealand butter. Britain complained to France over its sale of Exocet missiles to Argentina. COMECON feels the EEC is too closely linked to NATO. By 1988, however, a provisional agreement was signed to establish official relations between the EEC and COMECON.

11 Employment

Jobs would be created through Regional Aid in areas of high unemployment. In 1983 £2.7 million was allocated to job-creation schemes in Scotland.

11 Employment

Unemployment continues to rise in the EEC. By early 1984 there were 12 million people unemployed. By 1985, this had risen to 19 million. For young people under 25 years of age the rate was about 25 per cent.

12 Environment

The EEC takes steps to check pollution of the environment. There have been checks on the amount of waste dumped into the River Rhine, and in 1981 there was an agreement to limit the discharge of mercury from EEC chemical industries.

In 1984 the EEC approved a £6.4 million programme of research into acid rain and toxic waste, and £11 million for research into saving natural resources.

12 Environment

There is increasing radioactive pollution in the North Sea caused by nuclear waste from nuclear power industries in Britain, France and along the Rhine. In some parts of the Mediterranean beaches are closed in summer because of sewage pollution. There is also growing concern over the effects of acid rain on Europe's forests and lakes.

PART 3

World Co-operation

1. The United Nations

Introduction: Aims

It is April 1946 and the setting is a large building called the Palace of Nations in Geneva, Switzerland. A statesman is concluding a speech:

'From now on we owe to the United Nations all our loyalties and all our services . . . We part as we have met, delegates of governments, servants of a great idea; and as we break up from the last meeting of the League we all know that its soul goes marching on.'

With these words the President of the League of Nations brought to an end the first great experiment in world co-operation. The League had in fact died long before 1946. It had lost its importance ten years earlier in 1936 and became a forgotten dream in 1939 when the Second World War broke out.

But from the ashes of the Second World War and from the ruins of the League there was to emerge a second experiment in world co-operation. This was to be based not in Europe but in New York, USA. The location was new and so was the building but the aims behind the new organisation – the United Nations Organisation – were those of a long-held ideal of world co-operation.

Headquarters of the United Nations in New York

The aims behind the United Nations were set out in a Charter which was signed by 50 countries in San Francisco in June 1945.

To save succeeding generations from the scourge of war, which twice in our lifetime has brought untold sorrow to mankind . . . to reaffirm faith in fundamental human rights, in the dignity and worth of the human person, in the equal rights of men and women and of nations large and small, and to establish conditions under which justice and respect for . . . international law can be maintained for the promotion of the economic and social advancement of the peoples.

Thus the main aim of the United Nations is to provide a means by which the nations of the world can co-operate to bring about three major aims:

(1) to achieve international co-operation for the maintenance of world peace and security;
(2) to achieve international co-operation for the protection of human rights throughout the world;
(3) to achieve international co-operation for the promotion of economic and social progress throughout the world.

The Machinery of Co-operation

How were the aims to be achieved in practice?

The main parts of the United Nations can be seen in the chart below. You will notice that the total organisation is made up of a number of different parts, in fact the UN is sometimes described as a 'family' of organisations.

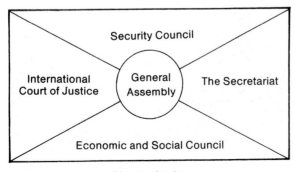

UN organisation

THE GENERAL ASSEMBLY

At the heart of the organisation is the General Assembly which is the UN's main forum for debate and discussion. It is made up of representatives of all member nations – at present 158 – and each member, large or small, has one vote. This means that a major power like the USA has no more voting strength than any other member.

The General Assembly decides the budget for the whole of the UN and it controls the other parts of the organisation. But its main function is as a forum for discussion of world problems, as a result of which it can make recommendations to member-nations. So it is in the Assembly that all of the UN's important projects (with the exception of peacekeeping) originate.

The General Assembly has been described as a 'world parliament' but unlike national parliaments it cannot pass laws and its recommendations cannot be enforced upon individual member-nations.

THE SECURITY COUNCIL

The Security Council is directly responsible for the peacekeeping role of the UN. It is composed of 15 members: five of these are permanent (China, France, the UK, the USA and the USSR) whilst the other ten are elected by the General Assembly for two-year terms.

The main function of the Security Council is maintaining international peace and security. In the event of conflict, the Council can demand the end of fighting and the withdrawal of any forces from territory which has been invaded; it can suggest ways to solve the dispute and if either of the parties refuses to carry out these demands, it can then impose economic sanctions on the offending country and even take military action against that country.

Each member of the Council has one vote and there must be a majority in favour of a decision to recommend action. But any one of the five permanent members can block this action by casting a 'No' vote – this is known as using their right of veto.

The use of the veto has tended to block any effective action by the Security Council, especially in the event of conflict involving the major powers. By 30 September 1975 the veto had been used a total of 141 times, of which the USSR accounted for 109 and the USA 11. (Note, however, that most of the Soviet vetoes were used in the very early years of the UN, when the USSR felt itself to be outvoted. From 1961 to 1975 the USSR used its veto only ten times whilst the USA cast all its 11 vetoes between 1970 and 1975, thus reflecting the changing composition of the UN.)

Because of the use of the veto and the deadlock in the Security Council, the General Assembly adopted a resolution in 1950 which has come to be known as the 'Uniting for Peace Resolution'. This states that in the event of deadlock in the Security Council the Assembly can intervene to recommend action. This happened in 1956–67 over the Middle East crisis, when the General Assembly sent in the United Nations Emergency Force.

It is worth noting that the Security Council does not have a permanent force to enforce its decisions and that there is little it can do if members do not carry out its decisions. This happened when the Security Council applied economic sanctions against Rhodesia, and several countries who were members of the UN ignored them and continued trading with Rhodesia (now Zimbabwe).

THE ECONOMIC AND SOCIAL COUNCIL

The Economic and Social Council is responsible for organising the action taken by the UN on the world's economic and social problems. It is also responsible for the promotion of human rights. Most of its work is carried out through its specialised agencies like the **FAO** and the **WHO**.

It is composed of 54 members elected by the General Assembly for three-year periods.

THE SECRETARIAT

The Secretariat is the international civil service of the UN and carries out the massive administration of the UN's work.

In charge of the Secretariat is the Secretary-General who is appointed by the General Assembly to run the UN. But throughout the history of the UN, the Secretary-General has not simply been an administrator but has become an important world figure. The post has been held by five men – Trygve Lie (Norway); Dag Hammarskjold (Sweden); U Thant (Burma); Kurt Waldheim (Austria) and the present holder **Javier Perez de Cuellar** (Peru).

THE INTERNATIONAL COURT OF JUSTICE

This is the main judicial organ of the UN and consists of 15 judges who are elected by the General Assembly and the Security Council. The Court has a permanent location in the Hague, Holland, and deals with problems of international law or international treaties.

Questions

1. Explain the three main aims of the UN.
2. What is meant by saying that the UN is a 'family' of organisations?
3. What is the main function of the General Assembly?
4. Describe the system of voting used in the General Assembly and explain why a country like the USA might object to this system of voting.
5. In what important way do the powers of the General Assembly differ from those of a national parliament?
6. Describe the powers and composition of the Security Council.
7. Give two reasons why the Security Council has not been effective in securing world peace.
8. What is the importance of the 'Uniting for Peace Resolution'?

UN Secretary-General Javier Perez de Cuellar (Peru), elected 1981

2. The United Nations in Action

The work done by the United Nations covers many different areas of the world, involves millions of people from many nations and costs an enormous amount of money every year. In this chapter we shall look at the three main kinds of work in which the UN is involved. These can be summarised in the following diagram:

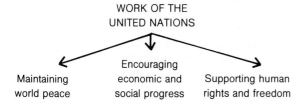

WORK OF THE
UNITED NATIONS

Maintaining world peace — Encouraging economic and social progress — Supporting human rights and freedom

Keeping the Peace

The most important job of the UN is to maintain international peace and security. This involves trying to prevent outbreaks of war if possible and, if war does occur, trying to bring it to an end as quickly as possible. It also involves trying to slow down the rate at which countries are developing the weapons of war. In doing these things the UN resembles a kind of world police officer, whose duty it is to patrol the world, keeping an eye open for trouble-makers and law-breakers, and taking action when necessary.

The UN has been involved, in its role as world police officer, in over 100 disputes since 1945. We shall look at some of the more important of these disputes and also at some of the problem areas where the UN might have been expected to act, but did not.

The Security Council has the main responsibility for maintaining international peace and security. The methods and machinery available to it for dealing with conflicts are shown below.

Fact-finding mission UN officials are sent to a problem area to investigate details of the problem and report back to the UN.

Military observers UN officials patrol a ceasefire line between countries in conflict to make sure they do not break the rules of the agreement, e.g. Kashmir.

Economic embargo UN member-nations stop trade in, for example, steel or oil with a country which attacks or acts against the interests of another country or group of people, e.g. Rhodesia.

Arms embargo Member-nations agree to stop supplying a country with weapons and ammunition if they think these will be used illegally against other nations or groups of people, e.g. South Africa.

UN Interim Force troops in Lebanon

Peacekeeping force An armed force, drawn from UN member-nations, patrols a trouble-spot and keep the forces of warring nations apart while attempts are made to find a solution to the problem, e.g. Cyprus, Middle East.

Questions

1. What do the UN's duties as 'world police officer' involve?
2. Describe the methods available to the Security Council in dealing with world trouble-spots.

Korea

After the Second World War Korea, formerly part of the Japanese Empire, was occupied by troops of the USA in the south and the USSR in the north. When the UN tried to hold elections for a National Assembly in 1947, the USSR refused and elections were held in the south only. In June 1950, when the South was attacked by North Korean forces, the Security Council condemned the attack, called for a ceasefire and asked for the assistance of UN member-countries to ensure the withdrawal of the North Korean forces.

When this decision was taken the Soviet Union was not represented since the Soviet delegation had walked out of the Security Council over its refusal to allow Communist China to take over China's seat in the UN: otherwise the Security Council would have found it impossible to take such a strong line.

Sixteen nations, under the command of the USA, sent troops to help the South Koreans, and five other member-countries supplied medical units.

(The USSR and China said the Security Council's decisions were illegal – can you say why?) Fighting continued until July 1953, when an Armistice Agreement was signed, but although the UN tried to find a permanent political solution to the problem, Korea has remained divided. A UN Commission for the Unification and Rehabilitation of Korea remained in the country until 1973 when it was dissolved. In 1974 the UN General Assembly urged North and South Korea to continue talking to try to unify the country. This possibility is now very remote.

Although the problem of Korea has still not been solved, the UN's action in co-ordinating military assistance to the South was eventually successful. It showed that the UN was capable of action to combat aggression, even if it did rely heavily on the United States' determination to ensure that South Korea would not fall to the communists.

Questions

1. How did the UN first become involved in Korea?
2. What help did the UN provide?
3. Was the Korean problem solved completely by the UN?
4. In what way was the UN action a success?

The Middle East

In his opening speech to the UN General Assembly in 1976, the former Secretary-General Kurt Waldheim said,

> 'Two major and long standing problems, the Middle East and Cyprus, continue to cause great anxiety.'

Details of the conflicts in the Middle East are given in Part One. The UN has been involved in the troubles of the area in three ways: firstly by taking military action to try to end hostilities between the Arab countries and Israel; secondly by devoting a great deal of its resources to helping the Palestinian refugees through the United Nations Relief and Works Agency (**UNRWA**); and thirdly by trying to find a permanent political solution to the problems of the area. The UN has been unable to prevent or halt the Gulf War between Iran and Iraq, and was totally ineffective when the Soviet Union intervened in Afghanistan. Although the UN was unable to stop war from breaking out in the Middle East, can it realistically be blamed for this? Could any organisation be expected to solve problems such as the Arab–Israeli conflict or the deep-rooted quarrel between Iran and Iraq? At the very least, the UN did

MILITARY ACTION	POLITICAL ACTION
1949 First Arab–Israeli War ended by truce called for by the Security Council, supervised by UN Truce Supervision Organisation.	**1947** General Assembly adopts a Partition Plan for Palestine.
1956 Suez Crisis ended with UNEF (United Nations Emergency Force) set up to preserve peace. Suez Canal cleared by UN.	**1967** Security Council adopts Resolution 242 as the basis of a just and lasting peace settlement.
1967 UNEF withdrawn at request of President Nasser of Egypt. Six-Day War – UN military observers sent to Middle East to observe ceasefire.	**1973** Security Council calls for negotiations for a lasting peace. Peace Conference on the Middle East set up in Geneva.
1973 Yom Kippur War – Security Council calls for ceasefire. UNEF II stationed between Israeli and Egyptian forces. Still in position in 1978.	**1974** General Assembly adopts resolution asserting 'the inalienable rights of the Palestinian people in Palestine' to national independence and sovereignty.
1978 United Nations Interim force in Lebanon (UNIFIL) forms buffer zone between Israeli army and PLO guerrillas following Israeli invasion of Southern Lebanon. Powerless to stop Israeli invasion of Lebanon in 1982.	
1984 UN peacekeeping force considered as alternative after withdrawal of the multinational peacekeeping force.	

take swift action after the Yom Kippur War, and its efforts to assist up to half a million Palestinian refugees in Lebanon have been remarkable.

In its attempts to bring about a permanent settlement to the Arab–Israeli dispute the UN has been less successful. The machinery of the UN has been ineffective in making any progress towards lasting peace in the Middle East and the prospects for a settlement of any of the major problems in this area are as remote in the 1980s as they have been during the last 40 years.

Questions

1. In what three ways has the UN been involved in the Middle East?
2. Copy the table showing UN military and political action in the area since 1947.
3. Why might the UN's involvement in the Middle East be considered both a success and a failure?
4. Briefly describe the UN's effectiveness in: (a) the Gulf War, and (b) Soviet intervention in Afghanistan.

Russians veto move for UN force

The Soviet Union today vetoed a United Nations Security Council resolution to send UN troops to Beirut to replace the multinational force. The vote was 13 in favour and two against – the Soviet Union and the Ukraine. There were no abstentions.

The main Soviet objection was that the draft failed to ensure there would be no further naval shelling or air attacks by the countries of the multinational force – particularly the US.

Under the resolution, the council would have decided to constitute a force drawn from UN members other than the five permanent members of the council. The force would have taken up position 'in the Beirut area, in co-ordination with the Lebanese authorities concerned, as soon as all elements of the multinational force have withdrawn from Lebanese territory and waters.'

Addressing the council, Mr Oleg Troyanovsky of the Soviet Union, said that despite the redeployment of the US marines, hardly a day went by without the Americans bombarding Lebanon. The situation had reached such a point that a pretext was no longer offered.

He quoted President Reagan as having said that even an accidentally fired shell would justify retaliation from the guns of the battleship *New Jersey*. – Reuter.

(*The Scotsman*, 1 March 1984)
© Reuter.

Cyrus

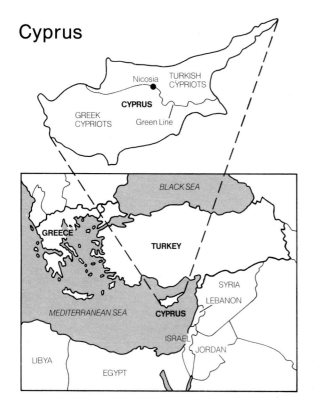

The island of Cyprus belonged to Turkey until 1914 when Britain took over its government until 1960. In that year Britain, Turkey and Greece agreed that Cyprus should become an independent sovereign republic. Because the majority of the people in Cyprus are Greek-Cypriots (about 78 per cent) and Turkish-Cypriots account for about 18 per cent, it was agreed that the President of Cyprus should always be a Greek-Cypriot and the Vice-President a Turkish-Cypriot, each elected by their own community for a period of five years at a time.

Unfortunately the Greek and Turkish Cypriots distrusted one another and this arrangement never really worked. Serious violence broke out between the two communities and the UN became involved in an attempt to stop the fighting. Since March 1964 the UN peacekeeping force in Cyprus (UNFICYP) has been stationed on the island to prevent further fighting between Greek and Turkish Cypriots. Since August 1974 UNFICYP has also had the job of maintaining the ceasefire between the Cyprus National Guard and the armed forces of Turkey, following the invasion of Cyprus by Turkish troops and the setting up of an area under Turkish control in the north of the island.

UNFICYP consisted of almost 7000 men in 1964, later reduced to less than 3000, but strengthened as a result of the events of 1974 to approximately 4400. Countries contributing troops or police include Australia, Austria, Canada, Denmark, Finland, Ire-

land, Sweden and the UK. Costs are met by the governments providing the troops and the government of Cyprus, as well as by voluntary contributions.

The UN has also been deeply concerned about the plight of refugees following the 1974 invasion. A UN High Commissioner for Refugees was appointed as co-ordinator of the UN humanitarian efforts to help some 200 000 people.

In January 1978 the UN Secretary-General, Kurt Waldheim, made a considerable breakthrough when he managed to arrange a meeting between the Greek and Turkish Prime Ministers, with a view to reaching a solution to the problem.

Questions

1. Describe the background to the violence which broke out in Cyprus in the 1960s.
2. What action has the UN taken in Cyprus?
3. Give a brief description of INFICYP.
4. What has the UN done to help refugees on the island?

The Congo

One of the UN's success stories happened in 1960 when the Democratic Republic of the Congo (now the Republic of Zaire), a former Belgian colony, was given independence. Disorder broke out and Belgium sent troops to the Congo to protect and evacuate Europeans. The new Congolese government, however, asked for UN military assistance to protect the Congo against 'external aggression'.

The Security Council called on Belgium to withdraw its troops, and in less than 48 hours after the Congolese government's call for help, UN troops, largely from neutral countries including Asian and African states, arrived in the Congo. UN civilian experts also arrived to help ensure the continued operation of essential public services.

During the next four years the Congo received a large amount of help from the UN; to restore and maintain its political independence; to help keep law and order; and to introduce a programme of training and technical assistance. The UN at one time had more than 20 000 people working in the Congo. After 1963 the UN force was gradually reduced and by June 1964 was completely withdrawn, although civilian aid continued.

Questions

1. Why did the government of the Congo ask for UN help?
2. What was the UN's reaction to this request?
3. The UN action in the Congo is considered to be one of its best successes. Give reasons why this view is justified.

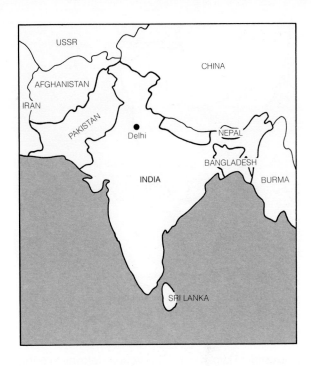

Once again, therefore, the UN machinery was unable to find a long-term solution to a problem area, and its main success was the help it gave to the refugees who returned to Bangladesh. Bangladesh joined the UN in 1974.

India and Pakistan

A dispute between India and Pakistan over Kashmir has been a threat to peace in Asia since 1947. The problem first came to the attention of the Security Council in 1948 when India complained that tribesmen and others were invading Kashmir and fighting was taking place. India claimed that Pakistan was helping the invading forces, but Pakistan denied this and made several complaints about India. The UN sent a Commission to the area and a ceasefire was agreed to, but the basic differences between the two countries were not settled and the problem cropped up again and again.

In 1965 fierce fighting broke out again between the two countries and the Security Council called for a ceasefire. A UN Military Observer Group (MOG) in Kashmir was strengthened and a new MOG set up between India and West Pakistan.

In 1971 trouble broke out once more over the civil war in East Pakistan, which later became the independent state of Bangladesh. Tension increased as millions of refugees fled into India. The UN gave a huge amount of help to these refugees but the two governments involved refused an offer of help in dealing with the problem.

Questions

1. What was the cause of the dispute between India and Pakistan in the late 1940s?
2. How successful was the UN's action at this time?
3. What action was taken by the UN when trouble flared up again in 1965 and 1971?
4. Assess the long-term effectiveness of the UN's action in this area.

The Falkland Islands

When the Argentine military government (junta) tried in 1982 to take possession of the Falkland Islands (known in Argentina as the Malvinas) from Britain and the British government sent a naval task force to recover the islands, the United Nations was once more by-passed.

The UN was powerless to prevent hostilities from the beginning, and once they had begun it played only a very minor part in bringing them to an end.

The former United States Secretary of State,

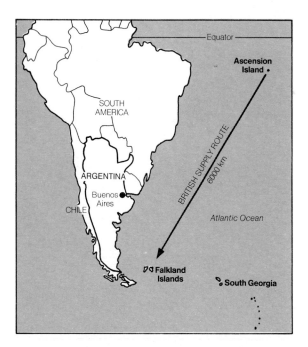

that each is an example, one from the 1960s, the other from the 1970s, of an event in which the UN might have been expected to become involved, but did not. They illustrate the fact that it is possible for a major crisis and a violent and destructive war to occur in which the UN is powerless to act. When the Superpowers are involved in a political situation in which they wish to act independently, outside the UN, they are perfectly able to do so. The exercise of the veto by the permanent members of the Security Council also illustrates the fact that the strength of the UN depends very much on the co-operation of its member-countries: if they are willing to act in the spirit of the UN Charter, much can be achieved, if not, the UN is powerless.

Questions

1. Why are Cuba and Vietnam significant events in the UN's attempts to keep world peace?
2. What weaknesses in the UN machinery do these events show up?
3. Why is the UN powerless if its members refuse to co-operate?

Disarmament and the UN

The statistics in the diagram opposite show the low priority which disarmament seems to have among the world's nations. It has been estimated that by the year 2000 almost 100 countries, including South Africa and some Middle East countries, will be capable of making nuclear weapons.

When the UN Charter was drawn up in 1945 the dangers of modern nuclear weapons were not fully recognised and disarmament was not made as important an aim as it has since become. Several important agreements limiting the development and use of nuclear weapons have been set up under UN influence, but the SALT talks between the USA and the USSR, which are the best hope for nuclear limitation, have taken place outside the UN.

In May/June 1978 the General Assembly held a Special Session – only the eighth in the UN's history – to debate the whole subject of disarmament. For five weeks more than 20 heads of state addressed the largest group of people ever brought together to try to reverse the increase in nuclear weapons. But two figures notable by their absence were Presidents Carter and Brezhnev. The failure of this Special Session can be seen in the continuing arms race and the growing number of countries with the potential to make nuclear weapons in the 1980s. By

Alexander Haig, was the key figure in efforts to bring about a diplomatic solution to the problem before the two countries went to war. The UN Security Council did call for an ending of the hostilities between Argentina and Britain, and diplomats from both countries made speeches in the UN, but these produced no visible results. The Security Council passed Resolution 502 calling for the removal of Argentine troops from the Falklands in order for a diplomatic solution to be found, but this was ignored. During and after the hostilities, the US government was the most important diplomatic channel.

The Falklands War illustrates once more the ineffectiveness of the UN machinery for preserving world peace in the face of two nations involved in a dispute who are determined on pursuing their own policies with little regard for the United Nations' machinery.

Questions

1. What was the cause of the dispute between Britain and Argentina in 1982?
2. How effective was the UN before and during the dispute?

Cuba and Vietnam

Details of the Cuban missile crisis and the Vietnam War are given in Part One. The reason why these two important events are dealt with together here is

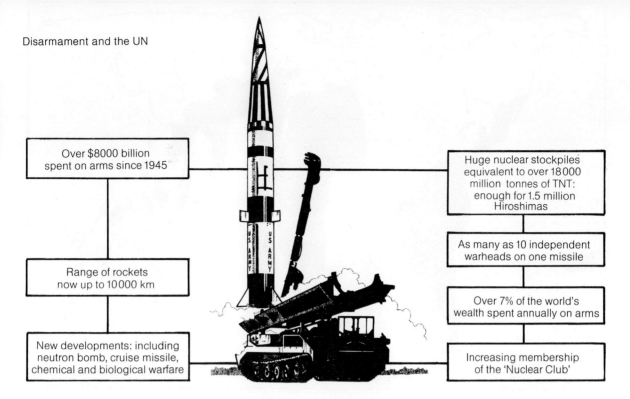

Over $8000 billion spent on arms since 1945

Range of rockets now up to 10 000 km

New developments: including neutron bomb, cruise missile, chemical and biological warfare

Huge nuclear stockpiles equivalent to over 18 000 million tonnes of TNT: enough for 1.5 million Hiroshimas

As many as 10 independent warheads on one missile

Over 7% of the world's wealth spent annually on arms

Increasing membership of the 'Nuclear Club'

1983 the US nuclear stockpile was equivalent to 9000 million tonnes of TNT – or to put it another way, one Hiroshima every 30 minutes since the Second World War, day and night, seven days a week for 38 years. The USSR's nuclear stockpile is now the same.

Questions

1. What evidence is there to show that many nations do not think disarmament is important?
2. Describe the action taken on disarmament by the UN.
3. How effective has this action been?

The War against Poverty

'The real problem of the modern world, the thing which creates misery, wars and hatred amongst men, is the division of mankind into rich and poor.'
Julius K. Nyerere, President of Tanzania

THE RICH AND POOR

The map on page 118 shows an unusual representation of the world. This map is the work of Dr Arno Peters, a German historian. Peters' map differs from the more usual map of the world – known as the Mercator map – in that it shows countries more accurately in relation to their true size. For example, on the Mercator map Greenland (2 million square kilometres in size) appears almost as big as Africa (30 million square kilometres). The Mercator map also shows a Europe which is unrealistically large and it is argued that this has emphasised the idea of Europe being the centre of the world.

The areas shaded on the map are the poorest areas of the world – the countries of Central America, Southern America, Asia, Africa and the Middle East. The richest countries are those of North America (USA and Canada), Europe, New Zealand, Australia, Japan, Israel and South Africa. The Peters' map helps to give a truer perspective of the relationship between the rich and poor nations, between the North and South.

The poor countries have traditionally been known as the Third World. They are also called the developing countries, whilst the richer are known as the developed countries. They have also been called the underdeveloped countries or less developed countries or the South (as part of the North–South division). Whatever term is used to describe the poor countries, there are a number of common problems which are generally taken to be characteristic of their condition.

The following description from Paul Hoffman, a UN official, sums up this view: 'Everyone knows an underdeveloped country when they see one . . .

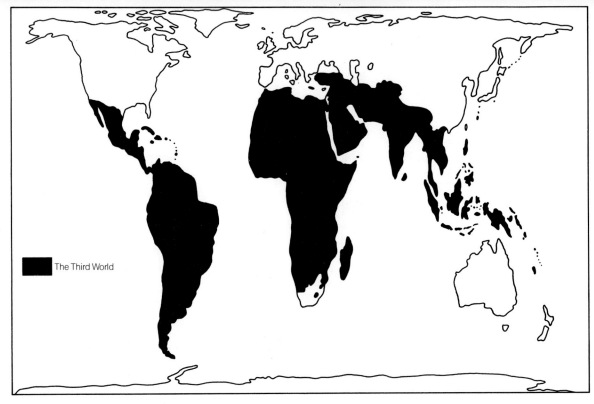

The Peters projection world map

characterised by poverty, with beggars in the cities, and villagers eking out a bare subsistence in the rural areas . . . usually has insufficient roads and railways . . . few hospitals . . . most of its people cannot read or write . . . may have isolated islands of wealth . . . exports to other countries usually consist almost entirely of raw materials, ores or fruits or some staple product. . . .'

Overpopulation, inadequate food supplies, poor medical facilities, poor educational standards and poor farming, a low level of industrialisation and a lack of trading leading to a very weak economy: these are some of the main features which when added together would give an 'Identikit' picture of a poor country.

Of course the poor countries do not provide one uniform group any more than do the rich countries. There is a great variety of levels of development. There are those countries which are the poorest in the world. They have been called the Least Developed Countries (LDCs). Among such countries are Afghanistan, Bangladesh, Botswana, Chad, Ethiopia, Haiti, Malawi, Nepal, Sudan, Uganda and Yemen. Above this group of countries are those which rely on one or two raw material exports for their wealth. And above them are the newly industrialised countries, such as Brazil, Taiwan and South Korea. Finally there are the oil-exporting countries of the Middle East, plus Venezuela and Nigeria.

No matter how one tries to describe the poor countries, there still exists a great contrast between the rich and poor countries in the world. It is the great challenge of the latter part of the twentieth century to close this gap. This challenge was clearly expressed in the Brandt Report *North–South, A Programme for Survival*, and it is one which has occupied a great deal of the attention of the United Nations. A major aim of the UN Charter is 'the promotion of the economic and social advancement of the peoples' of the world. In this unit we shall be examining the problems of the poor countries and the ways in which the United Nations tries to close the gap between rich and poor.

Questions

1. Which areas of the world make up the poor and the rich countries?
2. In what ways does the Peters' map help to give a new view of the relationship between the rich and poor countries?
3. What terms have been used to describe the poor countries of the world and what kind of problems do they share?
4. Describe the various levels of development which have been identified among the poor countries of the world.

OVERPOPULATION

The problem of too many people is one of the most serious facing the world today. This problem is most serious in the developing countries, which have about 70 per cent of the world's people.

It is estimated that there are about 4000 million people in the world. It is impossible to imagine this figure but there are just over five million people in Scotland and so the world's population is equal to 800 Scotlands.

It is not just the size of the world's population which is alarming but the speed at which it is growing. You can see this clearly from the graph of world population growth. It took until about 1830 to reach 1000 million people; 2000 million was reached by 1930; 3000 and 4000 million by about the late 1970s, i.e. the world's population is doubling within shorter periods of time. It is estimated that at present growth rates the world's population will reach 6500 million by the year 2000.

This population explosion has been caused by the fact that the world's death rate (the number of people who die within a certain period of time) has fallen dramatically, but the birth rate (the number of children who are born within the same period of time) has not fallen. This is especially true of the developing countries, where the advanced medical knowledge of the developed countries was introduced rapidly. In the developed countries the birth rate has fallen in line with the death rate.

Thus it is in those countries least able to afford it that the population explosion is taking place. By the year 2000 India will double its population to about 1000 million people. This means more food, more

Estimated rate of world population growth, 1750–2000

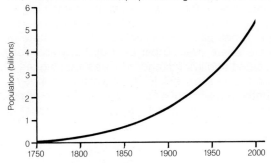

work, more schools, more hospitals, and more houses are needed. And this is only to cater for the extra population without making any progress on India's present problems. Mrs Ghandi, leader of India, once described her country as 'having to run fast to stay in the same place'.

A programme of birth control would obviously help solve the problem of overpopulation. But experience has shown that family planning is only successful when poverty is also attacked. Living standards need to be improved so that the poor do not need large numbers of children to help them farm and to ensure that they are cared for in their old age. A poor family in India still needs to have seven children to be sure of having one surviving son.

Estimated population growth (by region)

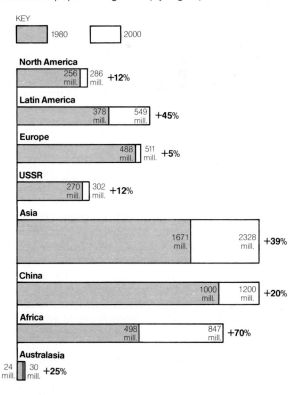

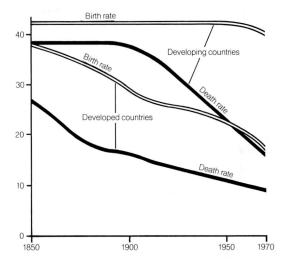

Birth and death rates per 1000 people for the developed and developing countries

Family planning has had little success in the Indian state of Bihar, where female literacy is less than seven per cent and medical services are very poor. It has been more successful in the state of Kerala where over 50 per cent of the women are educated and living standards are much higher.

And so we see the vicious circle of the developing country: poverty makes it difficult to reduce population growth whilst population growth makes it more difficult to solve poverty.

Questions

1. Where is the problem of overpopulation most serious?
2. What justification is there for describing the growth of world population as a 'population explosion'?
3. What is causing this population explosion especially in the developing countries? (You should refer to the graphs of birth and death rates on page 119).
4. What did Mrs Ghandi mean by describing the effects of overpopulation on India as 'having to run fast to stay in the same place'?
5. What evidence is there for the view that family planning is only successful when other features of poverty are attacked at the same time?
6. How does the problem of overpopulation illustrate the vicious circle of poverty affecting developing countries?

Queue for milk in Bangladesh

NOT ENOUGH TO EAT

It has been estimated that about half of the world's population is hungry. Of that figure about 500 million suffer from this seriously.

'Hunger' has two forms:

(a) undernourishment – insufficient food; and
(b) malnutrition – not enough of the right kinds of food.

Undernourishment can lead to death through starvation. We need food to give us energy to carry on our daily life. This energy is expressed in units called calories and the amount of calories we need depends on our age, our job, our sex and the climate we live in. If we eat more than we need the body stores the extra calories as fat. In the West many people count the calorie-value of their food very carefully in order to lose weight. Many people in the world never have to diet for they simply cannot get enough to eat and survive on less than 2000 calories per day. (An adult man needs an average

A British supermarket

basic requirement of 1700 calories for 24 hours, just to keep him alive. The British Medical Association recommend up to 3000 calories per day for an adult engaged in moderate work.) Others may get enough to eat in terms of quantity but suffer from deficiencies in the proteins, minerals and vitamins necessary for healthy growth. In particular, shortage of protein can lead to a number of diseases. Rickets and scurvy are two deficiency diseases which were once common in this country.

In the developing countries perhaps the most common disease is kwashiorkor, which strikes young children and is caused by lack of protein. An insufficient diet can also lead to a low resistance to infectious diseases: in some developing countries even measles can be a deadly killer.

A great many reasons can be given to explain why so many people, especially in the developing countries, suffer from hunger. Overpopulation, primitive farming techniques and climatic problems of drought are all important factors. The use of modern machinery and fertilisers, better quality seeds and improved irrigation will obviously improve food production. The use of these techniques has become known as the Green Revolution. During the 1960s food production did increase and countries such as India invested heavily in the new techniques.

However, a disastrous cereal harvest in 1972 and dreadful droughts a year later in Africa and India revealed that the world's food problem had still not been solved. In fact some people question whether the Green Revolution can meet the real needs of farmers in the developing countries: to use quality seeds properly, farmers need to buy fertiliser and new seeds every year; they need to have well-irrigated fields and extensive pest control. Very few peasant farmers can fill these requirements.

The reform of land ownership is often also necessary in order to increase food production. Many Third World farmers rent their land in return for a share in the crop (sharecropping) so that any improvement benefits the landlord as much as themselves. Co-operative farming is proving successful in many countries but traditional methods die hard.

It has been claimed that the world produces enough food to feed the entire population adequately, but the richer countries (which account for only 30 per cent of the world's population) use 60 per cent of the world's food. The developed countries, quite simply, may be eating too much. The eating of meat is an extravagant way of getting protein; it takes 4 kg of vegetable protein to feed animals to give 1 kg of meat protein. We could eat vegetable protein directly, e.g. pulses such as lentils and soya beans, which are very rich in protein. Already many of our foodstuffs consist of 'synthetic' meat made from spun soya beans. But the developed countries have a taste for meat which is unlikely to be sacrificed voluntarily.

Questions

1. What is the difference between malnutrition and undernourishment?
2. What are the results of malnutrition?
3. What do you understand by 'the Green Revolution'?
4. Why are some experts beginning to doubt that the Green Revolution will solve the world's food problem?
5. Why is the reform of land ownership important in increasing food production?
6. How are the developed countries contributing to the world food problem by their eating habits?

POOR MEDICAL FACILITIES

The National Health Service in Britain often comes under attack and people complain about overcrowded waiting rooms and long waiting lists for hospital treatment. But according to the UN magazine, *World Health*, the developed countries have a ratio of doctors to inhabitants in the range of one per 450 to one per 1000, while many developing countries have a ratio of one doctor for every 20 000 to 30 000 inhabitants.

Table 9 Health statistics for selected countries

	Mortality rate (per 1000 live births)		Life expectancy	
	Infant	Maternal	Male	Female
Bolivia	88.9	1.4	49.7	49.7
Egypt	118.5	0.9	51.6	53.8
Malaysia	45.1	1.7	63.1	66.0
Canada	20.8	0.3	68.6	74.2
Sweden	12.9	0.09	71.6	76.5
Britain	18.3	0.2	68.5	74.7

POOR EDUCATIONAL FACILITIES

An educated population is essential for a country to develop. Without this it must rely on foreign help. Doctors, engineers, agricultural specialists, etc. are needed. The mass of the people need to be literate (able to read and write) so that they can understand leaflets on family planning or new farming techniques and learn the basic skills needed in industry.

Unfortunately many developing countries are far from this educational standard (see Table 10).

Table 10 Illiteracy among men and women

	Area	Percentage illiterate
Adult men (over 15)	World Total	28
	Africa	63.4
	North America	1.1
	Latin America	19.9
	Europe	2.4
	Asia	37.0
Adult women (over 15)	World Total	40.3
	Africa	83.7
	North America	1.9
	Latin America	27.3
	Europe	4.7
	Asia	56.7

Questions

1. What major problem can be seen from the health statistics given in Table 9?
2. Why is education a crucial part in a country's development?
3. How serious a problem is illiteracy in the developing countries? (You will need to refer to the statistics on world illiteracy rates given in Table 10.)
4. From the case study, write a description of Bangladesh in your own words to show the life and problems of a developing country.

WHO CAN HELP?

The developed countries of the world supply help in the form of money as gifts or loans, equipment, foodstuffs, advice and training. Often this help is too small to make any real impact. Often it is not suitable to the needs of the developing country. High-technology machinery may not be appropriate for a developing country: a combine-harvester is of little use to a village if it cannot afford the diesel to run it or if there is no skilled mechanic to service it or if the fields are too small to make efficient use of it. There is a need to devise machinery suitable for the level of development of a country: this is known as 'appropriate technology'.

Aid is often offered in the form of 'tied aid', whereby the donor country insists on certain conditions before the aid is given. The conditions may be military or political but often they are economic:

Bangladesh

Every year 3 750 600 people are born in Bangladesh. What chances in life does each one of them have?

The hardest time comes at the beginning: there is a 13% chance of dying before the age of one, and a 25% chance of dying before the age of five. The most likely cause would be malnutrition or maybe dysentery, measles or whooping cough – the kind of childhood illnesses that cause little concern in a Western country. But with 9999 other people competing for the attention of one doctor and 5999 for each hospital bed, the chances of medical treatment are very slight. For a girl, the likelihood of an early death is 35–50% higher.

Having made it past the crucial early years, what about schooling? A child has a 56% chance of enrolment in a primary school, so has a better chance of becoming literate than his or her parents. There's a 78% chance that they are illiterate and in the mother's case the chances of literacy are very much slimmer.

In a country of 80 million people, 93% live in the countryside, 22 million people own no land from which to grow their food. The top 10% of landowners in the country own 34% of the land. So a Bangladeshi has a 65% chance of trying to eke out a living on wages of 5 to 8 *taka* a day (15–20 pence) or being dependent on someone else's wages. His or her early income will average out at £45 a year. It's a crowded country. The land area is small – 142 766 square kilometres, roughly the size of England and Wales. The population density – 559 per square kilometre – is higher than that of any other non-industrialised country in the world. A square kilometre of arable land supports 916 people, and though 83% of the cultivable land is under the plough, less than 5% is irrigated.

Travelling around the country is comparatively easy. On the waterways, including the three great rivers, the Ganges, the Brahmaputra and the Megnha, there are 4500 miles of navigable channels. There are also 3990 miles of road and 2600 miles of railway. But to catch a bus or ferry, the fare may be difficult to find.

In Bangladesh there is an 80% chance of being born a Moslem. As an inhabitant of one of the 65 000 villages, every 5 years one must take part in the elections for 10 out of 12 of the members of the Union Council, who have considerable local power. There are 4335 of these Councils, each covering an area of six or seven villages. Most government officials and decisions come from the *thana* or region, of which there are 410.

It's going to be a tough life, and probably not a long one. The chances of being permanently underfed are 54% and of protein deficiency 40%. Life expectancy is 47. But while it may be hard, there will be plenty to enjoy in a closely-knit family and community.

New Internationalist, No. 49, March 1977

a developed country will loan or give a developing country a sum of money on condition that it spends the money on machinery manufactured in the donor country, whether or not that country's goods are the best or cheapest on the world market. In these cases it is worth asking who is aiding whom.

Despite these serious limitations, aid has proved to be indispensable to the developing countries. Aid comes from three main sources:

(1) direct from the governments of developed countries (**bilateral aid**);
(2) from voluntary organisations such as Oxfam, Christian Aid and the Red Cross;
(3) from international organisations such as the EEC and the UN (**multilateral aid**).

Most of the UN help is channelled through its agencies. We can see the sort of aid given by examining the work of some of these agencies.

The War against Smallpox

'In just ten years smallpox has been transformed from a disease problem which afflicted more than ten million people annually, and was a threat to countries throughout the world, into a disease soon to be confirmed as extinct.'

This proud claim comes from the magazine *World Health* (March 1977), the journal of the UN agency the World Health Organisation (WHO), and marks the conclusion of a remarkable victory over a disease which has scourged humankind for thousands of years, and is the first time a human illness has ever been totally eliminated. The eradication of smallpox is possible because the virus causing the disease is passed only by humans and not by animals.

The WHO campaign against smallpox, which began in 1967, involved isolating victims and vaccinating those who had been in contact with a victim. By August 1975 there were only two countries in the world with any reported cases of smallpox: Bangladesh and Ethiopia. The campaign involved the help of over 30 countries to provide workers, vaccine and money. The leading contributors were Sweden, the USA and the USSR.

The War against the Desert Locust

Every year insects destroy enough food to feed millions of people. Among the most destructive of insects is the desert locust of the Middle East and North Africa. Individually, these insects do little damage, but at intervals they gather into swarms which may cover as much as 100 square kilometres and travel up to 65 kilometres a day, eating as much as 50 000 tonnes of vegetation every day and destroying every green thing in their path.

The UN agency the Food and Agricultural

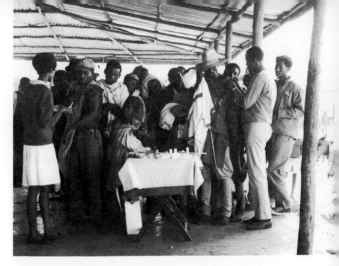
WHO team administering smallpox vaccine in Ethiopia

Organisation (FAO) began to co-ordinate campaigns against these plagues of locusts. International conferences were held and a special research centre was set up in Saudi Arabia to organise operations against the locust. Campaigns had to be organised every year, especially in 1957 and 1958, but gradually, through the use of poisonous sprays, dusts and baits, the FAO began to control the breeding of locusts and there were few serious swarms until 1978. Exceptional ecological conditions in late 1977 resulted in rapid breeding of the locust in Ethiopia and Somalia and the FAO's attempts to control the outbreak were seriously handicapped by the fighting in the Horn of Africa.

The War against Ignorance

Large-scale adult illiteracy is a major stumbling block in a developing country's attempts to solve its problems. In 1957 the United Nations Educational, Scientific and Cultural Organisation (**UNESCO**) launched a major ten-year project in 20 South American states with the aim of making free compulsory education available to all children in the area.

It was the first large-scale international project in education, and concentrated on increasing the number of teachers available. As a result of UNESCO's efforts 354 000 new teachers were trained and 12 million children were enrolled in primary school.

In 1960 UNESCO adopted a 20-year plan for educational development in Asia, involving 18 Asian countries. The aim was free compulsory education for at least seven years for over 160 million children by the year 1980. This required the training of more than five million teachers. UNESCO has set up similar programmes for Africa and for the Arab states.

THE BRANDT REPORT

As mentioned on page 118, the gap between the rich and poor countries was highlighted in a special Report, *North–South: A Programme for Survival*. This Report, published in 1980, was the result of a study carried out by a group of important people from the world of politics, banking, business and from the UN. The group was led by the former West German Chancellor, Willy Brandt.

The Brandt Report looked at questions of world interdependence. It considered questions of the environment, energy, food, health, employment, land reform and many others. The main recommendations dealt with the questions of trade, debt and aid, and it dealt with these in terms of the relationship of the North to the South.

The Report recommended that the rich industrial countries should not protect their products against competition from the Third World. This would help increase trade between the North and South and benefit all. The Report recommended controlling the activities of multinational companies to protect the interests of Third World countries. On the question of aid, the Report recommended that the rich countries should increase their government aid to 0.7 per cent of their GNP. The Report also highlighted the enormous problem of debt which faces many Third World countries. In 1981 the debt owed by Third World countries stood at some $525 billion and much of this was owed by a group of newly industrialised countries such as Brazil, Mexico, South Korea and Argentina. The size of this debt has become a threat to the future of the banking system in the West. The Brandt Report urged 'massive resource transfers' from the industrial North to allow Third World governments to keep paying interest on their debts. The Report stressed that it was in the interest of the North to do this to prevent default of payment causing possible bank collapse. The Report also called for the ending of hunger and malnutrition through increased aid for food production in the Third World.

Following the Brandt Report, the first North–South summit meeting was held in 1981 at Cancun in Mexico where leaders from 22 northern and southern countries, including the USA and China, met to discuss the kind of problems raised by the Brandt Report. Negotiation on such a world scale had been urged by the so-called Group of 77, which consists of the 122 developing countries in the United Nations. This Group want a fairer international economic order through a reform of North–South economic relations. Again this underlines, as did the Brandt Report, the interdependence of the North and South in one world economic system.

However, despite the Brandt Report, despite the Group of 77 and the Cancun Summit very little has changed in real terms and efforts to put world economic relations on a more secure basis have made little progress.

Questions

1. What do you understand by the terms 'appropriate technology' and 'tied aid'? Can you think of any device which may be very simple to make and operate but which could save a village in a developing country a great deal of time and work?
2. Explain the difference between bilateral and multilateral aid.
3. Name the main United Nations agencies involved in helping the developing countries and write a sentence about each one, summarising their work.
4. What is so unique about the WHO campaign against smallpox?
5. Describe the FAO campaign against the locust showing how this is a good example of international co-operation.
6. Outline the work and success of UNESCO in the campaign to establish primary education in the developing countries.
7. Summarise the main recommendations of the Brandt Report.
8. Explain what is meant by saying that the Brandt Report showed the interdependence of the North and South in the world economy.

Human Rights

Steve Biko

On 12 September 1977 the name of Steve Biko suddenly became world-wide news. Why? Because he was dead! Biko, a 30-year-old black South African, was the hero of millions of black people in that country and the founder of several important black organisations, including the Black Consciousness movement, which protest against the South African government's apartheid policy.

His death in a Pretoria prison made him the twentieth detainee to die in police custody in less than two years. The final post-mortem on Biko showed that he died as a result of head injuries leading to extensive brain damage. The post-mortem report stated that Biko had sustained at least a dozen other wounds and bruises, including rib injuries, and that these injuries had been suf-

THE WORK OF UN AGENCIES: A SUMMARY

Name of the agency	Main function	Activities

Food and Agricultural Organisation (FAO)	To raise levels of nutrition throughout the world and prevent world hunger by improving the efficiency of the production and supply of food	Organised the World Food Conference in Rome in 1974 to get international agreement on world food problems.
		    Helps to establish government agricultural services in the developing countries to bring modern agricultural programmes and scientific discoveries to the attention of farmers. Encourages developments in irrigation, fertilisers, high-yield crops, pesticides, livestock farming and animal diseases, fisheries and forestry work.
		    Helps governments train people to devise programmes to improve nutrition in their countries.

World Health Organisation (WHO)	To help promote the highest possible level of health throughout the world	Helps governments build up their own health services and provides them with technical assistance and aid.
		    Carries out research and collects information on problems of world health.
		    Co-ordinates and initiates campaigns aimed at wiping out major diseases in the world, e.g. tuberculosis, trachoma, leprosy, cholera. Malaria has been virtually cleared out in the Americas, North Africa, parts of Asia and the Western Pacific; greatly reduced in India and Pakistan, although it is still serious in Africa south of the Sahara.
		    Makes efforts to overcome the world-wide shortage of doctors, nurses and health workers. Because of the cost of health services, it has encouraged developing countries to develop 'primary health care', i.e. workers who can deal with simple illnesses and emergencies.

United Nations Educational Scientific and Cultural Organisation (UNESCO) 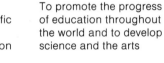	To promote the progress of education throughout the world and to develop science and the arts	Works in the fields of education, science, social science, culture and communication.
		    Encourages international co-operation to establish compulsory primary education throughout most of the developing world.
		    Encourages international co-operation in science.
		    Encourages international co-operation to safeguard the world's store of books and works of art. It works to save monuments; its most spectacular campaign was to save the ancient Egyptian monuments of Nubia from submersion by the Nile upon the completion of the Aswan Dam.

United Nations International Children's Emergency Fund (UNICEF)	To help children who are in need, especially the poorest children in the poorest areas of the world	Helps governments to set up projects in:
		    mother and child health, e.g. safe delivery of babies
		    mass disease-control campaigns – works alongside WHO
		    nutrition
		    family and child welfare services
		and organises emergency relief for children during disasters

International Labour Organisation (ILO)	To improve working conditions throughout the world	Set up an International Labour Code on many aspects of working conditions such as:
		    employment/unemployment
		    conditions of work
		    employment of children, young persons and women
		    industrial health, safety and welfare
		    industrial relations
		    migrant workers.
		These act as guidelines for the member-countries.

Steve Biko

fered over a period of time from eight days to twelve hours before his death. At the inquiry into his death evidence was given that Biko was driven naked in the back of a Land-Rover from Port Elizabeth to Pretoria, a 14-hour, 1200-kilometre trip. His medical equipment was 'a container of water'. The inquiry found that there was 'no evidence' to suggest that the police or prison authorities were in any way responsible for Steve Biko's death. This was not the first time that Biko, like many of his followers, had been persecuted. He had already been detained four times before and in 1973 he was 'banned': this meant that he was not allowed to continue his medical studies at Natal University and had to return to his place of birth, King Williams-town. He was not allowed to travel further than 16 kilometres from there without special permission, could not speak to more than one person at a time, could not be quoted and could not enter any publishing or educational premises.

Reaction to Biko's death was varied. The South African Minister of Justice, Police and Prisons, Mr Kruger, said: 'Biko's death leaves me cold. I feel nothing although one is sorry about any death. I suppose I would feel sorry about my own death.'

In October 1977 Mr Kruger took further action against the Black Consciousness movement by banning 17 organisations linked with the movement.

Reaction from abroad was different. The United States, Dutch and West German governments recalled their ambassadors from South Africa for consultations about the situation and the United Nations imposed a mandatory arms embargo on South Africa.

Fred Morris

'They began asking where I was taking my car and what I was doing with my friend Alanir. They weren't interested in the answers; they asked the questions and started hitting me, before I had a chance to answer. I was subjected to about 20 minutes of this kind of questioning, which was designed to disorientate and thoroughly intimidate me. I was kicked in the groin three times in succession, until I was laid out altogether, and then I was forced to get up again for more questions and beatings.

Then all of a sudden there was this complete silence and everybody left except for one guy. I heard him filling a bucket with water which he poured on my legs and on the floor around me. Then he came back with electrodes, fastening one to the second toe of my right foot and the other fastened with a spring-clip to the nipple of my right breast, cutting right into the flesh. I knew what I was in for because electric shock is their standard torture technique. He went back and sat down at what must have been a table and began asking the same questions – only this time with each question would come an electric shock.

The current would increase in voltage to the point of producing muscular convulsions and I would just be thrown to the floor. Then he would turn the current off, and if I didn't get up rapidly enough, even with my hands handcuffed behind my back on the wet floor with no clothes on, he would turn on the current with light doses, like a cattle prod. As soon as I would get on my feet again, it would be the same thing: more questions, turning on the shock, increasing the voltage until I would be thrown to the floor again.

I think the whole first session was about an hour and a half, counting the beatings and the shocks. By that time I was really just sort of in limbo, which is I think a physiological and psychological defence mechanism. You get to the point where it is not real. You are really not even there any more; you are just kind of hanging on. It was all sort of a big blur. And when they became aware of that, they stopped, because they don't want you to get to that position; you aren't hurting enough.'

This account of his torture in a Brazilian prison in September 1974 was written by the Reverend Fred Morris, a missionary of the United Methodist Church of the United States. He was arrested because he was suspected of having written an article for an

American news magazine which was uncomplimentary towards the Brazilian government.

Fred Morris was lucky. After three weeks of such treatment he was released and deported. Many others have never been seen again.

Alexander Solzhenitsyn

Born in the Soviet Union in 1918, Alexander Solzhenitsyn has a world-wide reputation as an author. He is also a leading campaigner for civil rights for the people of the USSR. Before he was expelled from the Soviet Union in 1974, he was an important member of a group who have become known as dissidents. They are a group of well-educated professional people including scientists, poets and authors who are concerned about the effects of some of the Soviet government's policies on the Soviet people.

Solzhenitsyn studied mathematics and physics before taking a course at the Moscow Institute of History, Philosophy and Literature. In 1941 he joined the Soviet army and served against the Nazis at the front until 1945, being decorated twice for bravery. But as a result of his criticisms of the Soviet system, he was sentenced to eight years imprisonment in 1945, followed by exile in Siberia between 1953 and 1956. In 1970 Solzhenitsyn was prevented from receiving the Nobel Prize for Literature. Finally, in 1974 he was expelled from the USSR and went to live first in Switzerland then later in the USA.

Soviet human rights campaigners like the exiled Solzhenitsyn and those still in the USSR are no longer pressing for the vague 'freedom' they hoped for 25 years ago. What they are demanding are basic human rights as laid down in the 1975 Helsinki Agreement – the right to lead normal, peaceful lives, unharassed by secret police.

These people, and many others like them, were victims of a problem which has become increasingly common in the 1970s and 80s – the violation of human rights. In 1977 the human rights organisation Amnesty International was awarded the Nobel Peace Prize for its efforts to bring the plight of the victims of discrimination to the attention of the world. Yet the problem, far from being solved, appears to be becoming worse.

Human rights are, or should be, everyone's concern. There is no country in the world in which someone's human rights are not in some way abused. It is more than 30 years since the United Nations pledged itself to fight against such discrimination and uphold human rights. On 10 December 1948 the UN General Assembly adopted the Universal Declaration of Human Rights. The 30 articles contained in this document are too long to reprint here, but some of the most important ones are given in the extract below.

Clearly, in spite of these optimistic hopes for the future of humankind, there are many areas of the world today where human rights are not respected.

UNIVERSAL DECLARATION OF HUMAN RIGHTS

THE GENERAL ASSEMBLY PROCLAIMS

All human beings are born free and equal in dignity and rights. They are endowed with reason and conscience and should act towards one another in a spirit of brotherhood.

Everyone has the right to life, liberty and security of person.

No one shall be held in slavery or servitude.

No one shall be subjected to torture or to cruel, inhuman or degrading treatment or punishment.

No one shall be subjected to arbitrary arrest, detention or exile.

Everyone has the right to seek and to enjoy in other countries asylum from persecution.

Everyone has the right to freedom of thought, conscience and religion.

Everyone has the right to freedom of opinion and expression.

At the Helsinki Conference on Security and Co-operaion in Europe held in 1975, 35 nations, including the USA and the USSR, agreed to maintain basic human rights. The agreements set up a programme of rights including reunification of families, marriages between citizens of different states, travel, tourism, circulation of information, cultural co-operation and so on.

More recent documents on human rights published by the United Nations include the covenants on human rights, which came into force in 1976, and are now legally binding on about 45 nations, including Britain. These agreements lay down the standards required of nations in fields such as conditions of work, trade unions, social security, protection of the family, standards of living and health, freedom of movement and equality before the law. But the influence of these covenants remains to be seen. Many UN member-states have not signed them, and although they cover many important subjects, they leave untouched the major violations of human rights in such countries as the USSR, South Africa, Uganda and South American countries, including Argentina, Chile and Uruguay.

Questions

1. Choose one of the case studies and explain why the events described are a threat to human rights.
2. What is the Universal Declaration of Human Rights?
3. Describe the agreements reached at the 1975 Helsinki Conference.
4. What subjects are covered by the UN covenants on human rights?
5. How effective has legislation on human rights been so far?

Terrorism

Closely associated with the problem of the denial of human rights is the problem of terrorism. National and international terrorism has been a feature of world politics since the late 1960s. Between then and now there has been a large increase in the number of incidents described as 'terrorist' (from under 100 a year to over 400 a year). These include bombings, shootings, hijackings and the taking of hostages.

Throughout the world there has been an upsurge in the number of groups prepared to take terrorist action in order to gain publicity for their problems. Some of the most active groups in recent years are shown in Table 11.

All of these groups have used the methods described as a means of attracting wider attention for their cause. Yet the label 'terrorist' is one which should be used only with great care. Many of the people who are described as terrorists see themselves as freedom fighters whose only aim is to achieve freedom and equality. In Lebanon, for example, the various groups such as the Druze seek political equality with the Christians. The boundaries between being an oppressed minority, a freedom fighter, a guerrilla fighter and a terrorist are blurred

Table 11 Active terrorist groups

Organisation	Active in
ETA (Basque Separatists)	Spain
IRA (Irish Republican Army)	Northern Ireland and mainland Britain
PLO (Palestinian Liberation Army)	Middle East
Baader-Meinhoff	West Germany
Red Brigades	Italy
Tupamaros	Uruguay

and often depend on whether the oppressed or the oppressor is speaking.

Terrorism and the use of terrorist tactics during the last 20 years have been largely unsuccessful in achieving their long-term aims, mainly because governments have refused to give in to their demands. Yet the number of terrorist acts continues to increase. The explanation for this apparent contradiction lies in the fact that even unsuccessful acts gain publicity. In addition, acts of terrorism will continue to increase until the underlying causes of the violence have been satisfactorily dealt with.

A UN International Congress, held in Geneva in 1975 and attended by some 1000 representatives, agreed on the need for international and multilateral action to reduce the number of incidents of international violence. However, it also agreed that until the causes were tackled there could be no reduction in international terrorism. In 1976 the General Assembly expressed deep concern over increasing acts of international terrorism which endangered or took innocent human lives or affected basic freedoms, and urged governments to seek just and peaceful solutions to the underlying causes which gave rise to such acts. So far this advice appears to have been ignored by many of the governments throughout the world.

Questions

1. Describe the methods used by 'terrorist' organisations.
2. What results do 'terrorist' groups hope to achieve?
3. Why is the use of the word 'terrorist' often a problem?
4. Describe the UN's views on the increase in terrorism since the 1960s and explain why terrorist acts have continued to increase in the 1980s.

3. Towards World Unity

United Nations Membership

> **How a country becomes a member of the United Nations**
>
> 1 The country must accept the aims of the charter, and be willing to carry out these aims.
> 2 The country must be peace-loving.
> 3 The country must be recommended by the UN Security Council.
> 4 The country must then gain a two-thirds majority vote in the General Assembly.

The United Nations had 51 founder members in 1945. By 1985 there were 159 member-countries. Why has there been such an increase in UN membership? What effect, if any, has this had on the UN?

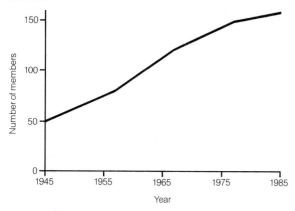

Increase in UN membership, 1945–84

INCREASING MEMBERSHIP

The increase in membership is mainly due to the fact that in the last 30 years many former colonies have become independent and applied to join the UN. As UN members, they are able to have a say in matters which affect them and also have access to UN information, expertise and aid.

Countries which have joined in the 1980s are:

Zimbabwe St Vincent and Grenadines
Vanuatu Belize
Antigua St Kitts and Nevis
Brunei

Belize: New Member of the UN

In September 1981 Belize (formerly British Honduras) in Central America became the 156th member of the UN. However, even as this tiny country (population 150 000) joined the UN, it was under threat from neighbouring Guatemala which claims part of the territory of Belize. There is a force of about 2000 British troops in Belize to maintain its independence.

EFFECTS OF INCREASING MEMBERSHIP

As the membership of the UN increases, many of the topics discussed and the decisions reached differ from earlier UN debates. Many of the newer members are Afro-Asian countries, many of whom are poor, lacking in industrial development, and they wanted discussion on topics which affect them directly. Previously, much discussion was dominated by the USA and the USSR, who were concerned about the Cold War and East–West confrontation. Much of the debate is now about economic items such as the gap in living standards between developed and developing nations, world trade, goods prices and supplies, and aid to less developed countries. Recently 100 countries stated that their main aim was a 'New International Economic Order' in the world, with much greater aid being given by rich to poor nations. In 1977 an arms embargo was placed on South Africa because of its apartheid policies.

A second effect of changing membership is that decisions reached by voting may not please some of the major countries, such as the USA and the USSR, who now cannot easily get a majority on their side in the Assembly or the Security Council. Previously the USA, with South American and West European support, could often win the voting.

A third effect has been that the Security Council membership has increased from 11 to 15 members. The ten elected members can now easily outvote permanent members provided the veto is not used.

A related effect of increasing membership is that the UN is now also involved in a whole range of debate and activities on world issues, such as outer space, development of the seabed, nuclear power for peace, the environment, Antarctica, international terrorism, stronger human rights programmes, world trade, and disarmament. Of these topics, disarmament has been described by the former UN Secretary-General Kurt Waldheim as the 'heart of the problem of international order'.

Many poor countries are more interested in developing a 'North–South dialogue' in which there should be discussion of ways in which the richer

Changing UN membership (approximate figures by region)

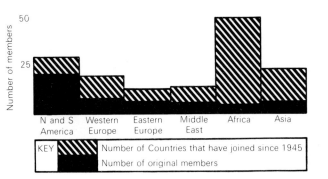

countries of the northern hemisphere can economically help the poorer countries of the southern hemisphere.

Sometimes the Superpowers themselves are criticised by the UN. In recent years the UN has voted against the Soviet Union over Afghanistan, and in 1983 the UN voted against the United States over the invasion of Grenada. The USA, angered by some of the voting decisions in UNESCO, withdrew from UNESCO in 1984.

The Non-members

Although membership of the UN is open to all independent sovereign states, there are some countries in the world who are not members of the UN. These include:

Switzerland   Taiwan   Tonga
North Korea   South Korea   Western Samoa

and some very small countries:

Monaco   Andorra   Liechtenstein

Use of the Veto on UN Membership

Both the United States and the Soviet Union have used the power of the veto in the UN Security Council to block membership of countries they do not like. The USA vetoed separate applications for membership by North Vietnam and South Vietnam before they became a united republic. Angola's application was at first vetoed by the USA because of Cuban troops in that country. The USA also vetoed the application of communist North Korea while the USSR used the veto to prevent the membership of non-communist South Korea.

China is formally admitted to the UN

China and the UN

At the end of the Chinese Revolution in 1949, the Chinese communist government ruled mainland China while the previous government fled to Taiwan. America did not recognise the communist government of China as the true government and supported Taiwan. In the UN America was able to get enough support to allow the Taiwan representative to sit as 'China' and keep communist China (with one fifth of the world's population) out. Finally, in October 1971, China was admitted to the UN and Taiwan was expelled.

Questions

1. How does a country become a member of the UN?
2. Which two regions of the world have had the biggest increase in membership of the UN?
3. What effects has increasing membership had on the UN?
4. Why are (a) Taiwan, (b) Switzerland, and (c) Monaco not in the UN?
5. When and why was the UN set up?
6. List some of the wide range of topics dealt with by the UN.

4. Unity: Problems and Achievements

Tackling World Problems

The vast scale of some of the problems the UN faces makes any solution difficult. The UN, through its specialised agencies such as the WHO and FAO, has helped the poorer countries considerably but is hampered by lack of finances and the fact that the aid given does not always reach those most in need. It cost £20 million over ten years to eliminate small-pox – the WHO programme to wipe out malaria, estimated cost £240 million, is slowing down due to shortage of funds.

A further problem in solving the world food shortage is that many poorer countries, like the developed countries, spend vast amounts of money which they can ill-afford on buying and producing arms and military equipment.

If there is to be a New International Economic Order (a fairer share of world resources and wealth) then the richer countries in the world must give greater help to the poorer countries. Failure in this could lead to serious confrontation between rich and poor countries.

FOOD: the facts

How many people are badly nourished?
2000 million people: about half the world's population.

How many are actually starving?
The Un Food and Agriculture Organisation estimates that 462 million are 'actually starving' and about half of them are children under five.

Where are they?
28 million in the developed countries, 36 million in Latin America, 30 million in the Near East, 67 million in Africa, and 301 million in the Far East.

What is the average number of calories required per day for a person to stay healthy?
It varies a lot, but 1900 calories per day is the recommended minimum.

Is enough food being grown to provide everybody in the world with this recommended minimum?
Yes. In fact enough is being grown to provide every person in the world with 3000–4000 calories per day.

But is there enough land and water in the world to grow food for a population which will be doubled in 30 years?
Easily. There are many estimates of the world's food potential and almost all of them see no difficulty in doubling world food production. For example, W. H. Pawley of FAO estimates that the earth's resources could feed 36 billion people (present population about 4 billion).

SHELTER: the facts

How many people are homeless?
No reliable figure for the homeless is known but the UN estimates the number of new houses required between 1970 and 1980 to be about 263 million: or 75 000 new homes every day for the next ten years.

How many people live in towns and cities and how many people live in the countryside?
At the beginning of this century, 85% of the world's population lived in rural areas. Today the figure is about 63%. By the year 2000 it will probably be less than 50% and, for the first time, more people will be living in towns and cities than in the countryside.

How many of the people in towns are squatters and slum dwellers?
16% of the people in Hong Kong, 30% of Guatemala City, 90% of Addis Ababa, 25% of Santiago, 33% of Calcutta, 33% of Nairobi, 46% of Mexico City, 38% of Lusaka, 50% of Dar-es-Salaam.

How many people have a safe water supply in or near their homes?
In Africa 77% of the urban population, in Latin America 76%, in South Asia 64%. But these figures are estimátes for the towns and cities only: the World Health Organisation says that 90% of the people in the rural areas of the Third World are using unsafe water all the time.

Nuclear plea by UN leader

The United Nations Secretary-General, Mr **Javier Perez de Cuellar**, gave warning today of a possible nuclear war and urged Soviet and American leaders to have the courage and sense to negotiate.

'They have to get the message that nobody has given them the right to decide our fate,' he said. The next war would be a nuclear conflict that would destroy not only countries involved, but those far away from the fighting.

During a year-end Press conference, the Secretary-General gave a sombre assessment of what he termed a turbulent 1983 marked by much violence and tragedy. He said the deterioration in international relations had caused widespread foreboding about the prospects for peace. 'The trend needs to be arrested before its effects become irreparable.'

Mr Perez de Cuellar said the most significant world problem was created by the remorseless build-up of nuclear weapons. 'The USSR and the United States owe it to themselves and to the entire human race to find ways of resuming in all earnestness their efforts to achieve an agreement on the limitation and reduction of both intermediate-range and strategic nuclear weapons.'

(*The Scotsman*, 22 December 1983)
© Reuter.

Further problems concern widespread poverty in Africa, racial conflict in South Africa, and the difficulty in achieving the independence of Namibia from South Africa. The problem of the Middle East is long-standing and difficult to unravel and, like Cyprus, the situation is potentially very dangerous since other opposing countries are involved. In both these areas, as in Cuba 1962, Biafra 1968–70, Vietnam, Angola, Iran/Iraq 1980, Falklands 1982 and Grenada 1983, the UN achieved little in terms of solving the problems of conflict.

The UN functions well in the works of its specialised agencies such as the WHO, FAO and UNESCO. These agencies set standards, link similar types of aid, supervise communications and provide information, specific knowledge and techniques for developing countries to improve their standards of living. Considering the size of the task involved in developing nations which have little money, the UN agencies have a special role in trying to raise their standards of living.

Questions

1. Can you name any regions to which the two major arms exporters send military supplies?
2. In what ways might it be said that the UN has not achieved its aims in (a) ending the 'scourge' of war, and (b) improving standards of living?
3. What warning did a former UN Secretary General give to the Superpowers?

'We, the peoples of the United Nations, determined to save succeeding generations from the scourge of war . . .'

. . . are spending more and more on military preparation so that the world's annual expenditure has now reached 300 billion (US) dollars – $800 millions a day.

We are employing 70 million of our world citizens as soldiers or in the manufacture of armaments and in researching to make weapons more effective to kill and overkill.

Terrifying weapons of deadly accuracy are poised at the ready, and the buttons are there to press to destroy vast areas of the globe.

'We, the peoples of the United Nations, determined to promote social progress and better standards of life in larger freedom . . .'

. . . live in a world where, more than 30 years after we made those pledges, 70 per cent of the people have to manage on 30 per cent of its wealth, while the 30 per cent who live in the rich world consume 70 per cent of its production.

The rich nations have pledged themselves to transfer annually to the poor nations through their governments just 0.7 per cent of their GNP; in fact they find that they can only afford to contribute about half of that mean, meagre target – a sum equal to about 6 per cent of what they can afford for military expenditure. UK official aid in 1982 amounted to 0.37 per cent of GNP.

Aspects of the UN's work:

Samples from 1983

Peacekeeping

The Secretary General reported that UNIFIL (UN Interim Force in Lebanon) had continued its efforts in southern Lebanon to protect and assist the local population, despite difficulties with increased local groups armed by Israel. The Security Council extended UNIFIL's mandate until 19 October.

The problems of peacekeeping were highlighted by deaths in the multi-national forces. UNIFIL itself has suffered 93 fatalities since March 1978. On 10 September Lebanon called on the Security Council to arrange and enforce a ceasefire.

South Africa

The Assembly rejected any linkage between Namibian independence and Cuban troop withdrawals from Angola, held that South Africa's occupation of Namibia constituted aggression and deplored all collaboration with it.

When South Africa raided Lesotho on 9 December the Assembly and the Security Council condemned it and the Council demanded compensation.

Afghanistan

Again the Assembly called for a withdrawal of foreign troops from Afghanistan, urged a political solution and reaffirmed Afghanistan's right to its own political and economic system. The Secretary General's personal representative plans to visit the area in January.

Grenada

The Council met on the evening of the invasion of Grenada. The USA vetoed the resolution which deeply deplored the intervention and called for an immediate withdrawal. The Assembly overwhelmingly passed a similar resolution and asked the Secretary General to report on the situation.

The General Assembly

In the general debate 150 speakers addressed the Assembly. Mrs Gandhi had specially urged government heads to participate in this forum for world problems. The overwhelming majority of speakers emphasised disarmament, the economic crisis and strengthening at the UN.

Human rights

The Human Rights Commission's annual session is considering general issues – torture, executions, mercenaries, minority rights, mass exoduses of refugees, the right to development and others, as well as specific countries – Bolivia, Chile, Guatemala, Iran, Poland, South Africa and Israeli-occupied territories.

The Human Rights Commission session concluded with a call for self-determination in Western Sahara, withdrawal of foreign troops from Afghanistan, release of civilian Palestinians and Lebanese detained by the Israelis in the invasion of Lebanon. It authorised a study of human rights in El Salvador.

Environment

The Gulf oil slick defied efforts of neighbouring states to implement their agreement to protect marine environment. Under the UN Environment Programme (UNEP) eight Gulf states agreed in 1978 to plan against pollution, but action to protect desalination plants and fishing was thwarted since two of the members were then at war and hesitated to allow the wells to be capped.

UNEP also collaborated in two environmental agreements. An international convention of transboundary air pollution came into force on 16 March for 35 countries – European states, the USSR, USA and Canada. It provides for collaboration particularly on acid rain.

Disarmament

No breakthrough occurred in disarmament. The Secretary General described the $800 000 million spent annually on armaments as 'an absurdity', when aid to developing countries equalled only 18 days of military spending. Negotiations continued outside the UN on intermediate nuclear and strategic weapons and at Vienna on conventional weapons.

Weapons

The General Assembly has asked its Disarmament Committee to concentrate on nuclear disarmament, especially a nuclear weapon test ban, and the elimination of chemical weapons.

On 10 February the US proposed that all chemical weapons should be destroyed within ten years of a treaty ban which includes verification. But the US administration has since sought funds for chemical weapon manufacture, turned down by Congress last year.

Nuclear waste

A two-year non-mandatory ban on dumping radioactive nuclear waste at sea has been agreed under the auspices of the UN International Maritime Organisation. The UK, which is responsible for about 90 per cent of such dumping, voted against it.

Iran–Iraq War

Iran warned the Assembly that any foreign 'misguided adventure' against its interests would result in halting oil from the Gulf. The Council called for an end to hostilities in the gulf area, asked the Secretary General to consult on verification, possibly with UN observers and urged an end to attacks against civilian targets.

United Nations Financial Problems

A major problem for the UN is how to get enough money to pay for all the different tasks it has to tackle. As world-wide problems of poverty and malnutrition increase, so the UN must try to find more money to help. At the same time, however, some member countries refuse to pay their full membership fee. This is based on an 'ability to pay' which is based mainly on national income level. In 1983 the USA, the biggest contributor to UN funds (about £90 million per year), refused to pay 'Law of the Sea' finances because it disagreed with UN decisions on this subject. The USSR also refused to pay about £20 million because it disagreed with certain UN peacekeeping missions. For various reasons, about a dozen other countries also withheld cash from the UN. Some countries though, such as Canada, Sweden, Libya, Kuwait and the Netherlands, pay more than they are required to. Despite this, however, the UN is short of money and has to cut back on projects for its specialised agencies and on development help for poor countries. The estimated budget deficit for 1983–5 was $285 million.

UN BUDGET
$685,315,089 (1983-85)

Who pays what?

159 countries are members of United Nations

	%
USA	25.00
USSR	10.54
Japan	10.32
West Germany	8.54
France	6.51
UK	4.67
Italy	3.74
Canada	3.08
Spain	1.93
Netherlands	1.78
Australia	1.57
Brazil	1.39
East Germany	1.39
Belgium	1.28
Sweden	1.32
Ukranian SS Rep	1.32
Others	15.62

UN BALANCE SHEET

Credits	Debits
The UN provides a place where many countries can put forward their views and be heard. This is especially important for the small and developing countries.	The use of the power of veto by some permanent members for their own purposes has sometimes blocked discussion and action on important issues. In 1983 the UK and the USA vetoed Security Council resolutions calling for a ceasefire in the Falklands War.
Its membership continues to increase, and no country has ever left the UN of its own accord.	The UN has not had much influence on the Cold War confrontation between the USA and the USSR. Both Superpowers continue to develop new weapons systems and to export weapons to other countries. At the 1982 Special Session of the General Assembly there was failure to agree on specific steps to halt the arms race.
The UN provides services to help to solve conflicts. The UN was successful in the Congo in 1960 in preventing further war and in helping to set up new organisations to run the country.	
UN Specialised Agencies (WHO, FAO) give a variety of aid to developing countries. Twenty per cent of UN money is applied to the task of development. WHO has been working to remove the disease of smallpox.	The UN has had little effect in preventing wars, e.g. Middle East, Vietnam, Angola, Cyprus, Afghanistan, Iran/Iraq, Falklands. By 1984 there was still fighting between various groups in Lebanon despite the presence of a UN force for some years.
There is concern for world problems, as shown by the UN conferences to try to settle issues of Disarmament, Food and Population, Law of the Sea, Antarctica and Outer Space.	The lack of a permanent UN military force can lead to delays in reacting to rapidly developing military situations.
The UN provides a forum for information and negotiation, if required, in crisis, e.g. organising disaster relief, and helping colonies to independence.	The UN has severe financial problems, and has not enough money to pay for the massive problems of solving issues such as world poverty, hunger, lack of human rights and peacekeeping.

Who's Who

Yuri **Andropov** (1914–84)   First Secretary of the Communist Party of the Soviet Union and leader of the Soviet Union from 1982 to 1984.

Yasser Arafat (b. 1929)   Leader of the Palestinian Liberation Organisation (PLO); spokesman for the Palestinian people at the UN.

Menachem Begin (b. 1913)   Prime Minister of Israel from 1977 until 1983.

Pieter Botha (b. 1916)   Elected Prime Minister of South Africa in 1978 after the resignation of Mr Vorster.

Willy Brandt (b. 1913)   Chancellor of West Germany from 1969 to 1974. Responsible for the policy of Ostpolitik. Winner of the Nobel Peace Prize and leader of the group responsible for the Brandt Report.

Leonid Brezhnev (1906–82)   First Secretary of the Communist Party of the Soviet Union and leader of the Soviet Union from 1964 to 1982.

Jimmy Carter (b. 1924)   President of the USA (Democratic) from 1976 until 1980.

Fidel Castro (b. 1926)   Cuban revolutionary leader; Prime Minister since 1959.

Konstantin Chernenko (1911–85)   First Secretary of the Communist Party of the Soviet Union and leader of the Soviet Union from 1984 to 1985.

Perez de Cuellar (b. 1920)   Peruvian Secretary-General of the United Nations since 1982.

Deng Xiaoping (b. 1904)   Vice-Chairman of the Chinese Communist Party. Formerly Vice-Premier of the People's Republic of China (1977–80).

Gerald Ford (b. 1913)   Became President of the USA (Republican) in 1974, following Nixon's downfall.

Colonel Gadafy (b. 1942)   Leader of the Socialist People's Republic of Libya since 1969. (also Gaddafi or Quaddafi)

Mikhail Gorbachev (b. 1931)   Became leader of the Soviet Union in 1985 after the death of Chernenko.

Ho Chi Minh (1890–1969)   Leader of North Vietnam till his death in September 1969. National hero of the Vietnamese communists for leading the struggle for a united independent Vietnam.

Saddam Hussein (b. 1937)   President of Iraq since 1979.

Lyndon Baines Johnson (1908–73)   Became President of the USA (Democratic) in 1963, following the assassination of John F. Kennedy. Stood down in 1968 because of the unpopularity of his handling of the Vietnam War.

John F. Kennedy (1917–63)   Elected President of the USA (Democratic) 1960; youngest and first Roman Catholic President; assassinated in Dallas, Texas, November 1963.

Ayatollah Khomeini (b. 1900)   Leader of the Islamic Republic of Iran since the fall of the Shah in 1979.

Nikita Khrushchev (1894–1971)   Secretary-General of Soviet Communist Party after Stalin's death in 1953; Prime Minister from 1958 until 1964.

Henry Kissinger (b. 1923)   US Secretary of State for Foreign Affairs 1973–6; founder of 'shuttle diplomacy'.

Vladimir Ilyich Lenin (1870–1924)   Russian revolutionary; leader of Bolsheviks; leader of Soviet Union from 1917 till his death.

Mao Zedong (1893–1976)   Became leader of the Chinese Communist Party in 1935, and leader of the Chinese People's Republic in 1949. His ideas and writing, e.g. *Thoughts of Chairman Mao* formed a major influence in China's development.

Karl Marx (1818–83)   German philosopher; founder of modern international communism; author of the Communist Manifesto.

Hosni Mubarak (b. 1928)   President of Egypt since 1981.

Robert Mugabe (b. 1928)   Elected Prime Minister of Zimbabwe (formerly Rhodesia) in 1980.

Richard Nixon (b. 1913)   Elected President of the USA (Republican) in 1969, and by a huge majority in 1972. The Watergate scandal led to his resignation from office in 1974.

Ronald Reagan (b. 1911)   President of the USA (Republican), elected in November 1980, re-elected in 1984.

Anwar Sadat (1918–81)   President of Egypt from 1970 until his assassination in 1981. Responsible for Middle East peace moves in 1977.

Robert Schuman (1886–1963)   French foreign minister responsible for the Schuman Plan for a common market in coal and steel in Europe.

Joseph Stalin (1879–1953)   Leader of Soviet Union from 1924 till his death; founder of collectivism and the Five Year Plans.

Tito (1892–1980)   Leader of Yugoslavia from 1945 to 1980. Pursued his own Yugoslavian version of communism – known as Titoism – and kept Yugoslavia free of Soviet influence.

Lech Walesa (b. 1943)   Leader and founding member of the Polish trade union, Solidarity. Winner of the Nobel Peace Prize.

Zhao Ziyang (b. 1919)   Premier of China since 1980.

Glossary

Apartheid (apartness)   The system of racial segregation in South Africa, in which there is separation of races in work, housing, education, sport, facilities, etc. The system in South Africa produces discrimination, especially against black South Africans.

Bantustans (Bantu homelands)   Areas of land set aside in South Africa for black South Africans. Intended to be independent nation states, but covering only 13% of South Africa, and dependent on the South African Government.

Black majority rule   Political control held by black people in a country where they form a majority of the total population.

Cadre   A specially trained member of the Communist Party who can operate as a leader and political adviser in local situations.

CAP   The Common Agricultural Policy of the EEC.

Cold War   The rivalry, of various types between the Soviet Union and the United States of America. At its coldest in the years immediately after the end of the Second World War.

Collectivisation   The process, favoured by communism, whereby peasant farmers give up their private plots of land to state control to be grouped into large collective farms.

COMECON   Council for Mutual Economic Assistance, set up in 1949 – communist equivalent of the Common Market. Includes Bulgaria, Czechoslovakia, East Germany, Hungary, Poland, Romania, the USSR and Cuba.

Common external tariff   The tariff rate set by the EEC for goods entering any EEC country from a non-member country.

Coup   The sudden overthrow of a government, often by military force.

Detente   The relaxation of international tension between the USA and the USSR and their respective allies.

Developed country   A country with an advanced industrialised economy – a 'rich' country.

Developing country   A country whose economy is based on agriculture and has not yet developed industrially – a 'poor' country.

Domino theory   A theory used by the USA in connection with their involvement in South East Asia and Central America. The countries of South East Asia and Central America were likened to a row of dominoes with South Vietnam (in SE Asia) and Cuba (in Central America) being the first in the row. If they fell under communist control then so eventually would the other

countries in the region – like a row of dominoes falling against each other.

ECSC   European Coal and Steel Community. Set up by Paris Treaty in 1951 to pave the way for economic unity by placing its six founder members' coal and steel in a single 'common market'.

Escalation   A term used by the USA during the Vietnam War to describe an increase in military involvement and effort.

EURATOM   European Atomic Energy Community. Set up by Treaty of Rome to promote the peaceful uses of nuclear energy on a Community scale.

FAO   Food and Agriculture Organisation. The specialised agency of the United Nations which deals with world problems of food supplies and improvement in farming throughout the world.

Gastarbeiter   The German name for the 'guest workers' who came from many countries in the 1960s and 1970s to work in West Germany.

Glasnost   The policy of openness introduced by Gorbachev in the USSR to encourage debate about the future of Soviet Communism.

GNP   Gross National Product: the value of the total annual production of goods and services of a country. Used as an indication of the wealth of a country.

Goulash communism   A term used to describe economic reforms in Hungary.

Green pound   The exchange rate for agricultural produce in transactions between Britain and other EEC countries.

Green Revolution   A term used to describe a revolution in agricultural methods used in Third World countries to bring about a dramatic increase in their crop yields. It involves great use of new strains of crops and relies heavily on modern fertilisers and pesticides.

Guerilla warfare   A 'hit and run' form of warfare favoured by (usually) a weaker native army against the much stronger regular armed forces of (usually) the government or an invader.

Hot-line   Telephone link set up between Washington and Moscow after the Cuban crisis to improve communications and reduce the possibility of similar emergencies in the future.

Human rights   Fundamental rights, such as freedom of movement and equality of opportunity, which belong to every human being, irrespective of race, colour, religion or political beliefs.